Handbook
of
TURFGRASS
INSECT
PESTS

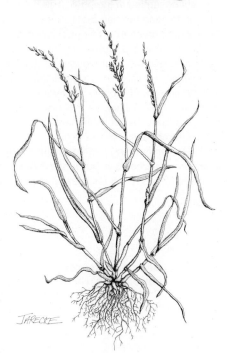

Edited by

Rick L. Brandenburg and Michael G. Villani

About the Handbook Series

Since the early 1900's, the Entomological Society of America has been at the forefront of publishing original entomological research. Traditionally, ESA publications have been directed toward entomologists, biologists, and agricultural scientists. In 1991, The ESA initiated the development of a series of handbooks on insect pests designed to make information on the biology, ecology, distribution, and management of arthropod pest species, and their principal natural enemies, readily available to extension specialists, area and county agents, pest management consultants, pest control operators, farmers, teachers of agriculture and their students, veterinarians, foresters, and master gardeners, as well as agricultural research scientists. Each handbook in the series focuses on pests of a particular commodity, pests which occupy a particular habitat type, or pests belonging to a particular taxa. To assist the nonspecialist in correctly diagnosing pest problems, each handbook contains keys to pest and injury identification, color photographs and graphic illustrations, as well as pest distribution maps.

The inaugural publication in this series, the *Handbook of Soybean Insect Pests,* was published in 1994. The *Handbook of Turfgrass Insect Pests* is the second handbook in the series. Users of this new handbook will be pleased to note the addition of life-sized silhouettes of each of the pests described in the book. The ESA Handbook Series Editorial Committee is committed to making the handbooks as user-friendly as possible, and welcomes suggestions for their improvement. The publication of this series is the result of efforts by many individuals who have generously volunteered their time and expertise. In particular we wish to acknowledge the contributions of the editorial committee: Rick Brandenburg, Ray Everngam, Mary Louise Flint, Roger Gold, Susan Heady, Gerald 'Skip' Jubb, Daniel Potter, Susan Whitney, and Victoria Yokoyama. We also extend a special thanks to Rick Brandenburg and Mike Villani, the editors of this handbook. Finally, we thank the nearly 30 authors and the ESA publications staff who contributed their expertise to the development of this handbook.

Additional handbooks are currently being written or are in the planning stage. The next to be published will be *The Handbook of Corn Insect Pests* and *The Handbook of Structural and Household Insect Pests.* Look for them to appear soon.

George G. Kennedy
Lowell 'Skip' Nault
Cochairs, ESA Handbook Series Editorial Committee
September 1995

Contents

Acknowledgments

This handbook is the second in a series produced by the Entomological Society of America. Incorporated in this handbook are the best concepts and ideas found in a variety of other sources. The editors are grateful to the full support of Lowell Nault and George Kennedy. We are most gracious for the freedom they provided us in the development of this book. We also thank the entire ESA Handbook Committee for their support, suggestions, and reviews.

We must recognize the authors whose outstanding contributions are contained in the individual chapters of this book. Maintaining the timetable and quality desired was possible only because a close-knit group of turfgrass entomologists was willing to make this book a priority. Their efforts are exemplary and are to be congratulated.

Our sincere thanks to Dr. James Baker for providing the majority of line drawings found in the key to invertebrate turfgrass pests as well as the life history tables and distribution maps found in most chapters. We hope you find the insect and mite line drawings, the raster pattern illustrations, and the life-size silhouettes, executed by Robert Jarecke, particularly useful. This added feature is new with this handbook. Luann Preston-Wilsey of Cornell University spent many hours managing this project and assured a consistent style throughout. Her perseverance over the past two years is both acknowledged and appreciated. In addition, our most sincere thanks to those individuals at North Carolina State University: Peter Hertl, Brian Royals, and Brenda Watson; and at Cornell University: Nancy Consolie, Wendy Heusler, and Paul Robbins who spent many hours reading text for accuracy, obtaining and confirming technical information, and providing a sounding board for ideas. Their willingness to put in an extraordinary effort over the past year and a half is a reflection, not only of their dedication and persistence, but to their overall commitment to a job well done.

We are most grateful for the many insect and mite photographs provided by the New York State Agricultural Experiment Station personnel, including staff photographers, Joe Ogrodnick and Gertrude Catlin (retired). The generosity of Dr. Haruo Tashiro (Professor Emeritus of Turfgrass Entomology at the New York State Agricultural Experiment Station) in allowing the use of his turfgrass insect slides provided us with first quality plates and greatly enhanced the appearance of the Handbook. Additional photographs were provided by David Shetlar, Mike Tolley and Patricia Cobb.

Our thanks are also extended to the staff of the Entomological Society of America for their work and to Eileen D'Araujo for copy editing the entire text. We also wish to thank Ray Everngam for his valuable support, guidance, and work behind the scenes to make this book a reality. Finally, the editors wish to thank our families who provided perhaps the most valuable contribution to this book; their support and patience.

Rick L. Brandenburg and
Michael G. Villani
March 1995

Contributing Authors

Steven R. Alm
Department of Plant Sciences
University of Rhode Island
Kingston, RI 02881

Frederick P. Baxendale
Department of Entomology
210 Plant Industry
University of Nebraska
Lincoln, NE 68583-0816

S. Kristine Braman
Department of Entomology
Georgia Station
Griffin, GA 30223-1797

Rick L. Brandenburg
Department of Entomology
P.O. Box 7613
North Carolina State University
Raleigh, NC 27695-7613

Wayne Buhler
Department of Entomology
Purdue University
West Lafayette, IN 47907

Patricia P. Cobb
205 Extension Hall
Auburn University
Auburn, AL 36849

Richard S. Cowles
Department of Entomology
Connecticut Agriculture Experiment Station
P.O. Box 1106
New Haven, CT 06504

Whitney S. Cranshaw
Department of Entomology
Colorado State University
Fort Collins, CO 80523

Robert L. Crocker
Agricultural Research and Extension Center
Texas A&M University
17360 Coit Road
Dallas, TX 75252

Timothy J. Gibb
Department of Entomology
Purdue University
West Lafayette, IN 47907

Clyde S. Gorsuch
Department of Entomology
109 Long Hall
Clemson University
Clemson, SC 29634-0365

Jennifer A. Grant
IPM Program
NYS Agriculture Experiment Station
Geneva, NY 14456

Paul R. Heller
501 ASI Building
Pennsylvania State University
University Park, PA 16802

J. Lee Hellman
Department of Entomology
1300 Symons Hall
University of Maryland
College Park, MD 20783

William G. Hudson
Department of Entomology
P.O. Box 1065
University of Georgia
Tifton, GA 31793

Michael G. Klein
USDA-ARS Horticultural Insect Laboratory
OARDC
Wooster, OH 44691

Rosa M. Marengo-Lozada
Department of Entomology
Texas A&M University
College Station, TX 77843

Joseph C. Neal
Department of Floriculture and Ornamental Horticulture
20 Plant Science Building
Cornell University
Ithaca, NY 14853-3134

William T. Nailon Jr.
Agricultural Research and Extension Center
Texas A&M University
17360 Coit Road
Dallas, TX 75252

Charles Peacock
Department of Crop Science
P.O. Box 7620
North Carolina State University
Raleigh, NC 27695

Daniel A. Potter
S-221 Agriculture Science Center North
University of Kentucky
Lexington, KY 40546-0091

Michael F. Potter
S-225H Agricultural Science Center North
University of Kentucky
Lexington, KY 40546-0091

James A. Reinert
Agricultural Research and Extension Center
17360 Coit Road
Texas A&M University
Dallas, TX 75252

David J. Shetlar
Entomology Extension
1991 Kenny Road
University of Ohio
Columbus, OH 43210-1090

Gail L. Schumann
Department of Plant Pathology
Fernald Hall
University of Massachusetts
Amherst, MA 01003

David R. Smitley
Department of Entomology
Michigan State University
East Lansing, MI 48824

Beverly Sparks
Entomology Extension
200 Barrow Hall
University of Georgia
Athens, GA 30824

Mike P. Tolley
DowElanco
3905 Vincennes Road, Suite 201
Indianapolis, IN 46268

Michael G. Villani
Department of Entomology
NYS Agriculture Experiment Station
Geneva, NY 14456

Patricia J. Vittum
Department of Entomology
Fernald Hall
University of Massachusetts
Amherst, MA 01003

W. H. Whitcomb
Department of Entomology and Nematology
University of Florida
Gainsesville, FL 32611

How to Use This Book

By Rick L. Brandenburg and Michael G. Villani

This handbook is designed to accommodate a broad field of users, including lawn care operators, superintendents, grounds maintenance personnel, sod producers, consultants, students, extension agents, and researchers. Our intent in this handbook is to provide basic information on turfgrass insect and mite pests, including identification, life history information, and management options. In addition to information on specific pests, general sections on important aspects of turfgrass management and pest management are provided. References for additional information are provided in most sections, and the sources of local information section at the end of the handbook provides addresses of entomology departments where management information for a specific area can be obtained. Authors are indicated after each section, and any unattributed sections are by the editors.

Insect and Mite Identification

Effective management of turfgrass insect and mite pests begins with accurate identification of the pests and reliable diagnosis of pest injury. Lists and keys are provided that will help to identify the most common insect and mite pests and the injury caused by these pests. The lists of pests by injury type and by scientific classification provide shorthand methods for accessing pest information. If you have some knowledge of the injury type or of the nature of the pest, you can use these lists to indicate which specific pests may be involved.

The injury and invertebrate pests keys provide a more comprehensive method for identifying a specific pest. You progress through the keys in steps. At each step you are presented with two choices, one of which should apply to the pest or the injury you are observing. The choice you make leads to another pair of choices, and so on. You progress through the appropriate series of choices until you have identified the insect or mite or the injury.

For additional verification of your identification, the lists and keys refer to the sections on specific pests. Information on specific pests is listed alphabetically by common name for easy reference. These sections include scientific classification, origin and distribution, description, pest status, injury, life history, management, and selected references. Also included in these sections are range maps, generation charts, detailed illustrations of pests at various life stages, including actual-size silhouettes, and color photographs of pests. A glossary is provided to assist with any unfamiliar terms.

General Information on Turfgrass and Turfgrass Pest Management

The beginning section on turfgrass provides an overview of the importance of turfgrass and of general production practices. The section on beneficial organisms discusses principles of natural and biological control involving predators, parasites, and entomopathogens. The section on turfgrass pest management provides a broad coverage of pest management issues as they relate to turfgrass pests. Sections on diseases, weeds, and their interactions illustrate how invertebrate pest management relates to other aspects of pest management in turfgrass.

An Introduction to Turfgrasses

By Charles Peacock

Most grass species used in turf areas (Table 1) are not native to North America, but have been introduced from Asia, Africa, and Europe (Beard 1973, Turgeon 1991). An exception is buffalograss (*Buchloe dactyloides*), which is found in the Great Plains and western United States. Turfgrasses result from selection pressure by humans and domesticated animals. Only those grasses that could withstand close cutting and the repeated grazing of animals survived. Most of those grasses were "forest-fringe" species from land cleared for farming.

Turfgrasses are herbaceous, perennial species capable of forming a dense sod. They are used for turf because of their adaptability. Grasses are able to tolerate frequent mowing because they have the following attributes: basal meristems that are protected during mowing, sheathing leaf bases with the oldest growth on the outside, short compact internodes, and deep fibrous root systems.

The quality of a given variety of turf depends on its genetic makeup, which dictates such factors as pest resistance, wear tolerance, and recuperative potential. Expression of these genetic factors varies depending on environmental and cultural influences. Six visual factors used to assess turf quality are as follows: (1) uniformity: the absence of bare areas or weeds; (2) density: the number of shoots per unit area (characteristic of each grass, but influenced by environmental and cultural factors); (3) texture: a function of leaf blade width (influenced by mowing height and difficult to separate from density); (4) color: variable because of its subjective nature, but considered by many turf managers to be the single best indication of quality; (5) growth habit: whether the growth is vertical or horizontal (growth habit partially determines how low the turf can be mowed; an upright growth is better from a mowing viewpoint); and (6) smoothness: quality of leaf ends, a surface feature influenced by the quality of mowing (Turgeon 1991).

Turf has many practical, recreational, and ornamental uses. One practical use of turf is to prevent erosion by stabilizing soil to the effects of wind and water. Grasses are extremely efficient in soil stabilization and erosion control because of their extensive fibrous root systems, which are well developed compared to those of other plants. Root biomass of grasses is several times that of other plants. Because they constantly regenerate root mass, over time grasses are great soil builders. Turf can also reduce glare and noise pollution and can have a cleansing effect on the air by absorbing dust and toxic emissions from vehicles. In addition, evaporation of water from leaf surfaces can cool the air. In areas provided for recreational activities and relaxation, turf is important and can greatly improve the quality of life. The grasses maintained in these areas also provide safety, by cushioning the impact of people involved in recreational activities, especially contact sports. The aesthetic value of turfgrasses is also important. Turf areas provide ideal settings for landscape details and can have a substantial impact on property values.

Turfgrass growth is influenced by many interdependent environmental factors, the most important of which are light, temperature, and moisture. Moisture can be managed to some extent, but tactics for dealing with light and temperature are limited. Warm-season turfgrasses differ from cool-season turfgrasses in the way they harvest the energy they have captured from the sun. As a result, warm-season grasses are better able to exist under conditions, or in locations, where temperatures and levels of sunlight are high. Where light is limited, shade-tolerant turfgrass varieties can be selected. In addition to variety selection, other management practices such as raising the mowing height, reducing irrigation, reducing nitrogen levels, and minimizing traffic can help in shady areas. Thatch accumulation affects exposure of turfgrass meristems to temperature extremes and should be kept to a minimum. In some cases, syringing and improving air movement may help when temperatures are high. Field observations on creeping bentgrass have found a significant improvement in stress tolerance where fans have been placed in areas with restricted air movement.

Cultural Practices

Mowing. Mowing is the periodic removal of a portion of turfgrass leaves and is the most basic cultural practice. It is detrimental to the plants and can decrease carbohydrate production and storage, decrease root growth, and increase water loss. However, turf species have been selected for their adaptability to mowing and persist even under constant defoliation. Advantages to mowing include controlling top growth, providing a uniform surface, and controlling weeds.

Mowing heights for each turf species must be maintained within a very specific range to maintain adequate leaf area for shoot growth and lateral stem production. Excessively short mowing can produce scalping and cause the turf to become thin and weed infested. High mowing can increase thatch accumulation. Mowing frequency is dependent on mowing height, shoot growth rate, turf use, fertilization and irrigation practices, and environmental conditions. In general, to prevent detrimental effects on grass growth and rooting, no more than 40% of the leaf area should be removed at one mowing.

Fertilization. To properly fertilize turf, it is necessary to have a basic understanding of how the soil provides nutrients, what affects nutrient availability, and how to control nutrients in different situations. Soil testing is an important aid in gathering this information and should be a part of every turf management program. Soil testing serves as a guideline in developing a sound fertilization program by providing information on pH, available nutrient levels, salt problems, and a wide range of chemical and physical characteristics. Most soil tests provide information about the nutrient levels present in a particular turf area and give recommendations, based on those levels, for appropriate fertilizer supplements. Soil samples should be taken 3–6 months before the most active growing season begins, to allow adequate time for applying lime and preparing the fertilization schedule.

If the soil is too acidic, a recommendation is made to add lime. If the soil is too alkaline, or basic, because of naturally occurring lime deposits such as those found in some coastal areas, there is little that can be done. Where the alkalinity has been created by an over application of lime, several approaches can be taken, including application of sulfur or of one of a selection of acid-forming nitrogen fertilizers such as ammonium sulfate or ammonium nitrate.

Macronutrients required by turfgrasses, also called major or primary nutrients, include nitrogen, phosphorus, potassium, calcium, magnesium, and sulfur. Nitrogen is the nutrient turfgrasses require in the largest amount, to maintain vigorous growth and sustain their perennial nature. However, because nitrogen levels change so rapidly in the soil, soil testing is not a reliable method for making nitrogen recommendations. Recom-

mended amounts of phosphorus, potassium, calcium, magnesium, and sulfur for fertilization, however, can be based on nutrient levels determined by the soil test. These levels are given within broad ranges and vary somewhat for different turfgrasses.

Calcium and magnesium are seldom a problem in soils that require lime. Dolomitic limestone, used to adjust soil pH, supplies both calcium and magnesium because it is a mixture of $CaCO_3$ and $MgCO_3$. If magnesium levels are adequate, use of calcitic limestone is suggested to increase soil pH. Where soil pH is at an optimum level but soil calcium is low, gypsum ($CaSO_4$) can be used to increase calcium levels. If, however, the soil is deficient in magnesium but requires no pH adjustment, then $MgSO_4$ (commonly called Epsom salts) can be used. A commonly used potassium source, Sul-Po-Mag®, is a mixture of potassium and magnesium sulfate and is an excellent source of potassium, sulfur, and magnesium. Sulfur is commonly supplied in potassium or nitrogen fertilizers and, naturally, through atmospheric deposition. When it is needed, it can be supplied in the sulfate form in nitrogen or potassium fertilizers.

Micronutrients required by turfgrasses include boron, chlorine, cobalt, copper, iron, manganese, molybdenum, and zinc. Of these nutrients, only copper, manganese, and zinc are routinely included in soil test reports. Soil tests provide reliable information on which to base fertilizer recommendations for these nutrients, which are most commonly deficient in the soil. Any deficiency of available manganese in the soil solution is highly dependent on pH and can usually be corrected by adjusting the soil pH. Iron is probably the most commonly deficient micronutrient in turf, but it is difficult to determine its availability by testing the soil. An analysis of chlorotic (yellow) plant tissue provides a good indication of iron deficiency and determines whether there is a need for corrective measures. Some grasses, such as bahiagrass and centipedegrass, routinely need iron applications in the spring when they first break dormancy. Cool-season grasses can benefit from iron applications at low rates during the summer months to stabilize turf color without forcing excessive growth.

Special consideration should be given when establishing new turf. This is the opportune time to incorporate lime, phosphorus, and potassium thoroughly into the root zone, because these nutrients move very slowly within the soil profile (applications made to the soil surface may move only 0.5–1 in [1.3–2.5 cm] in a year). By applying and thoroughly incorporating these materials into the soil before the turf is planted, liming materials and phosphorus fertilizers will be well distributed throughout the root zone and therefore available to the plants more quickly.

For established turf, the soil should be tested every 2–3 years to determine lime, phosphorus, and potassium requirements. A complete fertilizer with a ratio of nitrogen (N): phosphorus (P_2O_5): potash (K_2O) of 4:1:2 or 4:1:3 can be used in lieu of a soil test, but it is a poor substitute. Rates and schedules for fertilization vary depending on the type of grasses being grown. To reduce turf loss, avoid high nitrogen fertilization of cool-season grasses in late spring and summer and of warm-season grasses in fall and winter.

Irrigation. The water requirement of turfgrasses varies greatly depending on the turfgrass species, geographic location, solar radiation, relative humidity, wind movement, temperature, and soil moisture. Irrigation is important to ensure an adequate supply of moisture for turfgrass growth when there is insufficient rainfall. Lack of adequate water can lead to dormancy, injury, or death of the turfgrass. In many climates, although average annual rainfall should be adequate, timing of its occurrence does not always match turfgrass demand. In general, the cool-season grasses use more water than the warm-season species to produce a comparable amount of growth.

Supplementary Practices. Cultural practices that are important but not routinely scheduled include core cultivation, aerification, spiking, slicing, vertical mowing, topdressing, matting, use of wetting agents, and use of turf colorants. Core cultivation and aeration help to improve the physical characteristics of the soil by altering the bulk density and providing better water infiltration/percolation and air exchange. These practices are normally used on soils compacted by traffic or when layering has occurred as a result of improper topdressing programs. Opening channels within the turf profile greatly enhances rooting response by providing better oxygen/carbon dioxide exchange. This also creates a better environment for thatch decomposition. Vertical mowing is used to prevent grass from going to seed, to encourage more upright growth, and to remove excessive thatch. A topdressing of soil worked into the soil profile enhances thatch degradation by stimulating the growth of microorganisms.

Turf management includes development and implementation of cultural programs whose objectives are to maintain the turf in the healthiest possible condition and to minimize pest problems. Achieving these objectives requires a thorough understanding of turfgrass growth and development, interactions of the grasses with environmental factors, and a plan that integrates these practices into a total management program.

Table 1. Major cool-season and warm-season turfgrass species

Cool-season grasses		Warm-season grasses	
Common name	Species	Common name	Species
Colonial bentgrass	*Agrostis capillaris* Sibth.	Buffalograss	*Buchloe dactyloides* (Nutt.) Engelm.
Creeping bentgrass	*Agrostis palustris* Huds.	Bermudagrass	
Tall fescue	*Festuca arundinacea* Schreb.	Common	*Cynodon dactylon* L.
Fine fescues		Hybrid	*C. dactylon* L. x *C. transvaalensis*
Creeping Red	*Festuca rubra* ssp. *rubra* L.		Burt -Davy
Hard	*Festuca longifolia* Thuill.	Centipedegrass	*Eremochloa ophiuroides*
Chewings	*Festuca rubra* ssp. *commutata*		(Munro) Hack.
	Gaud.	Bahiagrass	*Paspalum notatum* Flügge
		Seashore paspalum	*Paspalum vaginatum* Sw.
Italian ryegrass	*Lolium multiflorum* Lam.	St. Augustinegrass	*Stenotaphrum secundatum*
Perennial ryegrass	*Lolium perenne* L.		(Walt.) Kuutze
Annual bluegrass		Japanese lawngrass	
Winter annual	*Poa annua* ssp. *annua* L.	(Zoysiagrass)	*Zoysia japonica* Stend.
Perennial	*Poa annua* ssp. *reptans* L.		
Kentucky bluegrass	*Poa pratensis* L.	Hybrid	*Z. japonica* x *Z. tenuifolia* Willd.
Rough bluegrass	*Poa trivialis* L.		

Selected References

Beard, J. B. 1973. Turfgrass: science and culture. Prentice-Hall, Englewood Cliffs, NJ.

Bruneau, A. H., J. M. DiPaola, G. L. Johnson, C. H. Peacock, W. M. Lewis, L. T. Lucas & R. L. Brandenburg. 1992. Temperatures and turf growth. North Carolina Cooperative Extension Service Fact Sheet.

Dudeck, A. E. & C. H. Peacock. 1992. Shade and turfgrass culture, pp. 269-284. *In* D. V. Waddington, R. N. Carrow and R. C. Shearman [eds.], Turfgrass. ASA, CSSA, SSSA, Madison, WI.

Jones, C. A. 1985. C_4 grasses and cereals. Wiley Interscience, New York.

Kneebone, W. R., D. M. Kopec & C. F. Mancino. 1992. Water requirements and irrigation, pp. 441-472. *In* Waddington, Carrow and Shearman [eds.], Turfgrass. ASA, CSSA, SSSA, Madison, WI.

Turgeon, A. J. 1991. Turfgrass management. Regents/Prentice Hall, Englewood Cliffs, NJ.

Status of Turfgrass Insect and Mite Pests in the United States

By Timothy J. Gibb and Wayne Buhler

Lawns in the United States occupy an area estimated at between 25 million and 30 million acres (10.1 million and 12.2 million hectares), 50,000 square mi, or roughly the size of the five New England states. Golf courses, athletic fields, and parks planted to turfgrass are becoming an increasingly important part of American recreational activities. Home lawns are a highly visible and valuable part of real estate. The already enormous area devoted to turfgrass in the United States continues to increase in direct correlation with population growth (Waddington et al. 1992).

In a 1988 survey conducted by the National Gardening Association, "gardening" was determined to be Americans' number one outdoor leisure activity and "lawn tending" the most popular gardening pursuit. More than 56 million Americans take part in their own lawn care. Between professional turfgrass management and homeowner lawn care, turf maintenance has become a $25,000,000,000 industry in the United States. Although turfgrass is widely grown, the economic value and management costs of turfgrass are often not appreciated. Consider the following facts. A typical town in the United States having a population of 170,000 people has:

• 1,338 acres (542 hectares) of turf in parks, cemeteries, and factory, school, and church yards, requiring 126 employees and $1.5 million to maintain
• 3,500 acres (1,418 hectares) of home lawns around 45,200 single family homes, costing $9 million to maintain
• 987 acres (400 hectares) of lawn around 19,600 apartments and condominiums, costing nearly $400,000 to maintain
• golf courses and bowling greens occupying another 600 acres (243 hectares) and requiring another $1.3 million to maintain.

In total, the 6,400 acres (2,592 hectares) of turfgrass in this town requires 166 professionals and over $13 million in maintenance costs (not including the time homeowners spend maintaining their own lawns) (Roberts & Roberts 1988).

A substantial portion of the maintenance budget, as well as time spent on lawn care, is devoted to insect/mite management (Danneberger 1993). Insects and mites may feed on all parts of the grass plant, including roots, stolons, stems, rhizomes, and foliage. Although a vast array of insect and mite species may potentially cause problems on turfgrass, only a small number of pests actually require control measures.

Successful management of turfgrass insect and mite pests depends, to a high degree, on the pest species, its population size, and the time of year that it begins to cause plant damage. Climatic conditions that define the regions in which cool- or warm-season turfgrasses are planted also define, to a certain extent, the species of insects and mites that may cause problems. Some insects and mites are adapted to regions with high temperatures where a lack of cold tolerance limits their survival. Others are adapted to areas of moderate temperature where precipitation and temperature define the limits of their survival. Within a specific geographic area, local weather conditions may further determine whether there will be an outbreak of a particular pest, in a given season.

A survey of turfgrass entomologists was conducted to determine which insect and mite pests are most damaging to turfgrass and which pests are perennial, as opposed to sporadic, in nature. The continental United States was divided into broad but similar geographic regions. Of the 26 insects and mites listed on the survey, seven were reported to be important turf pests throughout the country. Sod webworms were reported to be a common perennial problem throughout the continental United States with the exception of the Pacific Northwest, California, and the Southwest. Cutworms were reported as a perennial problem extending from the Northeast and eastern states throughout the Midwest and, occasionally, throughout the Northwest and the Pacific coast. Annual white grubs (masked chafers) were reported to be a perennial problem primarily in the midwestern states, Colorado, and Texas, and a sporadic problem in the Central Plains states, Florida, and California. Japanese beetles are serious pests throughout the eastern states and into the Midwest as far as Illinois. They are considered a perennial turfgrass pest wherever they occur. A smaller white grub, the black turfgrass ataenius, is considered a perennial pest in the New England states and a sporadic pest where it occurs in the Midwest, Central Plains, and California. Its pest activities are restricted to golf course fairways, tees, and greens. Chinch bugs are a common perennial pest in the Central Plains states, Texas, and Florida regions and are an occasional pest in the eastern and midwestern states depending on weather conditions. Billbugs are most commonly reported as sporadic pests in the northern states, from the Atlantic through the Midwest and western states, and into California.

Other perennial pests with much more localized distributions include the two-lined spittlebug, mole crickets, the red imported fire ant, and the green June beetle, which occur in the southern (primarily southeastern) states, and the annual bluegrass weevil, which occurs mostly in the Northeast. Other insect and mite pests not mentioned occur either as perennial pests in very localized areas or are considered very sporadic pests.

The distribution, abundance, and damage caused by a turfgrass pest varies depending on the geographic region in which it is found, local weather conditions, and cultural practices used to maintain the turf. Understanding the interactions between these factors is crucial to effective turf insect pest management.

Selected References

Danneberger T. K. 1993. Turfgrass ecology and management. Franzak and Foster G. I. E., Cleveland, OH.

Roberts E. C. & B. C. Roberts. 1988. Lawn and sports turf benefits. The Lawn Institute, Pleasant Hill, TN.

Waddington D. V., R. N. Carrow, & R. C. Shearman. 1992. Turfgrass monograph. American Society of Agronomy, Madison, WI.

Turfgrass Insect and Mite Pests by Injury Type

I. **Surface / Thatch Pests** (eat leaves and stems)

Armyworms (p. 24)
Cutworms (p. 46)
Sod webworms (p. 86)

II. **Surface / Thatch Pests** (discolor leaves and stems)

Bermudagrass and related eriophyid mites
(p. 29)
Chinch bugs (p. 38)
Clover and other noneriophyid mites (p. 42)
Greenbug (p. 60)
Mealybugs (p. 76)
Two-lined spittlebug (p. 88)

III. **Surface / Thatch Pests** (burrow into the stems)

Annual bluegrass weevil (p. 21)
Billbugs (p. 32)

IV. **Subsurface Pests** (attack the roots of grasses)

Asiatic garden beetle (p. 26)
Black turfgrass ataenius (p. 35)
Dichondra flea beetle (p. 48)
European chafer (p. 50)
Fall armyworm (p. 52)
Frit fly (p. 55)
Green June beetle (p. 57)
Ground pearls (p. 62)
Japanese beetle (p. 66)
Masked chafers (p. 70)
May and June beetles (p. 72)
Mole crickets (p. 78)
Oriental beetle (p. 81)

V. **Nuisance Pests** (live in turf habitat)

Chiggers (p. 91)
Cicada killers (p. 94)
Fleas (p. 91)
Harvester ants (p. 64)

Red imported fire ants (p. 84)
Ticks (p. 92)
Yellowjackets (p. 93)

Turfgrass Insect and Mite Pests by Scientific Classification

Phylum Arthropoda
  Class Arachnida
    Order Acari (ticks and mites)
      Family Argasidae (soft ticks)
        Ticks (p. 92)
      Family Ixodidae (hard ticks)
        Ticks (p. 92)
      Family Eriophyidae (eriophyid mites)
        Bermudagrass mite (p. 29)
      Family Tetranychidae (spider mites)
        Clover and other tetranychid mites (p. 42)
      Family Trombiculidae (chigger mites)
        Chigger (p. 91)

  Class Insecta
    Order Diptera (flies)
      Family Chloropidae (chloropid flies)
        Frit fly (p. 55)
    Order Orthoptera (grasshoppers and crickets)
      Family Gryllotalpidae (mole crickets)
        Mole crickets (p. 78)
    Order Siphonaptera (fleas)
      Family Ceratophyllidae (ceratophyllid fleas)
        Fleas (p. 91)
      Family Leptopsyllidae (leptopsyllid fleas)
        Fleas (p. 91)
      Family Pulicidae (pulicid fleas)
        Fleas (p. 91)
    Order Hemiptera (true bugs)
      Family Lygaeidae (seed bugs)
        Chinch bugs (p. 38)
    Order Hymenoptera (bees, ants, and wasps)
      Family Formicidae (ants)
        Red imported fire ant (p. 84)
        Harvester ants (p. 64)
      Family Sphecidae (digger wasps)
        Cicada killers (p. 94)
      Family Vespidae (wasps)
        Yellow jackets (p. 93)
    Order Homoptera (hoppers, scale, aphids, white flies psyllids, and cicadas)
      Family Aphididae (aphids)
        Greenbug (p. 60)
      Family Cercopidae (spittlebugs)
        Two-lined spittlebug (p. 88)
      Family Coccidae (soft scale insects)
        Ground pearls (p. 62)
      Family Pseudococcidae (mealybugs)
        Mealybugs (p. 76)
    Order Lepidoptera (moths and butterflies)
      Family Noctuidae (noctuid moths)
        Armyworm (p. 24)
        Cutworms (p. 46)
        Fall armyworm (p. 52)
        Sod webworms (p. 86)
    Order Coleoptera (beetles)
      Family Chrysomelidae (leaf beetles)
        Dichondra flea beetle (p. 48)
      Family Curculionidae (weevils or snout beetles)
        Annual bluegrass weevil (p. 21)
        Billbugs (p. 32)
      Family Scarabaeidae (scarab beetles)
        Asiatic garden beetle (p. 26)
        Black turfgrass ataenius (p. 35)
        European chafer (p. 50)
        Green June beetle (p. 57)
        Japanese beetle (p. 66)
        Masked chafers (p. 70)
        May and June beetles (p. 72)
        Oriental beetle (p. 81)

Key to Turfgrass Injury

by David J. Shetlar

1. a. Turf itself not normally damaged and not generally discolored (e.g., tunnels under sod, holes in turf, soil mounds, etc.) 2

   b. Turf damage appears as discoloration (e.g., browning, yellowing, streaking, or frosting) or has obvious feeding damage present (e.g., missing leaves or stems, ragged or chewed leaves). 13

2. a. Mounds of soil present (e.g., soil obviously brought to the surface) or tunnels under the sod (e.g., sod raised up into ridges). 3

   b. Soil not mounded or thrown into tunnels or ridges. 9

3. a. Tunnels running under the sod, periodic mounds may be built above the surface but these are associated with lateral tunnel(s). 4

   b. Soil mounds not associated with lateral tunnels, careful removal of mound usually reveals a hole going straight into the ground or ants present. 5

4. a. Tunnels 1–3 in (2.5–7.5 cm) in diameter; surface mounds usually 6–18 in (15–45 cm) in diameter. .... **Mammals (moles or pocket gophers)**

   b. Tunnels 0.5 in (12 mm) in diameter or less; surface mounds usually .... **1–2 in** (2.5–5.1 cm) in diameter as if something exited from the soil; usually in warm-season and transition turf zones. .... **Mole crickets (p. 78)**

5. a. Ants associated, mounds may be 1–3 in (2.5–7.5 cm) in diameter and resemble a small volcano with a hole in the middle (e.g., field ants), low and 1–3 ft (30–90 cm) in diameter with grass-cleared runways extending outward (e.g., harvester ants), or 6–18 in (15–45 cm) in diameter and resemble a rounded mountain (e.g., red imported fire ants and mound ants). Ants usually become active if nest or hole is disturbed. .... **Ants (pp. 64, 84)**

   b. Soil mounds not associated with ants, usually under 6 in (15 cm) in diameter. 6

6. a. Mounds built upward with mud not having turf leaves or stems incorporated, opening 1–2 in (2.5–5.0 cm) in diameter, usually near waterways or low, wet areas (e.g., road ditches). .... **Crayfish**

   b. Mounds with leaves and stems incorporated or mounds with loose soil. 7

7. a. Mounds 1–3 in (2.5–7.5 cm) in diameter, usually located within the turf canopy and thatch; mound material with leaves, thatch, and turf stems incorporated. .... **Earthworms, night crawlers**

   b. Mounds appear on top of turf canopy or as loose soil. 8

8. a. Mounds appear as extruded casings, as long sausages (Note: in sandy soils these extrusions may dry and fall into general mounds). .... **Earthworm castings**

   b. Mounds appear as loose soil, 1–3 in (2.5–7.5 cm) in diameter, with a 0.25–0.5 in (6–12 mm) open hole nearby. .... **Green June beetle grubs (p. 57),** .... **solitary wasps, shorttail crickets**

9. a. Turf spongy under foot, often can be pulled up easily. ...... **Scarab grubs (pp. 26, 35, 50, 57, 67, 70, 72, 81)**
    b. Soil under turf firm; turf merely thin, with clean holes or turf pulled back
       as in digging or scratching from some animal. 10
10. a. Turf sparse, close inspection of leaf blades usually reveals that something
       has chewed upon them (e.g., ragged edges). ....**Turf caterpillars (Armyworms [p. 24],**
       ....**cutworms [p. 46], webworms [p. 86])**
    b. Turf with holes or digging (scratching). 11
11. a. Holes present, appear as if pencil was stuck into turf and thatch in several
       locations. .... **Birds searching for insects**
    b. Holes or digging (scratching) otherwise. 12
12. a. Holes 0.5 in (12 mm) or smaller appear as if something broke through
       the turf from below, small amount of soil around hole rim. .... **Mole crickets (p. 78)**
    b. Turf ripped up, larger holes dug. .... **Animal digging** (e.g., raccoons, skunks, or
       armadillos digging for white grubs; squirrels depositing seeds; etc.)
13. a. Distinct brown, dead patches present. 14
    b. Turf alive, discoloration appears as yellowing, frosting (white color), or
       wilting of turf; or obvious feeding damage present. 21
14. a. Dead grass appearing as streaks or lines, often joining together to form
       larger general patches of dead turf. .... **Mole crickets (p. 78)**
    b. Dead patches more general in outline. 15
15. a. A pull on the dead patch indicates that the turf can be picked up like a
       loose carpet, soil spongy underneath. .... **Scarab grubs (pp. 26, 35, 50, 57, 67, 70, 72, 81)**
    b. Turf not loose like a carpet. 16
16. a. A sharp pulling of the grass stems from their tips, a "tug test", reveals
       that the stems break off easily and many of the stems are packed with
       a fine sawdustlike frass. .... **Billbugs (p. 32)**
    b. A "tug test" of the grass reveals that the stems are not broken and pulled
       out easily and are not packed with frass. 17
17. a. Dead patch consisting of mostly short stems and thatch, most of the leaf
       material is missing. ....**Turf caterpillars (armyworms [p. 24],**
       ....**cutworms [p. 46], webworms [p. 86])**
    b. Dead patch with stems and leaves present. 18
18. a. Dead turf appearing after snow melt, bases of grass stems still green,
       foliage appearing silvery or frosted; tiny black specks of fecal material
       on foliage visible with 10x hand lens, mainly cool-season turf. **Winter grain mite (p. 44)** (and other mites)
    b. Dead patches appearing during growing season. 19
19. a. Dead patches appearing as 1–3 in (2.5–7.5 cm) diameter spots, usually
       in spring or fall; small yellow-brown maggots with black head capsules
       present at base. .... **March fly**
    b. Dead patches larger and more irregular. 20
20. a. Dead patches usually yellow, turning to brown; appear in summer, usually
       under the shade of trees or along sides of buildings; ryegrass and
       bluegrass usually affected; small green aphids on grass blades
       surrounding dead areas. .... **Greenbug (aphid) (p. 60)**
    b. Dead patches usually yellow, turning straw colored, in full sun; appear in
       summer in cool-season turf, anytime in warm-season turf; ryegrass,
       bluegrass, and bentgrass in north; bermudagrass and St. Augustinegrass
       in south. .... **Chinch bugs (p. 38)**
21. a. Turf discoloration caused by feeding on the foliage (ragged edges on
       leaves or no discoloration present but foliage thin or ragged). 29

b. Turf yellowed, silvered, white frosted, or ashgray; no foliage damage evident. 22

22. a. Turf appears silvered, white frosted, or ashgray; usually in cool part of
   year or after snow melt; tiny black specks of fecal material on
   foliage visible with 10x hand lens, mainly cool-season turf. .... **Winter grain mite (p. 44) or**
   .... **Clover mite (p. 42)**

b. Turf appears yellowed or a green, wilted gray. 23

23. a. Turf turns a wilted gray-green, appears greasy, usually in afternoon sun. ....
   .... **Scarab grubs (pp. 26, 35, 50, 57, 67, 70, 72, 81)**

b. Turf yellowed, either on single blades and leaves or by general area discoloration. 24

24. a. Bases of yellowed turf with spittlelike material; warm-season turf. .... **Two-lined spittlebug (p. 88)**

b. No spittlelike material in soil/thatch area. 25

25. a. Individual grass stems or small groups of stems beginning to yellow; a
   "tug test" on these yellow stems reveals that they break off easily and
   are packed with sawdustlike frass or a small grub is present in the stem. .... **Billbugs (p. 32)**

b. Individual yellowed stems do not break off easily or yellowing is more
   general in pattern. 26

26. a. Small, pear-shaped insects present on leaves of yellowing turf. .... **Greenbug (aphid) (p. 60)**

b. Insects not easily visible on surface of leaves. 27

27. a. Inspection along leaf stems, under leaf sheaths, or along rhizomes and
   stolons reveals cottony or waxy coating present; removal of this material
   or crushing results in the production of pink to burgundy-colored liquid. ....
   .... **Various scales or Mealybugs (p. 76)**

b. No cottony or waxy material located on stems, under leaf sheaths, or
   along rhizomes and stolons. 28

28. a. Inspection at base of stems in area where turf is turning yellow reveals the
   presence of black and white, 0.13 in (3 mm) long bugs or red to orange
   nymphs (or both). .... **Chinch bugs (p. 38)**

b. No insects present at base of plants or in thatch; digging in soil under
   plants reveals 0.03–0.13 in (1–3 mm) diameter yellow to pinkish
   spheres with a pearly iridescence, some attached to roots or merely
   free in soil; usually on warm-season bermudagrass, centipedegrass, and
   zoysiagrasses. .... **Ground pearls (p. 62)**

29. a. Turf sparse, leaves generally removed; inspection at base of plants, in thatch,
   reveals numerous gray-tan maggots, 0.38–1.0 in (1.0–2.5 cm) long;
   usually Pacific Northwest turf. .... **Crane fly larvae**

b. Turf sparse, leaf margins often with ragged edges; short turf on golf course
   (i.e., putting greens) chewed down, close to soil. 30

30. a. Taller turf, leaf margins ragged, pelletlike frass usually present in thatch.
   .... **Turf caterpillars (Armyworms [p. 24],**
   .... **cutworms [p. 46], webworms [p. 86])**

b. Short turf (i.e., golf course putting greens and tees) with well-defined
   spots cropped down to soil level. .... **Cutworm (p. 46)**

Key to Invertebrate Turfgrass Pests

by David J. Shetlar

1. a. Body more or less divided into segments or distinct regions, with or without legs. 3
   b. Body not obviously divided into segments or body regions, no legs present,
      with or without shell. 2
2. a. Body round and worm-shaped, pointed at both ends, constantly wiggling
      but never shortening (Phylum Nematoda). .... **Roundworms**
   b. Body robust, often with a shell (snails) or without (slugs) (Phylum Mollusca). .... **Snails and Slugs**
3. a. Body without an obvious head capsule or mouth hooks (insect maggots
      often withdraw the mouth hooks); body usually consisting of numerous,
      similar ringlike segments; body never with legs or appendages
      (Phylum Annelida). .... **Earthworms**
   b. Body usually with obvious head (or cephalothorax) and trunk (thorax,
      abdomen) regions; body usually with external, jointed appendages
      (e.g., legs, antennae, palps, etc.) (Phylum Arthropoda). 4
4. a. Body with obvious legs. 5
   b. Body without obvious legs. 51
5. a. Four (4) pairs of legs present; no antennae (Class Arachnida). 6
   b. Never four pairs of legs present; usually three pairs or more than ten pairs
      present; antennae present. 7
6. a. Body regions (cephalothorax and abdomen) divided by a narrow waist
      (Order Arachnida). .... **Spiders**
   b. Body regions (cephalothorax and abdomen) broadly attached (Order Acari). .... **Mites and Ticks**
7. a. Body with head and trunk regions, more than five pairs of legs present
      (Note: caterpillars have false legs [prolegs] on the abdomen; the three
      true legs end in a single or double claw, the prolegs end in multiple hooks) (Fig. 1). 8

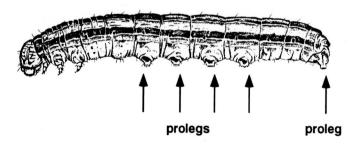

prolegs   **proleg**

Fig. 1. Prolegs on abdomen of caterpillar (7 a & b).

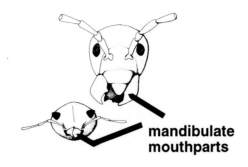

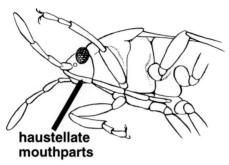

mandibulate mouthparts

haustellate mouthparts

Fig. 2. (Top) Example of mandibulate or chewing mouthparts (16 a). (Bottom) Example of haustellate or sucking mouthparts (16 b).

 b. Body with head, thorax, and abdominal regions; three pairs of legs present
   on thorax (Note: caterpillars may have two to six pairs of prolegs on
   the abdomen) (some insect larvae have no legs [go to 51]) (Class Insecta).
   Insects. 10
8. a. Legs attached to underside of trunk, appear to be joined into units of
      two pairs of legs per trunk segment, occasionally single pairs of legs
      are found about 1/3 of body length behind head (sexual organs);
      usually 30 pairs of legs or more (Class Diplopoda). ....**Millipedes**
   b. Legs not moved in units of two pairs. 9
9. a. Body with seven pairs of legs; sides of body extending over place where
      legs attach Class Crustacea, (Order Isopoda). ....**Sowbugs and Pillbugs**
   b. Body with 15 pairs of legs or more; front legs modified into pincherlike
      fangs under head (Class Chilopoda). ....**Centipedes**
10. a. Insects with wings, or at least short wings. 11
    b. Insects without wings (usually nymphs or larvae). 28
11. a. Wings cellophanelike (Note: wings may be colored or covered with scales
       or hair), not hardened or leathery; one or two pairs present. 12
    b. Front wings leathery, hardened, or even shell-like, at least at base; hind wings
       usually cellophanelike. 16
12. a. Only one pair of wings present (usually Diptera). 13
    b. Two pairs of wings present. 14
13. a. Pair of wings usually with four or more obvious veins; no waxy filaments
       attached to abdomen. .... **Flies, Gnats, Midges (p. 55)**
    b. One or two veins present in wings, if any; usually with two long waxy filaments
       attached to abdomen. .... **Scales and Mealybugs (p. 76)**
14. a. Wings covered with flat scales, mouthparts usually a coiled tube or absent
       (Order Lepidoptera).butterflies and moths.
       .... **Cutworms (p. 46), Armyworms (pp. 24, 52), Skippers, and Sod Webworms (p. 86)**
    b. Wings without scales but hairs may be present. 15
15. a. Body constricted between thorax and abdomen. ....**Ants (pp. 64, 84), Bees, Wasps (p. 93)**

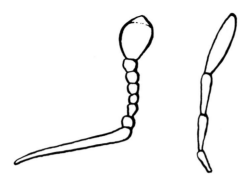

Fig. 3. Antenna ending in a distinct club (left) (19 a) and thread- or beadlike antenna that gradually tapers (right) (19 b).

      b. Body pear-shaped, not constricted; pair of small tubes (cornicles) arising
          from end of abdomen (Family Aphididae). .... **Winged Aphids, Greenbug (p. 60)**

16. a. Mandibulate or chewing mouthparts present (Fig. 2). 17
      b. Haustellate or sucking mouthparts present (Fig. 2). 25

17. a. Abdomen ending in a pair of forcepslike "pinchers" or cerci (Order Dermaptera). .... **Earwigs**
      b. Abdomen with no forcepslike cerci, either threadlike or absent. 18

18. a. Front wings without obvious veins, shell-like and joined together down
          the middle of the back when at rest (Note: rove beetles have short front
          wings and look like earwigs with no caudal pinchers) (Order Coleoptera).
          beetles. 19
      b. Front wings with obvious veins though wings may be leathery; usually
          held rooflike over body or overlapping (Order Orthoptera).crickets
          and grasshoppers. .... 23 (p. 78)

19. a. Antennae ending in a distinct club (swelling or knob) (Fig. 3). 20
      b. Antennae threadlike or beadlike, gradually tapering toward end (Fig. 3). 22

20. a. Front wing covers very short, most of abdomen exposed (Family Staphylinidae). .... **Rove beetles**
      b. Front wing covers covering most of abdomen. 21

21. a. Head ending in a distinct beak or snout (Family Curculionidae). .... **Weevils and Billbugs (pp. 21, 32)**
      b. No beak; antennal club consisting of flat plates (Family Scarabaeidae).
         .... **Scarabs (pp. 26, 35, 66, 81), Chafers (pp. 50, 70), White grubs (pp. 57, 72)**

22. a. Slender, elongate beetles, capable of making a "snapping" noise when
         turned over (Family Elateridae). .... **Click beetles, Wireworms**
      b. Variable-shaped beetles, not capable of making a "snapping" noise when turned
         over (Family Carabidae). .... **Ground beetles**

23. a. Front legs modified into large digging organs, like moles (Family Gryllotalpidae).
         .... **Mole crickets (p. 78)**
      b. Front legs not so modified. 24

24. a. Antennae short, not longer than body, usually only extending past thorax
         (Family Acrididae). .... **Grasshoppers**
      b. Antennae very long, usually longer than body and extending well past thorax
         (Family Gryllidae). .... **Crickets**

25. a. Forewings leathery in front, ending in a (usually clear) membrane; sucking
         beak arising from front of head (Order Hemiptera). True bugs. 26
      b. Forewings same texture and color throughout; sucking beak arising from
         back of head, between legs (Order Homoptera). Aphids, leafhoppers, etc. .... 27 (pp. 60, 62, 76, 88)

26. a. Width between eyes equal to or about equal to the widest part of body. .... **Bigeyed bugs**
      b. Width between eyes equal to half the widest part of the body, at most. .... **Chinch bugs (p. 38)**

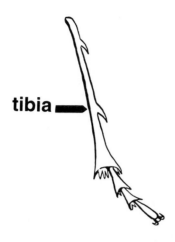

tibia

Fig. 4. Circlet of spines on hindleg tibia
(27 a).

27. a. Hind leg tibia with a circlet of spines; body usually oval or boat-shaped
       in outline (Family Cercopidae) (Fig. 4). .... **Spittlebugs (p. 88)**
     b. Hind leg tibia with simple row(s) of spines; body usually more wedge-shaped
       in outline (Family Cicadellidae) (Fig. 5). .... **Leafhoppers**
28. a. Insect body laterally compressed (flattened sideways); small, 0.04–0.08 in
       (1–2 mm); active jumpers and biters (Order Siphonaptera). .... **Fleas (p. 91)**
     b. Insect body round or flattened (top to bottom). 29
29. a. Antlike; body with distinct constriction between thorax and abdomen;
       antennae elbowed and ending in a distinct club; if antennae not elbowed,
       then body covered with hair (Order Hymenoptera). 30
     b. Body otherwise, abdomen usually broadly joined to thorax. 31
30. a. Thorax or abdomen (or both) covered with short hair; usually brightly
       colored with red, orange, or yellow; antennae not elbowed (Family Mutillidae). .... **Velvet ants**
     b. Thorax and abdomen bare or with few scattered hairs; usually brown,
       reddish brown, or black; antennae distinctly elbowed with club at end
       (Family Formicidae). .... **Ant workers (p. 64)**
31. a. Grublike, white to light tan, C-shaped larvae with tan to brown head
       capsules; body cuticle thin though may be covered with long and
       short hairs; prolegs not present (Family Scarabaeidae) (various larvae
       of scarabs) (Fig. 6). .... **Scarab grubs (pp. 26, 35, 50, 57, 67, 70, 72, 81)**
     b. Insects more elongate, not C-shaped; if grublike, then conspicuous leglike
       prolegs present on abdominal segments. 32

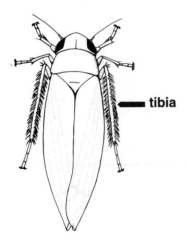

tibia

Fig. 5. Row of spines on hind leg of tibia
(27 b)

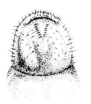

Fig. 6. Scarab raster patterns (31 b). (Top, Left to Right) Japanese beetle, European chafer, oriental beetle, black turfgrass ataenius. (Bottom, Left to Right) June beetle (*Phyllophaga anxia*), Asiatic garden beetle, northern masked chafer, and green June beetle.

32. a. Insects caterpillarlike; thick, round bodies with at least two pairs of prolegs (thick, leglike organs on the abdomen [see 7 a & b]) (Order Lepidoptera). Cutworms, sod webworms, armyworms, loopers, etc. 45
    b. Insects not caterpillarlike; without prolegs (see 7 a & b). 33
33. a. Insects with chewing mouthparts (see 16 a). 34
    b. Insects with sucking mouthparts (see 16 b). 39
34. a. Small insects, usually 0.06 in (2 mm) or less; a forked organ is attached to abdomen that allows the insects to jump when disturbed (Order Collembola). .... Springtails
    b. Larger, more than 0.06 in (2 mm); no forked jumping organ attached to abdomen. 35
35. a. Insects with jumping hind legs (e.g., crickets and grasshoppers). 36
    b. Insects that run or walk but do not jump when disturbed. 38
36. a. Front legs expanded into digging organs (Family Gryllotalpidae). .... Mole cricket nymphs (p. 78)
    b. Front legs normal, used for walking. 37
37. a. Antennae short, never extending beyond the thorax (Family Acrididae). .... Grasshopper nymphs
    b. Antennae long, extending beyond the thorax and often longer than the body (Family Gryllidae). .... Cricket nymphs
38. a. Abdomen ending in forcepslike cerci (Order Dermaptera). .... Earwig nymphs
    b. Abdomen with no appendage at tip or if an appendage is present, it is segmented or consists of a rigid forklike structure (Order Coleoptera). Ground beetles, rove beetles, lady beetles, etc. .... Beetle larvae
39. a. Tiny insects, usually less than 0.04 in (1 mm); tarsi one-segmented, ending in a balloonlike pad; mouthparts appear as a cone located between the front legs (Order Thysanoptera). .... Thrips nymphs
    b. Tarsi with two or more segments, ending in distinct claws; mouthparts appear as tubelike projection from front or rear of head. 40
40. a. Beak arising from front of head, usually folded under head and extending between legs; antennae always threadlike (Order Hemiptera). True bugs (e.g., chinch bug, bigeyed bugs, etc.) (Fig. 7). 41

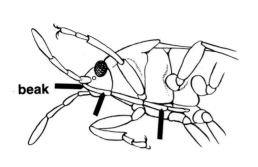
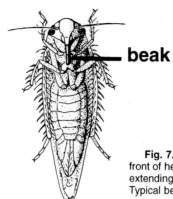

Fig. 7. (Left) Typical beak arising from front of head, folded under head and extending between legs (40 a). (Right) Typical beak arising at rear of head (40 b).

    b. Beak arising at rear of head under surface; antennae usually bristlelike, occasionally threadlike (Order Homoptera) (Fig. 7). 42

41. a. Width of head distinctly less than width of body; nymphs usually have distinct white band across back of abdomen. .... **Chinch bug nymphs (p. 38)**

    b. Width of head about same width as body or wider; nymphs usually completely tan, gray, or black. .... **Bigeyed bug nymphs**

42. a. Nymphs located within spittlelike mass; boat-shaped; hind tibia ending in ring of stout spines (Family Cercopidae) (see 27). .... **Spittlebug nymph (p. 88)**

    b. Nymphs not located within a spittlelike mass. 43

43. a. Nymphs very active; wedge-shaped; hind tibia used for jumping; antennae bristlelike (Family Cicadellidae). .... **Leafhopper nymphs**

    b. Nymphs pear-shaped or sac-shaped; hind tibia not used for jumping. 44

44. a. Nymphs pear-shaped; antennae long; tip of abdomen ending in a pair of tubelike structures; legs long and thin (Family Aphididae). .... **Aphids, Greenbug (p. 60)**

    b. Nymphs saclike; antennae short; legs short; body often covered with white, waxy coating; usually located under leaf sheath or at crown of plant (Family Pseudococcidae). .... **Mealybugs (p. 76)**

45. a. Caterpillar with a general covering of furlike bristles; thorax distinctly constricted behind head (Family Hesperiidae). .... **Skipper butterfly larvae**

    b. Caterpillar with a few scattered bristles or hairs; thorax not constricted. 46

46. a. Caterpillar with only two to three pairs of prolegs; moves in an inchworm manner (see 32). **Grass loopers**

    b. Caterpillar with four to five pairs of prolegs. 47

47. a. Crochets on prolegs (tiny hooks on end of proleg) arranged in two circles; body with distinct (and usually darkly pigmented) plates appearing as spots down the body, each with one or two hairs; caterpillars usually located within silken tubes in thatch (Family Pyralidae) (Fig. 8). .... **Sod webworms (p. 86)**

    b. Crochets on prolegs arranged in half circle or if in a circle three or more rings of hooks are present; body with distinct stripes or markings or with a general, overall coloration and texture (Fig. 8) 48

48. a. Crochets on prolegs arranged in circles, one series of large hooks and several of small hooks; pronotum distinctly hardened and darkly pigmented; body with a general, fine roughened surface; larvae usually in tightly woven tubes extending into the soil (Family Acrolophidae) (Fig. 8).

    .... **Burrowing Sod webworms (p. 86)**

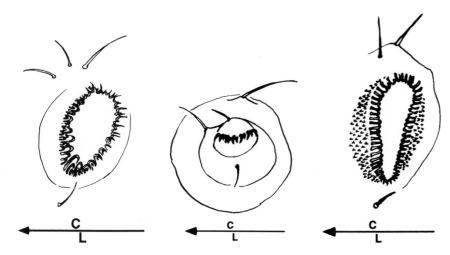

C
L

c
L

c
L

Fig. 8. (Left) Crochets (hooks on end of proleg) arranged in two circles (47 a). (Middle) Crochets (hooks on end of proleg) arranged in half circle (47 b, 48 b). (Right) Crochets (hooks on end of proleg) arranged in cricles, one series of large hooks and several small hooks (48 a).

    b. Crochets arranged in a half circle; larvae not usually with silken tubes
       (Family Noctuidae) (Fig. 8). Cutworms and armyworms. 49

49. a. Body generally of the same color and texture; only faint stripes down the
       body; under microscope, cuticle is covered with fine pebblelike surface. .... **Black cutworms (p. 46)**
    b. Body generally with distinct stripes. 50

50. a. Larvae with brown or bronze stripes; distinct dark brown pronotal plate
       with four white stripes; larvae usually in soil/thatch area in fall and spring. ...... **Bronzed cutworms (p. 46)**
    b. Larvae with various colored stripes; if brown striped, pronotum
       is not as above. .... **Various Armyworms (pp. 24, 52)**

51. a. Insect found under a white, oval waxy shell; usually located on stolons
       or at crown of bermudagrass plants. .... **Bermudagrass scales (p. 29)**
    b. Insect not located under a waxy shell. 52

52. a. Insect grublike, with a head capsule and plump body. 53
    b. Insect elongate, maggotlike or wormlike. 54

53. a. Grubs found as separate individuals; head capsule usually tan to brown;
       body thickest before tip of abdomen (Family Curculionidae). .... **Billbug or Weevil larvae (p. 32)**
    b. Grubs usually found in clusters; head capsule usually clear, same color as rest
       of body; body thickest at tip of abdomen (Family Formicidae). .... **Ant larvae (pp. 64, 84)**

54. a. Larva with a distinct, black head capsule; often found in clusters under
       dead patches of turf or in decaying thatch (Family Bibionidae). .... **March fly larvae**
    b. Larva without a distinct head capsule or head capsule easily withdrawn
       into front of body when disturbed. 55

55. a. Larva usually white, located within the stem of a grass plant; only small,
       black mouth hooks visible. .... **Frit fly larvae (p. 55)**
    b. Larva free-living, never within plant stems; larva usually gray or greenish
       brown; head appears as a small, black-pointed capsule, capable of being
       withdrawn into the front part of the body when disturbed (Family
       Tipulidae). .... **Crane fly larvae (=Leatherjackets)**

Pest Information

The following information is provided for specific insect pest species. This information follows a uniform format, but more information is provided for species that are of greater importance.

Common Name

Scientific Classification. The genus and species, followed by (Order: Family).

Origin and Distribution. An indication of whether the insect is native or introduced and its approximate distribution.

Description. Identification details for immatures and adults.

Pest Status. The economic importance of the pest.

Injury. How the pest injures turfgrass.

Life History. Details on the pest's life cycle with such information as number of generations, overwintering stage, number of offspring, and development time.

Management. General comments on approaches for managing the pest. Recommendations for specific management options in a given area can be obtained through sources listed in *Sources of Local Information.*

Selected References. Sources for additional information.

Range Map. A map of North America indicating the distribution of the pest. These distributions are only approximations, pests may sometimes occur outside the areas indicated on the map.

Generation Chart. An indication of the life cycle of the pest.

Illustrations. Life stage drawings, actual-size silhouettes, and color photographs of representative species.

Annual Bluegrass Weevil

Annual bluegrass weevil adult (courtesy NYSAES [G. Catlin]).

Scientific Classification. *Listronotus maculicollis* (Dietz), formerly *Hyperodes* sp. near *anthracinus* (Dietz) (Coleoptera: Curculionidae, Cylindrorhininae).

Origin and Distribution. The genus *Listronotus* is native to North, Central, and South America. *L. maculicollis* has been reported in several states in the northeastern United States. The center of distribution is metropolitan New York, including southeastern New York, Long Island, southwestern Connecticut, and northern New Jersey. Turf damage caused by the annual bluegrass weevil has also been reported in eastern and central Pennsylvania and all of the New England states.

Description. The annual bluegrass weevil adult is a relatively small weevil (0.125 in [3.2 mm] long) that is generally black or dark gray. It is covered with fine hairs and scales that wear off as the weevil ages. The thorax is about one-third as long as the abdomen, and the snout is relatively broad and short. (In contrast, billbugs, insects that are sometimes confused with the annual bluegrass weevil, have a thorax about one-half as long as the abdomen and the snout is relatively long and narrow.) The antennae are attached near the tip of the snout, but can be folded back along the side of the snout in a compact groove. Eggs are deposited between leaf sheaths of annual bluegrass plants. These eggs are about three times as long as they are wide (about 0.05 in [1.3 mm] long), rounded at both ends, and smoky gray. Usually a female places two or three eggs end to end inside the sheath. The larva is a typical weevil larva: creamy white, legless, sclerotized brown head capsule, slightly broader in the middle than at either end. There are five instars, each lasting about 5–7 days. All instars are similar in appear-

Annual bluegrass weevil mature larva (courtesy NYSAES [G. Catlin])

lantic States, Northeast, and perhaps the Midwest could experience infestations from annual bluegrass weevils.

Injury. The larva is the primary damaging stage, because it feeds inside the annual bluegrass stem during its early development and then on the crowns of plants as it matures. One larva can kill several plants during its lifetime. Damage first appears as a wilt, as the turf turns a straw color, but the turf does not respond to watering. Damage usually begins along the edges of fairways, particularly near woods, or on the perimeters of putting greens or tees. As the growing season progresses, damage may occur farther into the center of fairways, greens, or tees. Damage usually becomes apparent during late May or early June in the metropolitan New York area, with a second period of damage in late July or early August. Adults chew notches in the sides of grass blades, but this does not appear to be particularly detrimental to the plant.

Life History. In most years, the annual bluegrass weevil appears to be bivoltine in the metropolitan New York area and southern New England. In more northern latitudes, one generation may be the norm. Adults spend the winter in leaf or pine litter under trees relatively near the fairways. (White pine [*Pinus strobus* L.] appears to be a favorite overwintering site.) In the spring, adults begin to migrate across the roughs to the fairways, greens, or tees when *Forsythia* spp. is approaching full bloom. They begin laying eggs in early May (shortly before flowering dogwood, *Cornus florida* L., full bract). After 5–7 days, the larvae emerge. They complete their development through the five instars in about 4 weeks, so by early to mid-June, the bulk of the population is present as large larvae. The pupal stage lasts about 5–7 days, and young ("callow") adults emerge in late June or early July. The new adults are active on the surface of the turf, particularly on sunny days, for several days. They lay eggs around mid-July, and small larvae emerge a few days lat-

ance and differ only in size, ranging from 0.05 in (1.3 mm) (first instar) to 0.2 in (5.1 mm) (fifth instar). The first and second instars remain inside the plant tissue to feed, but later instars move along the exterior of the plant to the crown to feed. Later instars spend part of their time in the upper soil profile. The prepupa retains most of the larval characteristics, except that the thoracic segments are distended so that the prepupa does not have the same kinds of "folds" as the larva. The prepupa is a bit longer than the fifth instar and occurs only in the soil. The tip of the abdomen often rotates in a distinctive manner. The pupa has many of the characteristics of the adult. The snout and legs are tucked under the thorax, and the wings are folded along the side of the abdomen. When the pupa first emerges from the skin of the fifth instar, it is creamy white, but as it matures, the eyes, mandibles, tarsal claws, beak, and legs gradually darken.

Pest Status. The annual bluegrass weevil is a major pest of short-cut annual bluegrass (*Poa annua*) in the metropolitan New York area. Any closely mown annual bluegrass (less than 0.75 in [1.9 cm]) in the Middle At-

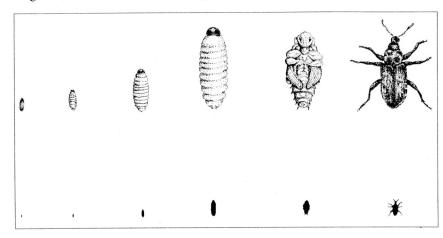

Egg, 1st, 3rd, and 5th larval instar, pupa, and adult of the annual bluegrass weevil. Silhouettes show actual size of each stage.

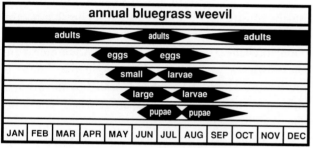

annual bluegrass weevil											
adults			adults			adults					
		eggs		eggs							
		small		larvae							
			large		larvae						
				pupae		pupae					
JAN	FEB	MAR	APR	MAY	JUN	JUL	AUG	SEP	OCT	NOV	DEC

er to repeat the cycle. The bulk of the population is present as large larvae again in early August. Most individuals pupate in late August, although a few pupae have been observed as late as September. Adults emerge in late summer and return to overwintering sites by the end of October. Every year there is considerable overlap of generations, so from mid-June through early September, all stages can be found at any given time. However, the overall distribution of the population is fairly constant and follows the pattern described above.

Management. To monitor annual bluegrass weevils, cut turf cores with a cup cutter (4.25 in [10.8 cm] diameter), break up the soil, and tear the thatch gently. Remove any insects with forceps and place them in a small dish or jar. All of the plant and soil material should be placed in a small dishpan, which then should be filled with lukewarm water. Any larvae, pupae, or adults that were not observed during the initial finger inspection will float to the surface of the water in 5–10 minutes. Adult weevils are attracted to light traps, particularly during the spring when they are moving from their overwintering sites to short-cut annual bluegrass. The tolerance level for annual bluegrass weevils varies depending on the general vigor of the turf, the amount of annual bluegrass present in an area, the height of cut, and de-

mands of the users. If a golf course has adequate water, particularly during the two most critical damage periods (early June and early August), the turf often can tolerate 30–50 larvae per square ft (0.09 m²) (three to five larvae per cup cutter plug). However, as a result of tournament schedules or user expectations, some managers are forced to use lower tolerance levels.

Traditional insecticides are currently the only recognized means of controlling or suppressing annual bluegrass weevil populations. Spring applications should be made between forsythia full bloom and dogwood full bract. These applications target adults as they begin to lay eggs. No degree-day model has been found to predict optimum timing for spring applications. In the metropolitan New York area, insecticide applications may also be made in early July, targeting the second-generation adults as they emerge and before they lay eggs. A degree-day predictive model is being developed to optimize the timing of that application, but in most years it will be within a week (before or after) of 4 July.

Selected References

Cameron, R. S. & N. E. Johnson. 1971. Biology of a species of *Hyperodes* (Coleoptera: Curculionidae), a pest of turfgrass. Search Agric., (Geneva, NY) 1(7).

Vittum, P. J. 1980. The biology and ecology of the annual bluegrass weevil, *Hyperodes* sp. near *anthracinus* (Dietz) (Coleoptera: Curculionidae). Ph.D. dissertation, Cornell University, Ithaca, NY.

Vittum, P. J. & H. Tashiro. 1987. Seasonal activity of *Listronotus maculicollis* (Coleoptera: Curculionidae) on annual bluegrass. J. Econ. Entomol. 80: 773–778.

—Patricia J. Vittum

Armyworm

Armyworm moth (courtesy NYSAES [G. Catlin]).

Scientific Classification. *Pseudaletia unipuncta* (Haworth) (Lepidoptera: Noctuidae). Former scientific names include *Cirphis unipuncta* and *Leucania extranea*.

Origin and Distribution. The armyworm is a native species, found throughout the United States and southern Canada east of the Rocky Mountains, with scattered populations along the Pacific coast. It is also found in Mexico, northwestern South America, and, sporadically, in western Europe.

Description. The pearly white, about 0.02 in [0.5 mm] diameter eggs are deposited in masses by the female moth. Young larvae are pale green. Mature larvae range from 1.4 to 2.0 in (35–50 mm) long with a yellowish or gray background color and distinct longitudinal stripes on the back and sides. The head capsule is honeycombed with dark lines. Armyworm larvae may be confused with fall armyworm larvae. Fall armyworm larvae have a distinct white inverted Y on the front of the head capsule and four distinct black dots on the dorsal side of each abdominal segment. Armyworm larvae lack teeth on the mandibles; fall armyworm larvae have well-defined mandibular teeth. Feeding habits may also be used to distinguish the two species. Armyworm larvae feed primarily on grasses and grains. Fall armyworm larvae feed on many herbaceous plants in addition to grasses. Pupation occurs in the soil or under organic material at a depth of 1 in (2.5 cm) or less. A small, silk-lined cell is usually constructed before pupation. The 0.5–0.7 in (13–17 mm) long pupa is initially reddish brown and gradually changes to black as it matures. Adult moths are pale brown to grayish brown. The wingspan is about 1.6 in (40 mm). The adults can be identified by the distinct white spot in the center of the front wing. The hind wing is a dirty white.

Pest Status. Armyworm larvae feed on a wide range of grasses. They are especially attracted to small grains, such as wheat, oats, barley, rye, and rice; pasture grasses of all types; large-stem grasses, such as corn, sugarcane, millet, and sorghum; some legumes; and fine turfgrasses. In most cases, turfgrasses are less likely to be attacked. A

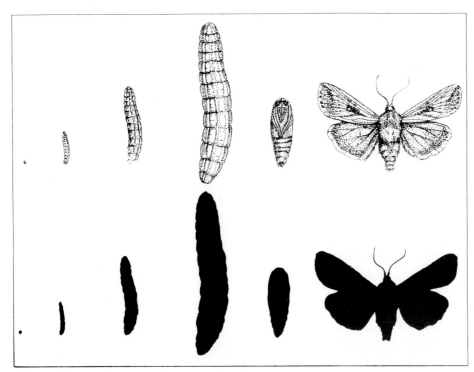

Egg, first, intermediate (third), and final larval instar, pupa, and adult of the armyworm. Silhouettes show actual size of each stage.

Lawn armyworm mid-instar larva (courtesy NYSAES, [H. Tashiro]).

wide variety of herbaceous plants may be attacked when food supplies are limited.

Injury. Young larvae begin to feed on tender foliage near the top of the plant. Feeding injury by the first two instars is characterized by skeletonized foliage. The third through sixth instars consume all or part of the leaf. When populations are high, feeding produces circular bare areas in fine turfgrass.

Life History. In the southern and middle portions of the United States, the armyworm overwinters as partially grown larvae or as pupae. In the northern portions of its range, the armyworm may overwinter as partially grown larvae (New Brunswick) or be present as migrant adults in the spring (New York and Ontario). Eggs are deposited in narrow, tight places such as the space between the sheath and blade of growing grass or in similar locations in dried, cut grasses and corn. The eggs are deposited in narrow bands of a few to several hundred. There are usually two to five rows of eggs. In the laboratory, an individual female may produce more than 14,000 eggs. The incubation period is temperature-dependent, ranging from 3 to 24 days in Tennessee and from 3 to 33 days in Ontario, under field conditions. The first instars consume the egg-shell before feeding on plant material. Larvae usually go through six instars, but may go through nine instars at low temperatures. The larval period ranges from 20 to 48 days (average 28) under summer conditions. The pupal stage averages 15 days in length (range, 7–40 days). Pupation occurs in the soil. Adult moths are active at night, with most flight activity occurring within 2 hours after sunset. The number of adult flights varies within the armyworm's range. There are four to five flights from Tennessee south, three flights in the middle portion of its range, and two flights

in the northern areas (New York and southern Canada). A wide range of natural enemies has been reported. Parasites and diseases usually act to keep populations in check. True to its common name, the armyworm periodically experiences population explosions and moves en masse, consuming the vegetation in its path. These population explosions usually occur after drought conditions.

Management. Because populations fluctuate so much from generation to generation and from year to year, it is difficult to provide specific action levels for the armyworm. Turfgrass managers need to be aware that armyworms prefer small grains and other types of "crop" grasses. Turf areas near susceptible field crops are at a higher risk. Turfgrass managers should also be very attentive during the season following a drought. The highest populations usually develop early in the year. If adult moths are observed in an area, turfgrass managers should begin scouting for larval activity. Because the larvae tend to remain concealed during the day, a detergent flush is a useful tool for sampling larval populations. One to 2 fluid oz (30–60 ml) of liquid dishwashing detergent per gallon (3.8 liters) of water should be used. The detergent solution aggravates the larvae and causes them to come to the surface. A gallon (3.8 liters) should cover a 4-ft^2 (3,716-cm^2) area.

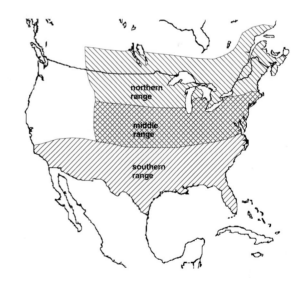

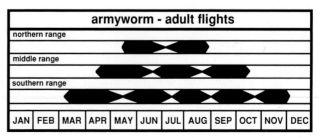

armyworm - adult flights											
northern range											
middle range											
southern range											
JAN	FEB	MAR	APR	MAY	JUN	JUL	AUG	SEP	OCT	NOV	DEC

Selected References

Breeland, S. G. 1958. Biological studies on the armyworm, *Pseudaletia unipuncta* (Haworth), in Tennessee (Lepidoptera: Noctuidae). J. Tenn. Acad. Sci. 33: 263–347.

Guppy, J. C. 1961. Life history and behavior of the armyworm, *Pseudaletia unipuncta* (Haw.) (Lepidoptera: Noctuidae), in eastern Ontario. Can. Entomol. 93: 1141–1153.

Pond, D. D. 1960. Life history studies of the armyworm, *Pseudaletia unipuncta* (Lepidoptera: Noctuidae), in New Brunswick. Ann. Entomol. Soc. Am. 53: 661–665.

—Clyde S. Gorsuch

Asiatic Garden Beetle

Asiatic garden beetle adult (courtesy NYSAES [G. Catlin])

Scientific Classification. *Maladera castanea* (Arrow) (Coleoptera: Scarabaeidae). First described as oriental garden beetle, *Aserica castanea* Arrow, but later named the Asiatic garden beetle.

Origin and Distribution. The Asiatic garden beetle, an introduced pest from China and Japan, was identified from samples collected in a nursery near Rutherford, NJ, in 1921. It is known to occur at many scattered points in Connecticut, Delaware, the District of Columbia, Maryland, New Jersey, New York, Pennsylvania, South Carolina, and Virginia. H. C. Hallock reported that, in New York State, it is generally distributed throughout Kings, Queens, and Nassau Counties, the western part of Suffolk County on Long Island, and in Bronx and Westchester Counties on the mainland. In New Jersey, it is uniformly present and abundant in Essex, Hudson, and Union Counties, as well as in parts of Bergen, Passaic, Middlesex, and Monmouth Counties. In the suburban area around Philadelphia, the insect is found in numbers in parts of Chester, Delaware, Montgomery, and Philadelphia Counties.

Description. Adults are chestnut brown, velvety in appearance, 0.31–0.43 in (8.0–11.0 mm) long, and 0.18–0.24 in (4.7–6.2 mm) wide. The elytra do not entirely cover the abdomen, and the last two segments are almost entirely exposed. Each segment on the undersurface of the abdomen has a row of short, yellowish hairs, and the underside of the thorax is partly covered with yellow hairs. On the upper surface of the body, hairs are present only on the outer margins of the elytra, on the lateral and sometimes the anterior margins of the prothorax, and on the forehead. These small, erect hairs on

Asiatic garden beetle grub showing diagnostic swollen stipe (courtesy NYSAES [J. Ogrodnick])

the head assist in recognizing this pest. Larvae (grubs) complete three instars and grow from 0.06 to 0.75 in (1.4–19.0 mm) long. They have a brown head capsule, white body, and three pair of legs. The larva's anal opening is Y-shaped, and there is a single transverse curved row of spines (crescent-shaped raster pattern) on the underside of the last segment (see p. 18 for rastral pattern), which, with the smaller claw on the third leg, distinguish this species from nearly all other similar white grubs. Another distinct larval characteristic is the lightly colored, enlarged bulbous stipe of the maxilla that is lateral to the mandibles.

Pest Status. The Asiatic garden beetle is a minor subsurface feeding pest of turfgrass but can cause economic damage to nursery and vegetable crops. It is primarily associated with metropolitan areas of New York, New Jersey, and Pennsylvania (Philadelphia). Mixed populations of the Asiatic garden beetle; the European chafer, *Rhizotrogus (Amphimallon) majalis* (Razoumowsky); and the Japanese beetle, *Popillia japonica* Newman, occur in Rochester, N Y, and mixed populations of the Asiatic garden beetle; the oriental beetle, *Exomala orientalis* Waterhouse; and the Japanese beetle occur on Long Island.

Injury. Adults feed sparingly on grass blades but feed on the margin of foliage, petals, blossoms, and flowers of more than 100 host plants, including ailanthus, aster, barberry (young shoots), chrysanthemums, dahlia, devils-walking-stick, phlox, rose, and sumac. Heavy beetle infestations can result in consumption of all leaf tissue, with only the midribs remaining. Beetle injury is most severe from mid-July through mid-August. Grubs feed on the young roots of weeds, flowers, vegetables, and turfgrass. Larval injury to turfgrass causes the plant to be unable to draw a sufficient supply of nutrients and moisture from the soil to maintain a good stand. Grub-infested areas of turfgrass appear to be wilting from lack of moisture.

Life History. The Asiatic garden beetle completes one generation annually. Adults appear from late June through late October. Peak activity occurs from mid-July through mid-August. During the day, beetles hide in areas where the ground is relatively cool and moist. Adults feed at night and are active night fliers when temperatures exceed 69.8°F (21°C). They are attracted to bright lights and have been observed gathering in large numbers on utility poles and window screens. Females burrow into the soil to lay white, ovoid, 0.04-in (1.0-mm) eggs at irregular intervals from early July through late October at depths varying from 0.5 to 3.9 in (1.25–10.0 cm). Females lay an average of 60 eggs in clusters of up to 19, loosely held together by a gelatinous material. Oviposition is affected by preferred host plants, types of ground cover, and texture and moisture content of the soil. Females prefer laying eggs in overgrown uncultivated areas where such weeds as daisy fleabane, goldenrod, plantain, orange hawkweed, ragweed, wild aster, and wild carrot abound. Eggs swell from soil moisture, become pearly white spheres, and hatch into 0.06-in (1.4-

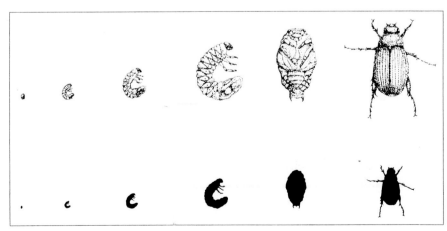

Egg, 1st, 2nd, and 3rd larval instar, pupa, and adult of the Asiatic garden beetle, Silhouettes show actual size of each stage.

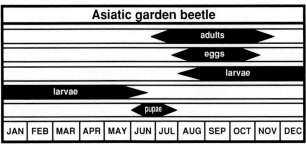

mm) larvae in 10 days. Young larvae feed on tender young roots and disintegrated vegetable matter. They continue feeding through the summer months, completing three instars. Seventy-five percent of the grubs overwinter as third instars at depths of 7.9–16 in (20.0–42.5 cm) in the soil. Overwintering grubs return to the top 4.9 in (12.5 cm) of soil in mid-April to resume feeding on plant roots. Feeding continues through early June, when the third instar grub constructs an earthen cell 1.5–3.9 in (3.7–10 cm) below the surface, spends 5 days in the prepupal stage, pupates (normally from mid-June through mid-July), and emerges as an adult 8–15 days later. Before emerging from the soil, young adults go through a hardening process, changing in color from a white tint to a distinct brown. Then they burrow through the soil to the surface to commence feeding. Very few natural enemies are associated with this pest. A wasp of the genus *Tiphia* is reported to parasitize grubs in Asia.

Management. Grub populations should be sampled in mid- to late August by taking square-foot (0.09-m²) samples. To accomplish this, make cuts on three sides of a square foot (0.09 m²). Turn the sod back to expose the soil, break the soil apart, closely examine both the soil and thatch, and count the grubs. Return the soil to the hole and replace the sod flap. The larval stage of this beetle may need to be controlled when 18–20 grubs per square foot (0.09 m²) are recorded. However, this management decision also depends on acceptable damage levels and overall condition of the stand. The Asiatic garden beetle has not been an important turfgrass pest in recent years. A shortage of soil moisture at the time eggs and small larvae predominate in the soil probably causes high mortality of these stages. Likewise, removal of preferred food sources (i.e., weeds) may assist in reducing beetle populations. Grubs of this pest may not be as damaging to turfgrass as related species, because they feed 2.0–2.9 in (5.0–7.5 cm) below the surface. However, management of this pest in the future may become increasingly difficult if mixed grub populations continue to develop. Minimal information is available on the success of entomogenous nematodes and "milky disease" to manage this species. Insecticides can be applied to manage grubs from mid-August through early September.

Selected References

Hallock, H. C. 1931. Recent observations on the distribution and abundance of *Anomala orientalis* (Waterhouse) and *Aserica castanea* Arrow in New York. J. Econ. Entomol. 24: 204–212.

———. 1932. Life history and control of the Asiatic garden beetle. U.S. Dep. Agric. Circ. 246.

———. 1936. Notes on biology and control of the Asiatic garden beetle. J. Econ. Entomol. 29: 348–356.

Tashiro, H. 1987. Turfgrass insects of the United States and Canada. Cornell University Press, Ithaca, NY.

—Paul R. Heller

Bermudagrass and Related Eriophyid Mites

Bermudagrass Mite

Scientific Classification. *Eriophyes cynodoniensis* Sayed (Acari: Eriophyidae).

Origin and Distribution. The bermudagrass mite is probably native to Australia, where bermudagrass has become a naturalized plant. However, the mite is now widespread, occurring in New Zealand, North Africa, and North America. In the United States, the bermudagrass mite was first found in Arizona, but soon spread throughout the southern states where bermudagrass is cultivated (California, New Mexico, Texas, Oklahoma, Alabama, Georgia, and Florida).

Description. The bermudagrass mite is whitish cream in color, wormlike in shape, and has two pairs of legs, as is typical of eriophyids. Adults are about 0.006–0.008 in (0.165–0.210 mm) long and just visible with a quality 15- to 20- power hand lens.

Pest Status. This mite is host specific to bermudagrass, *Cynodon* spp.

Injury. Infestations are easily recognized when signaled by plant injury. Infested grass first exhibits a slight yellowing of leaf tips followed by shortening of the internodes and leaves, producing a rosetted or tufted growth, or "witch's broom" effect. Severe infestations result in stand loss, and large dead areas soon become infested with weeds. Damage is usually amplified during hot, dry conditions.

Life History. Mites are active primarily during late spring and summer. Development from egg to adult re-

Bermudagrass mite injury   (courtesy NYSAES [H. Tashiro])

quires 5–10 days. After eggs hatch, they pass through two nymphal instars and molt to adults. All life stages live together, protected under the leaf sheath, and, often, 100–200 mites and eggs can be observed under a single leaf. Mites are spread on grass clippings and have been observed hitchhiking on other turf insects. Dispersal in the wind is also common.

Management. Chemical controls can be effective, but repeated applications are necessary. In southern Florida, where mites are active most of the year, cumulative treatment costs can be high. Cultural manipulation of the host by use of adequate irrigation and nutrition often can help the grass outgrow mite damage, because severe damage is usually linked to drought stress. The bermudagrass cultivars 'FloraTex', 'Midiron', and 'Tif-

Bermudagrass mites under leaf sheath (courtesy NYSAES [H. Tashiro])

Adult bermudagrass mite. Silhouette (in frame) shows actual size.

					Bermudagrass mite						
JAN	FEB	MAR	APR	MAY	JUN	JUL	AUG	SEP	OCT	NOV	DEC

dwarf' are resistant, but other standard varieties, including 'Tifway', are susceptible to this mite.

Zoysiagrass Mite

Scientific Classification. *Eriophyes zoysiae* Baker, Kono, and O'Neill (Acari: Eriophyidae).

Origin and Distribution. The zoysiagrass mite, native to Japan and Korea, was introduced to the United States in 1982. It is now established in Maryland, Texas, and Florida.

Description. Females are creamy white, elongate, wormlike, and 0.010–0.011 in (0.252–0.279 mm) long.

Pest Status. This eriophyid is host specific to several species of zoysiagrass, *Zoysia* spp.

Injury. Symptoms on zoysiagrass are similar to those caused by *E. cynodonis* infesting bermudagrass. Mites in all stages are found on unexpanded leaves, leaf sheath, and collar, and in the seed head. New leaf tips are twisted and caught in partially unrolled older leaves, resulting in terminal arches or "buggy whip" symptoms. Serious damage to the host is rare, but seed crop production may be limited by this eriophyid.

Life History. Life history is assumed to be similar to that of the bermudagrass mite, and all stages are present throughout the growing season of zoysiagrass.

Management. Control strategies are similar to those for other turfgrass eriophyids. However, although some grasses can outgrow their mite pests, well-managed zoysiagrass does not seem to outgrow zoysiagrass mite damage. Several resistant zoysiagrasses have been identified and are being released. 'Emerald' zoysiagrass is resistant to this eriophyid, but 'Belair', 'Meyer', and 'El Toro' are susceptible.

Buffalograss Mite

Scientific Classification. *Eriophyes slykhuisi* (Hall) (Acari: Eriophyidae).

Origin and Distribution. This native North American species occurs in the midwestern United States and probably throughout the host range of buffalograss, *Buchloe dactyloides* (Nutt.) Engelm., from Mexico to Canada.

Description. The female is white, wormlike, slightly arched in lateral view, and 0.007–0.009 in (0.190–0.237 mm) long.

Pest Status. Buffalograss mite is host specific to buffalograss, which occurs throughout the Great Plains.

Injury. Symptoms are nearly identical to those caused by *E. cynodoniensis* on bermudagrass. Tufting of the grass and thinning of stand usually becomes more pronounced in late summer, when the grass is under drought stress.

Life History. Because the symptoms of injury are very similar to those caused by *E. cynodoniensis*, the life cycle is also presumed to be similar.

Management. Control strategies are the same as for the bermudagrass mite, with emphasis on cultural control.

Grain Rust Mite

Scientific Classification. *Abacarus hystrix* (Nalepa), the grain rust mite, and *Aculodes mckenziei* (Kiefer) (Acari: Eriophyidae).

Origin and Distribution. Both *A. hystrix* and *A. mckenziei* feed on Kentucky bluegrass. These species are distributed throughout North America and Europe on numerous grass hosts.

Pest Status. Both of these eriophyids feed on Kentucky bluegrass whether it is grown for a seed crop or for turfgrass. *A. hystrix* is the primary vector of agropyron mosaic virus on winter wheat and also transmits ryegrass mosaic virus to perennial ryegrass.

Injury. These two eriophyids can cause reduced seed yield in Kentucky bluegrass. Ryegrass mosaic virus, transmitted by *A. hystrix*, causes stunting, reduced tillering, and leaf necrosis in perennial ryegrass and results in reduced seed yield.

Life History. The life histories are presumed to be similar to that of the wheat curl mite, *Eriophyes tulipae* Kiefer, with females producing up to 25 eggs in a lifetime. The life cycle may be completed in 8–10 days under favorable conditions.

Management. Burning of seed fields after harvest is the preferred control practice to reduce mite populations. No treatments are required in turfgrasses.

Eriophyes cynodonis

Scientific Classification. *Eriophyes cynodonis* (Wilson) (Acari: Eriophyidae).

Origin and Distribution. This eriophyid is known only in North America and has been found in California, Kansas, Alaska, and Florida.

Description. Mites are whitish or yellowish and resemble the bermudagrass mite. Adult length is 0.007 –0.008 in (0.170–0.211 mm) long.

Pest Status. This eriophyid is reported only on bermudagrass, *Cynodon* spp.

Injury. In plants injured by this species, terminal leaf blades extend fully, but the leaf tip fails to unfold. This results in a twisting of the folded terminal shoot and subsequent bending and twisting of the leaf blades. Serious damage to host vigor is unlikely, except that seed production may be limited.

Life History. The life cycle of *E. cynodonis* is similar to that of *E. cynodoniensis*.

Management. Control strategies are similar to those for *E. cynodoniensis* and may become necessary if seed production is affected.

Selected References

Baker, E. W., T. Kono & N. R. O'Neil. 1986. *Eriophyes zoysiae* Backer, Kono, and O'Neil (Acari: Eriophyidae), a new species of eriophyid mite from zoysiagrass. Int. J. Acarol. 12: 3–6.

Hall, C. C., Jr. 1958. A new eriophyid mite from Kansas. J. Kans. Entomol. Soc. 31(3): 233–235.

Jeppson, L. R., H. H. Keifer & E. W. Baker. 1975. Mites injurious to economic plants. University of California Press, Los Angeles.

Reinert, J. A. 1982. The bermudagrass stunt mite. United States Golf Association Green Section Record 20(6): 9–12.

Reinert, J. A., A. E. Dudeck & G. H. Snyder. 1978. Resistance in bermudagrass to the bermudagrass mite. Environ. Entomol. 7: 885–888.

Reinert, J. A., M. C. Engelke & S. J. Morton. 1993. Zoysiagrass resistance to the zoysiagrass mite, *Eriophyes zoysiae* (Acari: Eriophyidae). Proceedings International Turfgrass Society Research Journal. 7: 349–352.

Smilanick, J. M. & F. G. Zalom. 1983. Eriophyid mites in relation to Kentucky bluegrass seed production. Entomol. Exp. Appl. 33: 31–34.

Tashiro, H. 1987. Turfgrass insects of the United States and Canada. Cornell University Press Ithaca, NY.

—William G. Hudson, James A. Reinert, and Robert L. Crocker

Billbugs

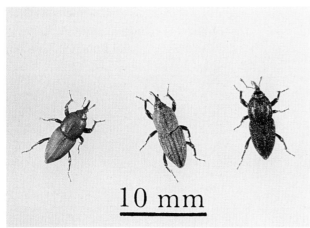

Bluegrass billbug callow and mature adults (courtesy NYSAES [G. Catlin])

Common Names. Bluegrass billbug, hunting billbug, Denver (or Rocky Mountain) billbug, Phoenician (or Phoenix) billbug.

Scientific Classification. *Sphenophorus parvulus* Gyllenhal, *S. venatus vestitus* Chittenden, *S. cicatristriatus* Fahraeus, and *S. phoeniciensis* Chittenden, respectively (Coleoptera: Curculionidae). Former scientific name for genus was *Calendra*.

Origin and Distribution. Billbugs are native to North America. The bluegrass billbug is most common in cool-season turf areas; the hunting billbug is most common in transition and southern turf areas; the Denver billbug is restricted to the Rocky Mountain region and northern Great Plains; the Phoenician billbug is found in southern California and Arizona.

Description. Eggs are white, elongate, kidney-shaped, and about 0.059 in (1.5 mm) long. They are deposited in small holes chewed into grass stems. Immatures are robust, light-colored larvae with a slightly tapered abdomen and brown head capsules. Billbug larvae have no legs, unlike true white grubs. Young larvae are about 0.051 in (1.3 mm) long and burrow in the pith of grass stems. Mature larvae may reach 0.236–0.394 in (6–10 mm) and are located in the thatch and soil. Pupae are at first cream-colored and then change to reddish brown before adult emergence. Their typical weevil snouts are evident, and their wing pads and legs are folded close to their bodies. Pupae are normally formed in a soil chamber 1–2 in (2.5–5.1 cm) deep. Adults are typical weevils with elongate snouts or bills, elbowed antennae, and hard wing covers. Adults are located in the turf canopy but are commonly found walking across sidewalks and driveways during sunny weather. Adult billbugs can be identified easily by referring to illustrations. Especially useful are markings on the prothorax and wing covers. The bluegrass billbug has fine, even pits on the prothorax and straight rows of double pits on the wing covers. The hunting billbug has a raised Y-shaped area surrounded by curved lines on the prothorax and rows of large and small pits on the wing covers. The Denver billbug is shiny black with heart-shaped rows of double pits on the wing covers. The Phoenician billbug has an M-shaped raised area on the pronotum. The species of billbug larvae cannot be identified without rearing them to adulthood. Several other species of billbugs may be associated with turfgrasses and sedges, but are of minor importance.

Pest Status. Billbugs cause some of the most commonly misdiagnosed problems associated with turfgrasses. Their damage is often mistaken for drought dormancy, chinch bug or white grub damage, delayed

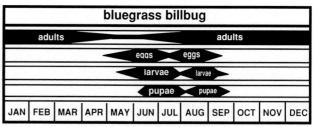

bluegrass billbug											
adults										adults	
				eggs		eggs					
				larvae		larvae					
				pupae		pupae					
JAN	FEB	MAR	APR	MAY	JUN	JUL	AUG	SEP	OCT	NOV	DEC

Hunting, Denver and Phoenix billbugs											
			adults								
					eggs						
larvae										larvae	
			pupae								
JAN	FEB	MAR	APR	MAY	JUN	JUL	AUG	SEP	OCT	NOV	DEC

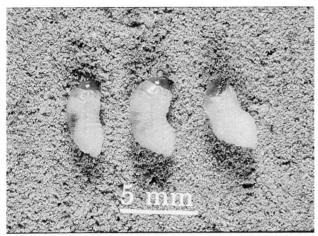
Bluegrass billbug mature larva (courtesy NYSAES [G. Catlin])

spring greening, or damage from one of a variety of diseases. The bluegrass billbug is one of the top three pests of Kentucky bluegrass and of perennial rye. The hunting and Phoenician billbugs commonly thin out poorly maintained bermudagrass or kill patches of zoysiagrass. The Denver billbug prefers cool-season turfgrasses.

Injury. In cool-season turf, billbug larvae burrow down grass stems and seed stalks to the crown of the plant. This kills individual stems and, eventually, larger clumps of turf. Early damage looks like dollar spot disease. Heavier infestations result in patchy areas of dead turf and even death of extensive areas. The stems of damaged turf break off easily and are filled with fine, sawdustlike frass. Most damage occurs in June and July. In transition and warm-season turf, the hunting and Phoenician billbugs may have larvae and adults present all year. When populations are not checked, most damage to bermudagrass appears in the spring as dead patches or areas that are slow to green up. Stems and rhizomes are easily broken and may exhibit numerous, irregular feeding spots. In southern sod production, billbugs can damage the sod to the extent that it will not hold together when cut.

Life History. The bluegrass billbug has a single generation per year, although a limited part of the population may attempt a second generation. Adults overwinter in the turf and surrounding areas. In April and early May, the adults become active, feed, and lay eggs in grass stems. Spring oviposition may continue for a month. The eggs hatch in 10–14 days and the first instars burrow up and down the grass stem. Larvae move from stem to stem until no longer able to fit within the stem walls. At that time, they burrow into the grass plant crown or even exit the plant entirely. From late June through July, pupae are formed in cells deeper in the soil. The new adults emerge from mid-July through August. Callow adults are reddish brown but soon turn slate gray. Adults may appear brown to black, but the brown coloration is usually caused by a coating of soil. The new adults puncture and feed through small wounds in turf stems, but this produces no noticeable damage. The hunting, Denver, and Phoenician billbugs appear to have one major generation per year, but adults and larvae may be found at any given time. Most of the population overwinters as partially mature larvae and finishes development in the spring. The new adults mate, feed, and oviposit over an extended period of time. Usually, bermudagrass grows so rapidly during the hot summer months that billbug damage often goes undetected. By the time of fall dormancy, billbug populations may be high enough to damage most of the roots and stolons. However, damage at that time is usually mistaken for dormancy. Denver billbugs, like hunting billbugs, prefer cool-season turfgrasses throughout their life cycle, with all stages present year round. Billbugs are known to be attacked by a wasp egg parasitoid, *Patasson calendrae* (Gahan) (Mymaridae). The adults are suscepti-

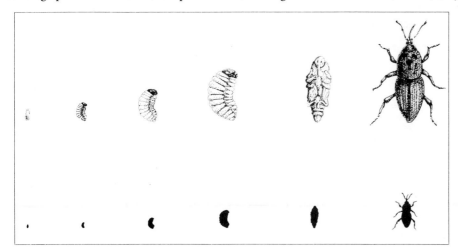
Egg, 1st, 3rd, and 5th larval instar, pupa, and adult of the bluegrass billbug. Silhouettes show actual size of each stage.

ble to *Beauveria* fungal infections, which may lower populations substantially in rainy years. Birds also readily pick up the adults as they cross sidewalks.

Management. A range of control options can be used to manage billbugs in turf. For long term-cultural control, select resistant turfgrass cultivars. Bluegrasses and ryegrasses have been identified with resistance to the bluegrass billbug. Perennial ryegrasses and fescues with endophyte fungal enhancements are highly resistant to billbug attack. Bermudagrasses and zoysias that are resistant to hunting billbug attack have also been identified. Billbug damage is most evident when there is a lack of turf fertility and soil moisture. Low to moderate billbug infestations can be masked by keeping a moderate fertility level and irrigating during the time that the billbug larvae are emerging from the grass stems to feed at the crowns. The entomopathogenic nematodes *Steinernema* and *Heterorhabditis* have been shown to control billbug larvae and adults effectively. Augmenting nematode levels by spraying them at a rate of 1.0 billion infective juvenile nematodes per acre (0.4 ha), followed by immediate irrigation, has produced satisfactory billbug reduction. Other biological controls, such as the fungus *Beauveria*, are not commercially available at present. Chemical control strategies can be used to control either larval or adult billbugs. Bluegrass billbug adults are susceptible to residual surface insecticides applied in late April and early May. Hunting, Denver, and Phoenician billbug adults are more numerous in late May and may be controlled at that time. The adults of these three billbug species may require two applications, one in early May followed by a second treatment in mid-June. Billbug larvae can be treated as if they were white grubs. Insecticides should be applied when the billbug larvae are small and actively feeding at the base of turf plants. The optimum time to apply bluegrass billbug larval controls is between 1,330 and 1,485 degree-days. Control of adult billbugs is most appropriate where billbugs are a perennial problem. Larval control can be performed where infestations are increasing.

Selected References

Johnson-Cicalese, J. M., G. W. Wolfe & C. R. Funk. 1990. Biology, distribution and taxonomy of billbug turf pests (Coleoptera: Curculionidae). Environ. Entomol. 19: 1037–1046.

Kelsheimer, E. G. 1956. The hunting billbug, a serious pest of zoysia. Proc. Fla. State Hortic. Soc. 69: 415–418.

Kindler, S. D., E. J. Kinbacher & R. Staples. 1982. Evaluation of Kentucky bluegrass cultivars for resistance to the bluegrass billbug, *Sphenophorus parvulus* Gyllenhall, pp. 19–22. *In* H. D. Niemczyk & B. G. Joyner [eds.], Advances in turfgrass entomology. Hammer Graphics, Pi-

qua, OH.

Tashiro, H. 1987. Turfgrass insects of the United States and Canada. Cornell University Press, Ithaca, NY.

Vaurie, P. 1951. Revision of the genus *Calendra* (formerly *Sphenophorus*) in the United States and Mexico (Coleoptera, Curculionidae). Bull. Am. Mus. Nat. Hist. 98(2): 29–186.

—David J. Shetlar

Black Turfgrass Ataenius

Larva, pupa, callow adult and mature adult of Black turfgrass ataenius (courtesy NYSAES [H. Tashiro])

Scientific Classification. *Ataenius spretulus* (Haldeman) (Coleoptera: Scarabaeidae).

Origin and Distribution. The black turfgrass ataenius is native to North America and has been reported in 41 of the 48 contiguous states. It was first described as a turfgrass pest in Minnesota in 1932. It was next reported as a turf pest on fairways in widely separated areas of New York State in 1969–1970 and on fairways in southern Ohio in 1973. Since that time, it has been reported as a damaging turf pest in at least 12 midwestern and northeastern states, as well as in Ontario, Canada. Its current distribution suggests that it is most prevalent in the midwestern states, with additional substantial activity in some of the Central Plains and northeastern states. Most damage occurs on golf course turf, particularly fairways and, occasionally, greens and tees.

Description. The adult black turfgrass ataenius is a relatively small beetle, 0.1–0.2 in (2.5–5.1 mm) long and half as wide. It is shiny black with fairly distinct striations (longitudinal ridges) on the elytra. The beetles can fly short distances and are attracted to black-light traps. The adult is similar in size to the annual bluegrass weevil, but is more flattened dorsoventrally and does not have an elongated snout. Cream-colored, nearly spherical eggs are laid in the soil in clusters of 10–15 eggs, usually in the top inch (2.54 cm) of soil. Eggs are less than 0.05 in (1.3 mm) long when mature, but can be seen with the naked eye in contrast to the dark soil. Larvae are typical scarab grubs: cream-colored, C-shaped when at rest, with brown head capsule and three distinct pairs of legs. However, they are much smaller than the grubs of other scarab species that are active in turf. When feeding actively, they often appear to be grayer than many other white grub species. Third instars are very similar in size and coloration to first instars of the European chafer and occur at about the same time of year. First and second instars are very small (no more than 0.15 in [3.8 mm] long), but can be seen without magnification. Black turfgrass ataenius larvae can be recognized by a pair of distinct padlike structures on the tip of the abdomen, just in front of the anal slit (see p. 18 for rastral pattern). The pupa resembles that of the European chafer, although it is much smaller. Wings and legs are evident, although folded fairly close to the body. Young pupae are cream-colored, but those from which adults are about to emerge are light brown. Pupae are about 0.2 in (5.1 mm) long and 0.1 in (2.5 mm) wide and occur in the top inch of soil, usually near the thatch/soil interface.

Pest Status. The black turfgrass ataenius can be a major problem on golf courses in parts of the Midwest, Northeast, and Middle Atlantic states. Although they often are not widespread (i.e., they do not affect all of the golf courses in a given area), they can cause severe damage where they do occur. In some cases, outbreaks of this pest can be traced to the use of chlordane in the 1960s or early 1970s, when some populations apparently developed resistance to chlordane. In addition, the in-

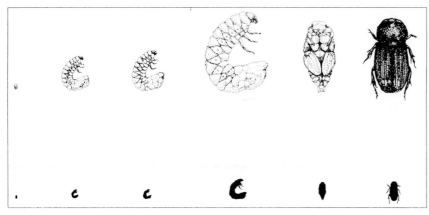

Egg, 1st, 2nd, and 3rd larval instar, pupa, and adult of the black turfgrass ataenius. Silhouettes show actual size of each stage.

Normal (l) and milky disease infected Black turfgrass ataenius grubs (courtesy NYSAES [H. Tashiro])

secticide probably had detrimental effects on some of the beneficial organisms that might have provided various degrees of suppression of the pest. However, more recently, outbreaks of the black turfgrass ataenius have occurred regardless of chlordane history.

Injury. The black turfgrass ataenius is primarily a golf course pest, attacking fairways, greens, tees, and collars. Symptoms are wilting and gradual thinning of turf, even in the presence of adequate water. Wilting is most apparent when the damaged area is viewed by looking directly into the sun. Injury is similar to that caused by other species of white grubs: direct feeding on roots and root hairs and some feeding in the lower thatch. As a result, heavily infested turf has a severely stunted or damaged root system and can be lifted from the soil because all connecting roots have been destroyed. The black turfgrass ataenius feeds on a variety of turfgrass species, including annual bluegrass, Kentucky bluegrass, and bentgrasses.

Life History. The black turfgrass ataenius has one or two generations per year, depending on location and weather conditions. As a general rule, two generations occur in Ohio and farther south, and one generation and a partial second generation may occur in western or central New York and southern New England. Northern New England normally experiences only one generation per year. Adults overwinter within 1 or 2 in (2.5–5.1 cm) of the soil surface, usually under leaf litter along fairways or under trees in nearby wooded areas. In areas where two generations occur (for example, southern Ohio) adults begin to migrate to their turf sites in late March. Often large numbers of adults can be seen on putting greens or in flight on warm sunny days in April or early May. Egg laying begins in early May and contin-

ues into the middle of June. Early eggs hatch and larvae are present from late May through mid-July, as they pass through three instars. Larvae are active in the upper soil zone (top inch [2.5 cm]) or in the lower thatch profile. By late June and early July, the largest larvae begin to burrow a little deeper into the soil (1–3 in [2.5–7.6 cm]), where they pupate. Young adults emerge from these pupae in mid-July and begin to lay eggs for a second generation in late July or early August. Larvae from this second generation are present in August and September and can cause as much damage as the first generation. Pupation occurs in late August or September, and the new adults return to their overwintering sites in September or October. As with annual bluegrass weevils, there is considerable overlap between generations. During the growing season, notably between June and September, any stage can be found at a given time. Many turf managers have observed that black turfgrass ataenius populations remain high for 3 or 4 years and then decline, apparently naturally. In some cases, a bacterial "milky disease" has been observed in declining populations, but the exact dynamics of the population and the decline are not well understood. Much of the activity of the black turfgrass ataenius appears to be closely related to the phenology of indicator plants, at least in the Midwest. For example, first-generation eggs are laid at the

black turfgrass ataenius											
southern Ohio											
adults			eggs	grubs		pupae	adults	eggs	grubs	pupae	adults
southern New England											
adults			eggs	grubs		pupae	adults	eggs	grubs	pupae	adults
northern New England											
adults				eggs	grubs		pupae			adults	
JAN	FEB	MAR	APR	MAY	JUN	JUL	AUG	SEP	OCT	NOV	DEC

time vanhoutte spirea (*Spiraea vanhouttei* [Briot.] Zab.) or horse chestnut (*Aesculus hippocastanum* L.) is in full bloom. First generation larvae begin to appear when multiflora rose (*Rosa multiflora* Thunberg) is in full bloom. Summer adults appear when summer phlox (*Phlox paniculata* L.) is in full bloom. Second-generation eggs are laid when rose of Sharon (*Hibiscus syriacus* L.) is in full bloom. These phenological events can be useful in tracking the development of black turfgrass ataenius populations.

Management. Adult black turfgrass ataenius can be monitored with black-light traps, particularly in April and early May and again in the summer during their dispersal flights. Larvae can be monitored by taking soil samples similar to those used to sample other white grub species. Perhaps the most efficient method is to use a cup cutter (4.25 in [10.8 cm] diameter) to collect cores to a depth of about 2 in (5.1 cm), and carefully break up the soil. Inspect the lower thatch areas as well, for evidence of larvae or their feeding damage. There is little information available on tolerance levels, other than the observation that more than 200 grubs per square foot (0.09 m²) resulted in visible damage to the turf. The tolerance level for black turfgrass ataenius larvae depends on many factors relating to the overall vigor of the turf. Cool-season golf course turf that is not under other stresses (water, desiccation, mowing height, nutrition, compaction) probably can tolerate at least 30 - 50 grubs per square foot (0.09 m²) and, in many cases, may tolerate even higher populations. However, if other stresses are present, the tolerance level may have to be reduced. Standard petrochemical insecticides are currently the only recognized means of controlling or suppressing black turfgrass ataenius populations. The traditional approach has been to apply materials targeted against the small grubs, shortly after oviposition has been completed. As a general rule, insecticides that have shown efficacy against Japanese beetles and other similar white grubs show similar levels of activity against black turfgrass ataenius larvae. These applications (made at horse chestnut or vanhouette spirea full bloom) should be watered in thoroughly to enhance efficacy. The other approach, which was first developed at Ohio State University in the late 1970s, involves applying an insecticide when adults become active in the spring, before they have an opportunity to lay eggs. In this case, an insecticide that remains bound in the thatch can be beneficial, because adults remain in the thatch for much of this period. Also, such applications should not be watered in heavily. Efforts to use biological control agents to control black

turfgrass ataenius grub populations have had mixed success. Some field trials in Rhode Island indicated that *Steinernema carpocapsae,* currently the most readily available species of entomopathogenic nematode, could suppress grub populations. However, the trials involved application rates 10 times higher than the currently recommended (and commercially viable) rate. In many cases, natural infestations of a bacterial 'milky disease' appear to become established 3 or 4 years into an infestation, providing marked suppression of populations.

Selected References

Niemczyk, H. 1979. Controlling the black turfgrass ataenius. Golf Course Manage. (April): 29-31, 34, 37.

Niemczyk, H. D. & G. S. Wegner. 1982. Life history and control of the black turfgrass ataenius (Coleoptera-Scarabaeidae), pp. 113-117. *In* H. D. Niemczyk & B. G. Joyner [eds.], Advances in turfgrass entomology. Hammer Graphics, Piqua, OH.

Wegner, G. S., & H. D. Niemczyk. 1979. The ataenius of Ohio. Ohio J. Sci. 79: 249-255.

1981. Bionomics and phenology of *Ataenius spretulus*. Ann. Entomol. Soc. Am. 74: 374-384.

—Patricia J. Vittum

Chinch Bugs

Scientific Classification. *Blissus leucopterus* complex. The *B. leucopterus* complex consists of three species of chinch bugs, the hairy chinch bug (*B. leucopterus hirtus* Montandon), the southern chinch bug (*Blissus insularis* Barber), and the common chinch bug (*B. leucopterus leucopterus* [Say]). To distinguish among these species, it is best to look at whole populations, because morphological similarities and variation within species make identification of individuals extremely difficult. All three species even have the same number and size of chromosomes. The three species can be differentiated by using Leonard's (1968) key to adults of the eastern species of *Blissus*.

Hairy Chinch Bug

Scientific Classification. *Blissus leucopterus hirtus* Montandon (Hemiptera: Lygaeidae: Blissinae). First described as a species, *B. hirtus* Montandon, later treated as a variety, and, recently, as a subspecies of *B. leucopterus* (Say).

Origin and Distribution. The hairy chinch bug is distributed across the eastern Canadian provinces of Nova Scotia, Newfoundland, Prince Edward Island, New Brunswick, Quebec, and Ontario, and from the northeastern United States to the Middle Atlantic states south to Virginia, and west to Minnesota.

Description. Adults are 0.04 in (1.0 mm) wide, 0.12 –0.14 in (3.0–3.6 mm) long, and black with shiny white wings that rest held flat over the body and with a black spot near the middle of the costal margin of each forewing. Legs are red to yellowish red, and the abdominal sternum is dark brown, with straw yellow setae. Hairy chinch bugs occur as macropterous or brachypterous adults. Adult females are larger and more robust than males. Nymphs complete five instars, growing from a width of 0.009 to 0.038 in (0.23–0.96 mm) and from a length of 0.035 to 0.117 in (0.9–2.97 mm). Nymphal instars undergo distinct color changes. First and second instars are bright red with a distinct white band on the anterior two abdominal segments; third instars are orange with mesothoracic wing pads appearing; fourth instars are orange brown with wing pads extending over the abdomen to the posterior area of the first abdominal segment; and fifth instars are black with developing wing pads easily visible, extending at least onto the second abdominal segment.

Hairy chinch bug adult (courtesy D. J. Shetlar).

Pest Status. The hairy chinch bug is a serious but periodic surface-feeding pest of cool-season turfgrasses (e.g., perennial ryegrass, Kentucky bluegrass, red fescues, bentgrasses) and zoysiagrass. Pest infestations frequently occur in turfgrass with thick thatch that are exposed to full sunlight during periods of hot, dry weather. The hairy chinch bug is a major home lawn pest and occasionally infests golf courses and sod farms.

Injury. Aggregations of adults and nymphs suck sap from stems and crowns of susceptible grasses. Extensive feeding causes grass to first turn yellow and then reddish brown. Injury is caused mainly by the withdrawal of plant fluids from both the phloem and xylem tubes and by clogging of the conducting tissues. Symptoms of hairy chinch bug feeding resemble drought injury or sun scald.

Life History. The hairy chinch bug produces two generations a year in southern New England, in the Middle Atlantic states, including New Jersey and Long Island, NY, and westward through Ohio. It produces one generation in upstate New York and southern Ontario, Canada. Overwintering adults start to emerge from protected leaf litter and dense thatch sites when a threshold temperature of 44.6°F (7°C) is reached. Adults feed and mate during a 2-week spring period before oviposition. Adult females then start laying eggs in leaf sheaths and in the ground on the roots of host plants. Females lay an average of 20 eggs per day for 2 to 3 weeks. In New Jersey, peak oviposition occurs from early May through early June when white clover (*Trifolium repens* L.), field chamonide (*Anthemis arvensis* L.), and birds-foot trefoil (*Lotus corniculatus* L.) are in early bloom. Eggs hatch within 1–4 weeks, depending on field temperatures. Upon hatching, nymphs commence feeding and complete five nymphal instars in about 4–6 weeks. Fifth-instar nymphs are very active from early to mid-July. Maximum adult emergence occurs when sumac (*Rhus copallina* L.) has well-developed inflorescences, but before anthesis. These adults lay eggs (mid-July through late August) that hatch into second-generation (summer) nymphs that complete development by late summer or early fall. Adults seek out protected areas for hibernation. Numerous mortality factors affect hairy chinch bug populations. The pathogenic fungus *Beauveria bassiana* (Blas.) Vuillemin can affect every stage of the pest. Infected individuals become covered with a soft white mycelium that later sporulates on the surface of the dead insect. Dampness favors fungal development. Predatory mesostigmatid mites (*Pergamasus crassipes* [L.]) and the lygaeid *Geocoris bullatus* (Say) assist in regulating pest populations. Egg mortality can be caused by a scelionid hymenopterous parasite (*Eumicrosoma benefica* Gahan), desiccation, or predation by a ground beetle (*Amara* sp.). Wet thatch conditions can result in failure of nymphal establishment.

Management. Several sampling schemes are available to detect hairy chinch bug populations. One method is the flotation technique. To employ this technique, cut off both ends of a 1-gal (3.8-liter) can, drive the can several inches into the soil, and fill it with water, maintaining a depth of 0.6–0.8 in (1–20 mm). All stages of the hairy chinch bug should float to the surface within 5–7 minutes. Fifteen to 20 immature insects per square foot (0.09 m²) can cause substantial damage and may warrant control. Vacuum sampling can be accomplished with any of a number of vacuum devices, including so-called "wet-dry shop vacs" and back-pack leaf blowers. Some leaf blowers must be modified to harness the air intake or to prevent passing the bugs through an impel-

ler. A series of quick transects can quickly determine whether chinch bugs are a problem. Populations can be managed by selecting chemical, cultural, or biological control strategies. Insecticide treatments can provide excellent control of hairy chinch bugs, but they do not prevent pest migration from untreated sites. Also, concern about the repeated use of insecticides and the resulting side effects (e.g., insecticide resistance, enhanced biodegradation, reduction of nontarget organisms, human exposure) has brought about the need for alternative, environmentally friendly cultural and biological control strategies. Hairy chinch bug populations can be suppressed through the use of endophyte-enhanced or tolerant cultivars. Adults and first- and second-instar nymphs reared on endophyte-infected ryegrass have substantially lower survival rates. Thus, the future development and deployment of pathogenic fungus, endophyte-enhanced turfgrass cultivars, biorational insecticides, and natural enemies may assist in reducing hairy chinch bug populations. Degree-day models are being developed to provide information on the optimum time to treat this pest. A sequential sampling plan has been developed in Canada (Guelph, Ontario) to manage univoltine hairy chinch bug populations. Results suggest that the optimum period to control this insect is when peak numbers of third-instar nymphs are active. This period can be predicted by a temperature accumulation in the thatch of 750–950 degree-days above a 44.6°F (7°C) threshold. Sampling for treatment/nontreatment decisions (i.e., 30+ nymphs per 35 in² [225 cm²] requires treatment) of univoltine populations should be initiated at 897 degree-days accumulations and terminated at 950 degree-days. In comparison, in New Jersey, two generations of the hairy chinch bug

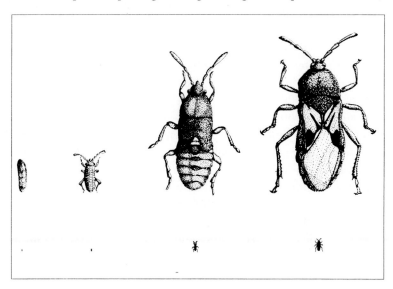

Egg, first stage nymph, final stage nymph, and adult of the hairy chinch bug. Silhouettes show actual size of each stage.

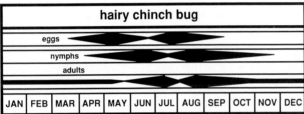

Southern chinch bug nymph (courtesy D. J. Shetlar).

occur annually. The temperature threshold selected for egg development with bivoltine populations is 59°F (14.6°C). Results from a New Jersey study, based on two generations per year, determined that egg hatch of the first generation was completed by 115 degree-days (in early June), and second-generation egg hatch was completed near 850 degree-days (after mid-August). Likewise, peak adult presence occurred at more than 1,159 degree-days (during mid-October).

Southern Chinch Bug

Scientific Classification. *Blissus insularis* Barber (Hemiptera: Lygaeidae: Blinninae).

Origin and Distribution. The southern chinch bug is distributed throughout South Carolina, Georgia, and Florida and west through Alabama, Mississippi, Louisiana, and Texas. Damaging po;ulations also occur in California, Mexico, and throughout the Caribbean Archipelago. Distribution of the southern chinch bug parallels the range of its primary host, St. Augustinegrass.

Description. Southern chinch bug adults are oblong, oval, and black with shiny white wings. They are slightly more than 0.04 in (1.0 mm) wide and 0.12–0.14 in (3.0

–3.6 mm) long. Populations include both macropterous (long-winged) and brachypterous (short-winged) adults. Females are slightly more robust than males. Mature fifth-instar nymphs are 0.12 in (3.1 mm) long.

Pest Status. St. Augustinegrass is the primary host of the southern chinch bug, but it will feed on other turfgrasses, including zoysiagrass, bermudagrass, bahiagrass, and centipedegrass. There have also been reports of southern chinch bugs feeding on crabgrass, torpedograss, and Pangolagrass.

Injury. Chinch bugs have piercing-sucking mouthparts and, as they suck the sap from crowns, stems, and stolons, they also inject a toxin that causes the grass to yellow and die. The insects feed in aggregates and, early in the infestation, in localized areas of the lawn. However, as the infestation progresses, the damaged areas, if left uncontrolled, coalesce and cause complete kill of a St. Augustinegrass lawn. Damage shows up first in sunny, drought-stressed, or heat-stressed areas of the lawn.

Life History. In northern Florida and Louisiana, there are three or four generations of the southern chinch bug per year. In the lower third of Florida and on the Caribbean Islands, seven to 10 generations per year are common. By midsummer, populations of 500–1,000 per 1.1 ft² (0.1 m²) are common and as many as 2,300 insects per 1.1 ft² (0.1 m²) have been recorded. Migration from one lawn to another is accomplished primarily by walking. After hatching from their eggs, chinch bugs pass through five nymphal instars. The first and second instars are bright orange, third and fourth instars are darker red, and the last instar is black and closely resembles the adult. In southern Florida, all stages are present throughout the year. However, in the northern range of the southern chinch bug, adults compose 80–90% of populations during the winter months.

Management. Twenty to 25 chinch bugs per square foot (0.09 m²) can cause economic damage. Population levels can be determined using the sampling techniques described in the section on the hairy chinch bug. Chemical control has been widely used for the southern chinch bug. As many as 12 applications of insecticides have been used annually in southern Florida to control this chinch bug; however, two to four properly timed applications often provide season-long control. Long-term heavy use of pesticides has led to complete resistance to organophosphate insecticides and partial resistance to carbamate insecticides in parts of southern Florida. Resistant cultivars of St. Augustinegrass ('Flora-tam', 'Floralawn', 'FX33', and 'FX10') have been developed as management tools. In addition, a whole complex of natural enemies present in the turf provides considerable control of the southern chinch bug, unless these enemies are repressed by pesticide use.

Common Chinch Bug

Scientific Classification. *Blissus leucopterus leucopterus* (Say) (Hemiptera: Lygaeidae: Blissinae).

Origin and Distribution. The common chinch bug is present from the east coast to the western plains. Its distribution overlaps that of *B. l. hirtus* and that of *B. insularis,* and populations have been identified in Alabama, Arkansas, Colorado, Georgia, Illinois, Indiana, Iowa, Kansas, Kentucky, Louisiana, Michigan, Minnesota, Mississippi, Missouri, North Carolina, North Dakota, Ohio, Oklahoma, South Carolina, South Dakota, Tennessee, Texas, Virginia, West Virginia, Wisconsin, and Wyoming.

Description. A member of the *B. leucopterus* complex, the common chinch bug can be distinguished from the southern chinch bug and the hairy chinch bug on the basis of several minute characters (Leonard 1968).

Pest Status. The common chinch bug is primarily a pest of corn, sorghum, millet, rye, and many bunchgrasses. It feeds on several turf species, including both cool-season and warm-season species. Large numbers of these chinch bugs often migrate from maturing grain fields into turf areas of bermudagrass and Kentucky bluegrass and cause damage overnight, even though these grasses are not their preferred hosts.

Injury. Damage is similar to that of the southern chinch bug.

Life History The life stages are similar to those of the other species in the *B. leucopterus* complex. The common chinch bug overwinters in bunchgrasses and usually migrates to grain fields or turfgrass in early spring.

Management. Insecticides may be required for control, but annual controls are usually not needed except where the common chinch bug occurs in mixed populations with one of the other *B. leucopterus* species.

Other *Blissus* spp. (Hemiptera: Lygaeidae: Blissinae)

There are 20 species of *Blissus* Burmeister that occur in the United States and Canada. Several of the other species are occasionally reported as pests of turfgrass. However, an undescribed species has been reported that damages only buffalograss. It has only been reported in Nebraska, but may be distributed elsewhere across the range of buffalograss, which reaches from Canada to Mexico.

Selected References

Baxendale, F. P. 1992. Insects and related pests of turfgrass, pp. 16–35. *In* F. P. Baxendale, & R. E. Gaussoin [eds.], Integrated management guide for Nebraska turfgrass. Univ. Nebr. Publ. EC 92-1557-S.

Blatchley, W. S. 1926. Heteroptera or true bugs of eastern North America. Nature Publishing, Indianapolis, IN.

Henry, N. J. & R. C. Froeschner [eds.]. 1988. Catalog of the Heteroptera or true bugs of Canada and the continental United States. E. J. Brill, Leiden.

Leonard, D. E. 1966. Biosystematics of the "*leucopterus* complex" of the genus *Blissus* (Heteroptera: Lygaeidae). Conn. Agric. Exp. Stn. Bull. 677: 1–47.

1968. A revision of the genus *Blissus* (Heteroptera: Lygaeidae). Ann. Entomol. Soc. Am. 61: 239–250.

Liu, H. J. & F. L. McEwen. 1979. The use of temperature accumulation and sequential sampling in predicting damaging populations of *Blissus leucopterus hirtus*. Environ. Entomol. 8: 512–515.

Mailloux, G. & H. T. Streu. 1981. Population biology of the hairy chinch bug (*Blissus leucopterus hirtus* Montandon: Hemiptera: Lygaeidae). Ann. Entomol. Soc. Que. 26: 51–90.

Niemczyk, H. D. 1982. Chinch bug and bluegrass billbug control with spring applications of chlorpyrifos, pp. 85-89. *In* H. D. Niemczyk, & B. J. Joyner [eds.], Advances in turfgrass entomology. Hammer Graphics, Piqua, OH.

Painter, R. H. 1928. Notes on the injury to plant cells in chinch bug feeding. Ann. Entomol. Soc. Am. 21: 232–241.

Reinert, J. A. 1978. Natural enemy complex of the southern chinch bug in Florida Ann. Entomol. Soc. Am. 71: 728–731.

Reinert, J. A., & S. H. Kerr. 1973. Bionomics and control of lawn chinch bugs. Bull. Entomol. Soc. Am. 19: 91–92.

Reinert, J. A. & K. M. Portier. 1983. Distribution and characterization of organophosphate-resistant southern chinch bug (Heteroptera: Lygaeidae) in Florida. J. Econ. Entomol. 76: 1187–1190.

Reinert, J. A., B. D. Bruton & R. W. Toler. 1980. Resistance of St. Augustinegrass to southern chinch bug and St. Augustine decline strain of Panicum mosaic virus. J. Econ. Entomol. 73: 602–604.

Schread, J. C. 1970. Chinch bug control. Conn. Agric. Exp. Stn. Circ. 233: 1–6.

Tashiro, H. 1987. Turfgrass insects of the United States and Canada. Cornell University Press, Ithaca, NY.

—James A. Reinert, Paul R. Heller,
and Robert L. Crocker

Clover and Other Noneriophyid Mites

Clover mite adult (courtesy NYSAES [H. Tashiro])

Clover Mite

Scientific Classification. *Bryobia praetiosa* Koch (Acari: Tetranychidae).

Origin and Distribution. The clover mite is widely distributed throughout the northern United States and Canada. Apparently native to Europe, it is found in essentially all of the North Temperate Zone.

Description. The clover mite is small (less than 0.04 in [1 mm] in length), similar in size to other spider mites. Its color is a general dark green with orange red

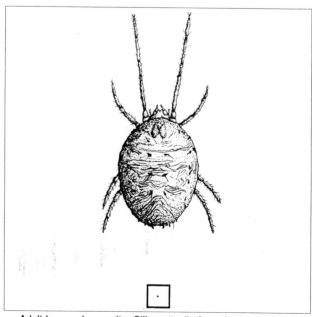

Adult brown clover mite. Silhouette (in frame) shows actual size.

markings, sometimes becoming a general brick red color. A distinguishing characteristic for adults is the unusually long front pair of legs that extend in front of the body. Under magnification, clover mites have distinctive flattened setae on the body. Eggs are bright red, spherical, and are laid on the bark of trees and other plants and on the walls of buildings. This species is closely related to the brown mite (*Bryobia rubrioculus* [Scheuten]), a species that restricts its feeding to various trees and shrubs.

Pest Status. The clover mite is generally a minor turfgrass pest, limiting injury to turfgrass in close proximity to sun-exposed sides of various landscape features. However, clover mite populations that develop on turfgrass can be important nuisance pests of buildings adjacent to turfgrass areas, because of mass indoor migrations during fall and early spring.

Injury. The clover mite feeds in a manner typical of other spider mites, rupturing the epidermal cells and removing the cell contents. Damaged areas of the leaf appear silvery and may occur in a pattern of meandering streaks, particularly on broadleaf plants. Turfgrass damage is restricted to the early, cooler seasons and is highly concentrated in areas within 6.5 feet (2 m) of the south and west (i.e., sun-exposed) sides of buildings, trees, and shrubs.

Life History. The clover mites is a cool-season species that produces a dormant egg stage during the warm months. With the return of cool temperatures in early fall, eggs hatch. The newly hatched clover mite larvae are minute, crimson-colored, and six-legged. After they feed and develop, the mites shed their skin (molt) and change to the subsequent protonymph and deutonymph stages. The other spider mite species discussed here have similar life cycles. In warmer regions, the clover mite may spend the winter in both egg and actively feeding adult or nymphal stages, producing two or three overlapping generations. In cooler climates, eggs are the only wintering stage, with eggs hatching in late winter. For molting and egg laying, clover mites generally move to solid upright objects such as tree trunks or building foundations. Mites may also use these locations during unfavorable conditions such as after a mowing or during excessive (hot or cold) temperatures. The continued return of mites to these locations produces the localized injury patterns.

Management. One of the most important means of limiting clover mite injury is to provide adequate water to lawn areas that have a high risk of injury, such as warm, dry areas along sun-exposed sides of buildings.

Adequate watering suppresses winter populations and helps susceptible lawn areas better tolerate injury. Other cultural practices that improve the overall health of the lawns are useful in limiting damage. Treatments for clover mite control should involve spot applications to sites used by clover mites for feeding and egg laying. These include lower foundation walls and tree trunks as well as adjacent turf. Spot treatments may often be further limited to the sun-exposed areas. Relatively few pesticides are labeled for control of clover mites.

Brown Wheat Mite

Scientific Classification. *Petrobia latens* (Müller) (Acari: Tetranychidae).

Origin and Distribution The brown wheat mite is a circumpolar species found throughout temperate areas of the world. It is most common and damaging to cool-season turfgrass grown in drier climates.

Description. The brown wheat mite shares with the clover mite the characteristic long front pair of legs. It is also generally similar in color and size. However, upon close inspection under magnification, the general body shape of the brown wheat mite is rounded rather than flattened. The brown wheat mite also lacks the flattened setae found in the clover mite.

Pest Status. The brown wheat mite is a minor pest of turfgrass, with outbreaks limited to drought-stressed turfgrass grown in drier climates.

Injury. Although brown wheat mite damage is associated with drought, injury is not so strictly confined to areas around buildings or trees, as occurs with the clover mite. Peak feeding injury by the brown wheat mite typically occurs during midspring and is often confused with damage caused by drought.

Life History. The brown wheat mite also is a cool-season mite, with peak populations occurring in spring and fall. During the summer, most mites produce dormant (diapausing) eggs that do not hatch until the return of cooler weather. Dormant eggs are also produced during the winter months. During favorable conditions of moderate temperatures and drought stress, the mites are active and a life cycle can be completed in less than 2 weeks. Several generations are produced during a season. Like the clover mite, the brown wheat mite typically leaves its host plant to lay eggs on nearby surfaces. Soil particles or other solid surfaces in the area of the plant serve as oviposition sites.

Management. Turfgrass under drought stress during spring is susceptible to injury by the brown wheat mite, particularly such sites as highway medians and south-facing slopes. Adequate winter and spring watering are important in limiting infestations of the brown wheat mite. Under conditions that promote turfgrass growth, the plants can usually outgrow injury. The brown wheat mite appears to be fairly susceptible to many pesticides.

Banks Grass Mite (Timothy Mite, Date Mite)

Scientific Classification. *Oligonychus pratensis* (Banks) (Acari: Tetranychidae).

Origin and Distribution. The Banks grass mite is widely distributed throughout the western and southern United States, ranging into Central America, Mexico, the Caribbean Archipelago, Hawaii, and Africa.

Description. The Banks grass mite differs considerably in appearance from the other turf-damaging mites. It is smaller and a lighter green, with the young stages even paler in color. During periods when the mites have run out of food or environmental conditions are otherwise unfavorable, they may temporarily turn a bright salmon color.

The Banks grass mite lacks the elongated front pair of legs characteristic of the previously discussed species. It is closely related to the spruce spider mite (*O. ununguis* [Jacobi]), a common pest of evergreens, but differs greatly in its feeding habits. One distinguishing behavioral trait is that the young mites, when crowded, climb to the top of the grass blade. Clusters of these pale yellow mite nymphs may be observed during heavy infestations. Some silk, produced by the mites during heavy infestations, may also be observed. The young mites are dispersed by the wind, sometimes for long distances.

Pest Status. The Banks grass mite is a pest of many grass species and can be a serious turfgrass pest during outbreaks, capable of rapidly killing large turfgrass areas during a short period. It is the most serious arthropod pest of turfgrass in Colorado. St. Augustinegrass, bermudagrass, bluegrass, and zoysiagrass are among the turfgrasses damaged by this species. It is also reported as a pest of wheat, sorghum, corn, and sugarcane.

Injury. The Banks grass mite appears to be more destructive to turf than are the other spider mite species. In early stages of feeding injury, there is small white flecking (stippling), similar to that of other mites. On St. Augustinegrass, this injury resembles symptoms of mildew or St. Augustine decline and often resembles symptoms of severe drought on other grasses. A slight purpling of the injured grass blade may be observed during outbreaks in the cool season. Dead grass takes on a brownish yellow color and the blades are stiff. During favorable conditions for the mite, severe injury to the turf can progress rapidly. Almost all serious injury by the Banks grass mite is related to drought stress.

Life History. The Banks grass mite overwinters as an adult female, near the base of the plants. During these dormant periods, the mites may be a bright salmon color. When weather conditions again allow activity, in late winter or early spring, the mites resume feeding and lay eggs. Eggs are relatively small and are pearly white when first laid, but later turn light straw-colored. Under favorable conditions, the life cycle can be completed in 8–25 days. Continuous, overlapping generations are produced throughout the growing season. High temperatures in late summer favor feeding and reproduction, which, in turn, cause serious damage to turf. Under laboratory conditions, populations have doubled in as little as 36 hours. Copious amounts of webbing are characteristic of this mite. The Banks grass mite spends much of the time feeding and resting at the base of the grass plant. This can make the mites somewhat difficult to detect and inhibits effective control.

Management. Water management is critical to management of the Banks grass mite. Outbreaks almost always originate in drought sites on a lawn, although they then may spread to other areas. Providing adequate water to "hot spots" in a landscape (e.g., south-facing slopes, areas around the base of trees and shrubs) often can prevent outbreaks from developing. The Banks grass mite is more difficult to control chemically than are the other spider mites affecting turfgrass. Also, some pesticides may aggravate outbreaks, presumably because of disruptions of biological control agents. For example, higher populations have been associated with application of chlorpyrifos in sorghum. Resistance to this mite has been shown in *Zoysia tenuifolia*, but genotypes of *Z. matrella* and *Z. japonica* were highly susceptible.

Pest Status. Although widely distributed throughout North America, damaging populations of the winter

Winter Grain Mite (Blue Oat Mite, Pea Mite)

Scientific Classification. *Pentheleus major* (Dugès) (Acari: Penthaleidae).

Origin and Distribution The winter grain mite is widely distributed in both the North and South Temperate Zones.

Description. The winter grain mite is somewhat larger (females average 0.04 in [1 mm] long) than the previously discussed mites. The mites have a generally dark

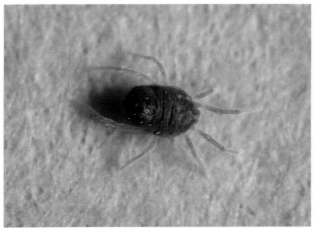

Winter grain mite adult female (courtesy NYSAES [H. Tashiro])

green-black body, with a red marking (the anus) on the back. The legs are reddish and of approximately equal size.

Pest Status. Although widely distributed throughout North America, damaging populations of the winter grain mite on turfgrass have only been reported in some eastern states, where it has occasionally damaged Kentucky bluegrass, fine fescue, perennial ryegrass lawns, and bentgrass greens. It also has been reported as a dam-

aging pest in grass seed fields in the Pacific Northwest. The species is largely limited to loose sandy or loamy, rather than hard clay, soils and is sensitive to moisture changes during its development. The species has a wide host range. Although preferring small grains and grasses, it has also been reported to damage legumes, vegetables, flowers, cotton, peanut, and various weeds.

Injury. Feeding injury by the winter grain mite often causes the tips of affected plants to become blanched and die back. Symptoms may resemble those associated with winter desiccation, for which it is easily mistaken. Difficulties in diagnosis also occur because damage occurs very early in the year, typically in late winter. At that time, the mites tend to hide within the thatch during the day, emerging only at night to feed.

Life History. Development of the winter grain mite is slightly different than that of the spider mites, involving a unique deutovum (prelarva) stage. This is an intermediate stage following egg hatch during which the developing mite occurs within a membrane in the egg-shell. Continuous, but not excessive, moisture is needed during this stage to allow development of the larval stage. The winter grain mite is a cool-season species, with optimal development when temperatures range from about 44.6 to 64.4°F (7–18°C). In the eastern United States, peak populations typically occur in March and decline in April. Two generations are usually produced annually, with the spring generation developing from overwintered eggs. As temperatures rise to about 73.4°F (23°C), eggs fail to hatch and oversummer until the return of cool weather. A fall generation occurs at that time. Most feeding by the winter grain mite occurs during the evening. During sunny periods, the mites take cover in the thatch or under foliage, resuming feeding during cool or cloudy periods.

Management. Little information is available regarding control of the winter grain mite . Some evidence suggests that use of the insecticide carbaryl can aggravate problems by destroying predatory mites. The presence of adequate humidity is critical to development of this species.

Selected References

Cranshaw, W. S. **1988.** A review of Rocky Mountain turfgrass insects. Am. Lawn Appl. March 1988.

Jeppson, L. R., H. H. Keifer & E. W. Baker. **1975.** Mites injurious to economic plants. University of California Press, Berkeley.

Krantz, G. W. **1978.** A manual of acarology, 2nd ed. Oregon State University Book Stores, Corvallis.

Malcolm, D. R. **1955.** Biology and control of the timothy mite, *Paratetranychus pratensis* (Banks). Wash. Agric. Exp. Stn. Tech. Bull. 17.

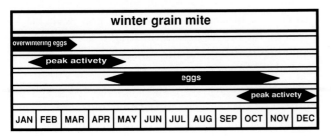

winter grain mite											
overwintering eggs											
peak activity											
				eggs							
								peak activity			
JAN	FEB	MAR	APR	MAY	JUN	JUL	AUG	SEP	OCT	NOV	DEC

Streu, H. T. & J. B. Gingrich. 1972. Seasonal activity of the winter grain mite in turfgrass in New Jersey. J. Econ. Entomol. 65: 427–430.

Tashiro, H. 1987. Turfgrass insects of the United States and Canada. Cornell University Press, Ithaca, NY.

—Whitney S. Cranshaw and James A. Reinert

Cutworms

Black cutworms male moth (courtesy NYSAES [H. Tashiro])

Common Names. Black cutworm, bronzed cutworm, variegated cutworm.

Scientific Classification. *Agrotis ipsilon* (Hufnagel), *Nephelodes minians* Guenée, and *Peridroma saucia* (Hubner), respectively (Lepidoptera: Noctuidae).

Origin and Distribution. The cutworms listed above are found throughout North America, although the bronzed cutworm prefers cooler climates and the black cutworm is a worldwide pest.

Description. Eggs are usually round, 0.02–0.03 in (0.5–0.75 mm) in diameter, flat on the lower surface, bluntly pointed at the top, and, often, have sculpturing, lines, and ridges on the surface. Larvae are mostly hairless except for a few scattered bristles. In addition to three pairs of true legs, caterpillars have five pairs of fleshy prolegs on the abdomen. Most cutworms have characteristic markings on the head and body that aid in species identification. Full-grown cutworm larvae are 0.2 in (6.0 mm) wide and 1.4–2.0 in (35–50 mm) long. Most cutworms coil into a spiral when disturbed. Pupae are brown, reddish brown, or black and 0.5–0.9 in (13–22 mm) long. The antennae, wing pads, and legs are firmly joined together, but the abdomen is free to twist around if the pupa is disturbed. Adults are generally dull-colored moths with wing spans of 1.4–1.8 in (35–45 mm). At rest, the wings are folded flat over the abdomen. The black cutworm adult is gray with black markings, the bronzed cutworm adult is a mottled burgundy brown color, and the variegated cutworm adult ranges from brown to gray.

Pest Status. Black cutworms are perennial problems on the close-cut bentgrass turf of golf course greens and tees. Bronzed and variegated cutworms are occasional

Black cutworm mature larva (courtesy NYSAES [H. Tashiro])

pests in mixed-grass lawns.

Injury. Cutworms are semisubterranean pests. They usually dig a burrow into the ground or thatch (or use an aeration hole) and emerge at night to clip off grass blades and shoots. This feeding damage often shows up as circular spots of dead grass or depressed spots that resemble ball marks on golf greens. The bronzed cutworm is active in the fall and spring and can completely destroy lawns by clipping off all grass stems at ground level.

Life History. Black, bronzed, and variegated cutworms overwinter as larvae or as pupae in the northern states. In southern turf, these species remain active all year. In the northern states, black and variegated cutworms may have two to four generations per year; in the southern states three to seven generations may occur. The bronzed cutworm has a single generation per year. Females mate and feed at night in trees, shrubs and weeds that are in bloom. Mated females seek out crops or grasses and lay eggs on leaf blades. A single female may lay 300–2,000 eggs over several days. Under optimum conditions, these eggs hatch in 3–10 days, and the young larvae begin to feed on the turf leaves. Cutworms excavate holes into the thatch or ground or occupy aeration holes. These holes are rarely lined with silk, as are those of sod webworms. From this retreat, the larvae venture forth at night to feed on plant material. In comparison, armyworms do not build a hiding place in the thatch or soil, and older armyworms feed continuously during the day and night. Most cutworms take 20–40 days to complete their larval development. The pupae may be located in the cutworm retreat or, occasionally, in the thatch. The pupa takes about 2 weeks to mature. Developmental times may be greatly lengthened during the cooler parts of the season.

Management. These pests are generally controlled by using one of the contact or stomach insecticides. However, if populations are high in surrounding areas, such as in field crops, continual reinfestations may occur. Biological controls and resistant turf can also be used. Cutworms can be difficult to locate, so use a soap flushing solution to determine population pressure. If a disclosing solution test indicates considerable activity (three to eight or more larvae per square yard (0.8 m²), a pesticide application may be needed. Irrigation after the applica-

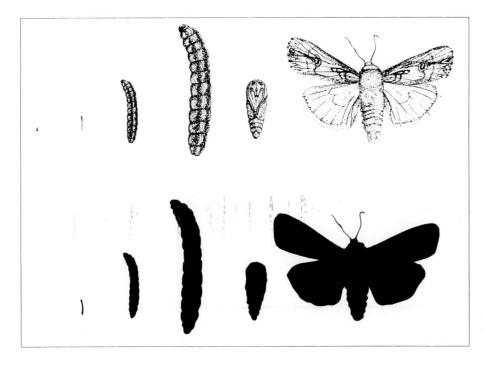

Egg, first, intermediate (third), and final larval instar pupa, and adult of the black cutworm. Silhouettes show actual size of each stage.

47

black and variegated cutworms											
northern range											
			2-4 generations								
southern range											
			4-6 generations								
JAN	FEB	MAR	APR	MAY	JUN	JUL	AUG	SEP	OCT	NOV	DEC

tion is not recommended.

The bacterium *Bacillus thuringiensis* is available commercially and may control cutworms if enough material is ingested by first to third instars. Do not wash the material off the turf foliage after the application.

Entomopathogenic nematodes in the genus *Steinernema* have been used effectively to manage black cutworm larvae in golf course putting greens at a rate of 1.0 billion nematodes per acre (0.4 ha). Irrigate immediately after making the application. In lawns and golf fairways, endophyte-enhanced turfgrasses can be used to suppress cutworm populations.

Selected References

Rings, R. W. 1977. An illustrated field key to common cutworms, armyworms, and looper moths in north central states. Ohio Agric. Res. Dev. Cent. Res. Circ. 227.

Rings, R. W., F. J. Arnold, A. J. Keaster & G. J. Musick. 1974. A worldwide annotated bibliography of the black cutworm *Agrotis ipsilon* (Hufnagel). Ohio Agric. Res. Dev. Cent. Res. Circ. 198.

Rings, R. W., B. A. Baughman & F. J. Arnold. 1974. An annotated bibliography of the bronzed cutworm, *Nephelodes minians* Guenée. Ohio Agric. Res. Dev. Cent. Res. Circ. 200.

Walkden, H. H. 1950. Cutworms, armyworms, and related species attacking cereal and forage crops in the Central Great Plains. U. S. Dep. Agric. Circ. 849.

—David J. Shetlar

Dichondra Flea Beetle

Dichondra flea beetle adult (courtesy NYSAES [H. Tashiro])

Scientific Classification. *Chaetocnema repens* McCrea (Coleoptera: Chrysomelidae).

Origin and Distribution. The origin of the dichondra flea beetle is unknown; however, it is currently of economic concern in all areas of California where dichondra is grown.

Description. Dichondra flea beetle larvae are white, have fine bristles and a light brown head capsule, and are found in the soil up to a depth of 4.7 in (12 cm). Last, or fourth, instars are 0.16–0.24 in (4–6 mm) long with head capsules about 0.01 in (0.25 mm) wide. Pupation takes place throughout the 4.7-in (12-cm) feeding zone. Pupae are about 0.06 in (1.4 mm) long and remain in

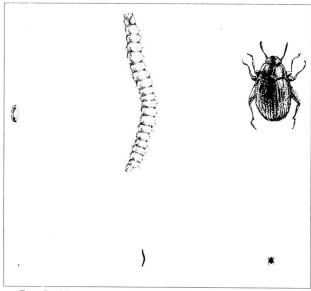

Egg, final larval instar, and adult of the dichondra flea beetle. Silhouettes show actual size of each stage.

this stage about 5 days. At emergence, the teneral adults are white, but, within 1 day, develop a very dark reddish bronze color, with reddish yellow antennae, front, and middle legs. They are ovoid, about 0.06 in (1.5–1.7 mm) long, and have the greatly thickened hind femora typical of flea beetles. Adults may be distinguished from other species in the same genus using the key provided by McCrea (1973).

Pest Status. The dichondra flea beetle is not known to feed on any grasses or economic crops. However, injury to dichondra turf has required multiple applications of broad-spectrum insecticides, and decline of dichondra turf has generally led to replacement with other plant material.

Injury. The larval stage causes the greatest injury. Larvae feed on small roots and the outer surfaces of larger roots. This injury causes the plants to wilt and die, often resulting in the simultaneous decline of large patches of dichondra turf. Adults feed on dichondra leaves, producing distinctive crescent marks. Often, severely skeletonized plants wither; however, this is most likely caused by below-ground larval feeding damage. Signs of damage are generally observed between May and October.

Life History. Eggs (0.02 in [0.5 mm] long) are laid in the sod near the soil surface and require 3 days to hatch. Larval development takes 22–25 days, and the pupal stage lasts 5 days. The teneral period is known to be 1 day, the interval before mating and egg laying, but, adult

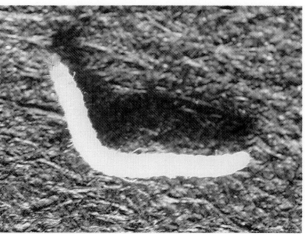
Dichondra flea beetle mature larva (courtesy NYSAES [H. Tashiro])

longevity, and the fecundity for this pest are unknown. Host range, outside of dichondra, has not been investigated, so alternative weedy hosts are not known. Also, although it is known that the dichondra flea beetle overwinters as an adult, development models have not been pursued, and it is not known how many generations may develop under particular local conditions. Natural enemies, diseases, and susceptibility to entomopathogenic nematodes have not been investigated.

Management. Adult feeding activity does not seriously affect the health of the plants; however, the feeding marks allow adult flea beetle activity to be monitored readily. Another monitoring technique is to place turf cores in a Berlese funnel to determine larval population densities. Insecticide labels rarely include dichondra as a site or the dichondra flea beetle as a pest. However, broad-spectrum insecticides have been recommended for adult control, probably because adults are the most accessible life stage.

Selected References

Jefferson, R. N., F. S. Morishita, A. S. Deal & W. A. Humphrey. 1967. Look for turf pests now. Calif. Turfgrass Cult. 17(2): 9–11.

McCrea, R. J. 1973. A new species of the flea beetle genus *Chaetocnema* found on dichondra in California. Pan-Pac. Entomol. 49: 61–66.

—Richard S. Cowles

dichondra flea beetle											
overwintering adults				4 to 6 generations						adults	
JAN	FEB	MAR	APR	MAY	JUN	JUL	AUG	SEP	OCT	NOV	DEC

European Chafer

Male (left) and female (right) European chafer adults (courtesy NYSAES [G. Catlin])

Scientific Classification. *Rhizotrogus* (*Amphimallon*) *majalis* (Razoumowsky) (Coleoptera: Scarabaeidae). The European chafer was referred to as *Amphimallon majalis* before 1978.

Origin and Distribution. The European chafer is native to western and central Europe. It was discovered in the United States in 1940 when a grub was found in a nursery in Newark, N.Y. The species has been reported in New York, New Jersey, Connecticut, Pennsylvania, Massachusetts, Rhode Island, Ohio, Michigan, Delaware, and southern Ontario.

Description. European chafer adults are 0.5 in (13–15 mm) long. Males and females are a uniform fawn brown. A narrow band of light yellow hairs extends from the caudal margin of the pronotum to the anterior margin of the elytra. The elytra are heavily striated and light-ly punctated. The last abdominal segment protrudes beyond the elytra. The antennae club of males is twice as long as that of females. Larvae are typical C-shaped white grubs, reaching a maximum size of 0.2 in (6 mm) wide and 0.9 in (23 mm) long. They can be distinguished from other Scarabaeidae larvae by a Y-shaped anal slit and by two parallel rows of palidia that diverge gradually toward the posterior (see p. 18 for rastral pattern).

Pest Status. The European chafer may be the most serious grub pest of home lawns and low-maintenance turf. Although not as widespread as the Japanese beetle, the European chafer grub is more damaging to turf in areas where both are found. The European chafer is slightly larger than the Japanese beetle grub, it feeds later into the fall, and it starts feeding again earlier in the spring.

Injury. European chafer grubs feed most heavily on grass roots from August to November and from April to June. Even during the winter months, grubs may resume feeding during warm spells. Turf damage caused by grub feeding injury to roots is most severe under drought conditions, when water-stressed grass plants cannot grow new roots to replace injured ones. In heavily infested areas, entire lawns may turn brown and die during prolonged periods of dry weather in the fall or spring.

Life History. The European chafer has a 1-year life cycle. A small proportion of the population (<1%) may require 2 years to complete development. In Michigan and in New York State, adult beetles emerge from the soil sometime between the middle of June and early July. Emergence may be 3 weeks earlier in Ohio, Pennsylvania, and New Jersey. European chafer beetles fly on

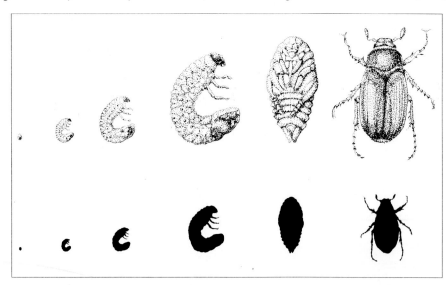

Egg, 1st, 2nd, and 3rd larval instar, pupa, and adult of the European chafer. Silhouettes show actual size of each stage.

warm (>65°F [18°C]) evenings for several hours after sunset. Adult activity peaks within 2–3 weeks of first emergence. Eggs are deposited 2–4 in (5–10 cm) below the soil surface. First-instar grubs emerge from their eggs in early August, molt, and become second instars by the middle of August. By the first of September, nearly all grubs are second instars (0.5 in [13 mm] long), and, by the first of October, most grubs are third instars (0.75 –1.0 in [19–25 mm] long). They continue feeding on turf roots into November until the soil surface freezes. Overwintering third instars remain just below the frozen soil. An average of 24% of the grubs do not survive the winter. Survivors return to the surface as soon as the ground thaws, feeding on grass roots again in late winter and spring. By the first of June, almost all of the grubs move down to a depth of 2–10 in (5–25 cm) to pupate. They remain as pupae for about 2 weeks before emerging as adults. Wet soil during pupation may cause high mortality. Natural control of the European chafer by predators, parasites, and pathogens is excellent in Europe but poor in the United States. Several parasites have been released in the United States with little success: four species of flies (Tachinidae) and two wasp species (*Tiphia femorata* [F.] and *T. morio* [F.]). Natural enemies reported in the United States include two species of ground beetles (Carabidae) that feed on grubs and eggs,

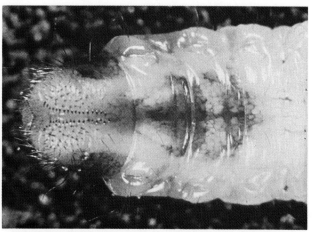

European chafer raster (courtesy NYSAES [G. Catlin])

a protozoan (*Adelina* sp.), the milky spore bacterium (*Bacillus popilliae* Dutky), and a rickettsia (*Rickettsiella popilliae* [Dutky]).

Management. Damage thresholds have been estimated at five to 10 grubs per square foot (0.09 m^2) for low-maintenance turf and 15–20 per square foot (0.09 m^2) for daily irrigated turf. Frequent irrigation may be more effective than insecticides for preventing damage caused by grub injury. Insecticides are most effective when applied in August or early September when grubs are less than 0.5 in (13 mm) long. Liquid insecticide sprays should be followed immediately with 0.5 in (13 mm) of irrigation to move the insecticide into the thatch and root zone. Granular formulations are more practical for low-maintenance turf. European chafer grubs may not be as susceptible to insecticides as Japanese beetle grubs. In tests that included both species, chlorpyrifos, isofenfos, and dycarb were more toxic to the Japanese beetle than to the European chafer. The reverse was true for diazinon. Two pathogens, *Bacillus popilliae* and *Steinernema carpocapsae* (Weiser), have been developed into microbial control products with limited success, so far. *B. popilliae*, the bacterium that causes milky spore disease of some white grubs, infects European chafer grubs in laboratory tests. In New York State, 7–22% of the grubs at two study sites were infected with *B. popilliae*. In Connecticut, however, not one European chafer grub was found to be infected, while, in the same locations, 10% of all Japanese beetle grubs were infected with *B. popilliae*. Currently the only nematode products available for control of grubs are made from cultures of *Steinernema carpocapsae*. Unfortunately, *S. carpocapsae* does not infect European chafer grubs as readily as do *Heterorhabditis heliothidis* (Khan, Brooke, and Hirschmann) or *Steinernema glaseri* (Steiner).

European chafer												
3rd instar larvae				pupae	adults							
					eggs	1st instar	2nd instar	3rd instar larvae				
JAN	FEB	MAR	APR	MAY	JUN	JUL	AUG	SEP	OCT	NOV	DEC

Selected References

Hanula, J. L. & T. G. Andreadis. 1988. Parasitic microorganisms of Japanese beetle (Coleoptera: Scarabaeidae) and associated scarab larvae in Connecticut soils. Environ. Entomol. 17: 709–714.

Tashiro, H. 1987. Turfgrass insects of the United States and Canada. Cornell University Press, Ithaca, NY.

Tashiro, H., J. G. Gyrisco, F. L. Gambrell, B. J. Fiori & H. Breitfeld. 1969. Biology of the European chafer *Amphimallon majalis* (Coleoptera Scarabaeidae) in northeastern United States. N. Y. State Agric. Exp. Stn. Bull. 828.

Villani, M. G., R. J. Wright & P. B. Baker. 1988. Differential susceptibility of Japanese beetle, oriental beetle, and European chafer (Coleoptera: Scarabaeidae) larvae to five soil insecticides. J. Econ. Entomol. 8: 785–788.

Wright, R. J., M. G. Villani & F. Agudelo-Silva. 1988. Steinernematid and heterorhabditid nematodes for control of larval European chafers and Japanese beetles (Coleoptera: Scarabaeidae) in potted yew. J. Econ. Entomol. 81: 152–157.

—David R. Smitley

Fall Armyworm

Fall armyworm moth female (courtesy D. J. Shetlar)

Scientific Classification. *Spodoptera frugiperda* (J. E. Smith) (Lepidoptera: Noctuidae).

Origin and Distribution. The fall armyworm is a continuous resident of Central America and tropical South America and the West Indies. During mild winters, it may overwinter in coastal areas of southern Florida and Texas. Each spring, the fall armyworm spreads from these areas into the United States east of the Rocky Mountains and westward into southern New Mexico, Arizona, and California.

Description. The larva, the injurious stage, is green, brown, or almost black. The dark head is marked on the "face" with a yellow inverted "Y." There is a longitudinal black stripe along each side of the body and a faint, narrow middorsal stripe. There are four black dots on the dorsal side of each abdominal segment. Fully grown larvae may be 1.38–1.97 in (35–50 mm) long. The pupa is about 0.5 in (13 mm) long and is found in the soil. It is reddish brown and darkens to almost black as it ages. Adults are moths with a wingspan of about 1.50 in (38 mm). Their front wings are dark gray mottled with light and dark markings. There is a white blotch near the tip of each front wing. The front wings of the male moth are more vividly marked than those of the female. They have a light diagonal marking about midway on each of the distinctly gray front wings. The female moth is usually more brownish gray and has the same diagonal markings, although they are not as distinct. The back wings of both sexes are white. Fall armyworm moths resemble their close relatives, the cutworm moths. Fall armyworm eggs are small, circular, and about 0.20 in (5 mm) wide. Females produce about 1,000 eggs, laid in clusters of 50 to several hundred. Eggs are greenish white when newly deposited, but darken to almost black just before hatching. Egg clusters resemble patches of gray cotton because they are covered with fuzzy scales from the female's body.

Pest Status. The fall armyworm has a wide host range, but preferred hosts are grasses. The fall armyworm is most commonly associated with damage to bermudagrasses in the southern United States. However, the fall armyworm also feeds on fescue, ryegrasses, bentgrasses, bluegrass, and various small grain and grass crops. Infestations are usually associated with lush, green, dense grass. Problems most commonly occur in late summer and fall after populations have increased during the season.

Injury. Larvae feed on all above-ground plant parts. Younger larvae skeletonize the tenderest leaf tissue. Older larvae may consume most or all of the leaf tissue. Larvae move in groups from areas where grass has been consumed into areas with new food sources. Bermudagrasses usually regenerate, with proper management, after fall armyworm feeding. However, if the growing tips of cool-season grasses such as fescues and bluegrasses are destroyed, permanent damage may result.

Life History. Fall armyworm moths are most active at night and are attracted to lights. Favorite egg deposition sites for female fall armyworm moths include light-colored objects adjacent to turf, such as flags on golf greens, light-colored undersurfaces of foliage on landscape plantings, goal posts and metal fences on athletic fields, light-painted surfaces of structures, and metal gutters. Eggs hatch in 2–10 days; most eggs in a mass hatch at about the same time. Young larvae feed on the remains

of their eggshells and then spin down to the turf on silken threads. Fall armyworms may feed at any time of day, but on turf they appear most active early in the morning and in late afternoon. After 2–3 weeks, fully grown larvae burrow into the soil to pupate. Moths emerge in 10–14 days. It is probable that continuously breeding populations of the fall armyworm occur in both South Florida and South Texas. However, fall armyworm populations in other areas of the United States are dependent upon moths carried by weather fronts to areas far north of continuous breeding zones. In years when migrating moths are established in those areas, only one fall armyworm generation occurs in the most northern part of its range. Four or more generations may occur farther south and westward. Naturally occurring parasites are important in reducing fall armyworm populations. There are indications that wet springs do not favor development of these beneficials.

Management. Flocks of birds feeding consistently in turf areas or holes pecked in the turf by birds may indicate fall armyworm presence. If no larvae are seen on the grass, the turf should be examined for green fecal pellets and larvae. Soap flushes can be used to bring larvae to the top of the turf. During flights, moths may be numerous around lights at night. Light-colored surfaces adjacent to turf areas should be examined for egg masses. Although there are several overlapping generations of the fall armyworm in the more southern areas each year, peaks in moth emergence and egg laying can be observed. The decision to treat for fall armyworms depends on the kind, condition, and expected use of the turf. Except for home lawns and golf greens and tees, infested

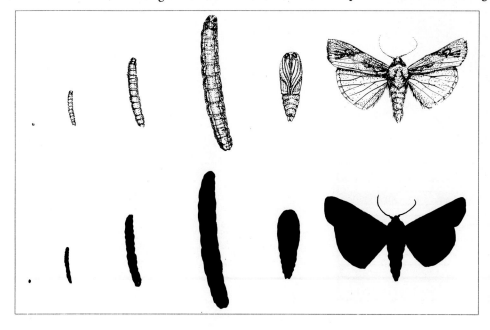

Egg, first, intermediate (third), and final larval instar, pupa and adult of the fall armyworm. Silhouettes show actual size of each stage.

Pest Information

Fall armyworm mature larva (courtesy NYSAES [G. Catlin])

age by spray applications. Light irrigation several hours before treatment may help to increase larval activity near the turf surface. Applications of biorational and chemical control products should be made during periods when larvae are active near the turf surface, usually early morning or late afternoon.

Selected References

Baker, J. R. [ed.]. 1982. Insects and other pests associated with turf: Some important, common, and potential pests in the southeastern United States. N. C. Agric. Ext. Serv. AG-268.

Barfield, C. S., J. L. Stimac & M. A. Keller. 1980. State-of-art for predicting damaging infestations of fall armyworms. Fla. Entomol. 63(4): 364–374.

Luginbill, P. 1928. The fall armyworm. U.S. Dep. Agric. Tech. Bull. 34.

Tashiro, H. 1987. Turfgrass insects of the United States and Canada. Cornell University Press, Ithaca, NY.

—Patricia P. Cobb

areas of less than 1,000 ft² (92.9 m²) are seldom treated. Injury to nonstoloniferous grasses such as fescue and ryegrasses is likely to result in more serious damage. Established turf of bermudagrasses will usually recover, if properly managed, but will be damaged in appearance until regrowth occurs. Mowing before a treatment is applied may mechanically destroy a few larvae; in addition, it reduces the depth of the turf and ensures better cover-

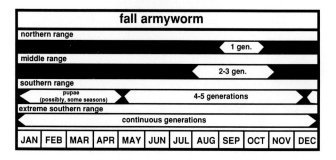

Frit Fly

Frit fly adult male (courtesy M. Tolley)

Scientific Classification. *Oscinella frit* (L.) (Diptera: Chloropidae). Formerly known as *Musca frit* L.

Origin and Distribution. Origin of the frit fly is uncertain. The frit fly is widely distributed across North America and throughout the Northern Hemisphere.

Description. Larvae, the injurious stage, are small (up to 0.12–0.20 in [3–5 mm] long), light yellow maggots that have three instars. Larvae have two conspicuous black mouth hooks. Larvae are found within the base of grass stems or between the leaf sheath and stem; on occasion, they also mine leaf tissue. Eggs are white and up to 0.03 in (0.7 mm) long. Eggs are placed between the leaf sheath and stem; on occasion, eggs can also be found on the leaves and on the outside of stems. Pupae are cigar-shaped and are, at first, yellow but eventually turn a dark brown. Pupae are up to 0.12 in (3 mm) long and are found at the base of grasses between

the leaf sheath and stem. Adults are small, shiny, black flies about 0.04–0.08 in (1–2 mm) long; males are smaller and have smaller abdomens than females. Adults have a large triangle pattern on the head. *Rhopalopterum carbonarium* (Loew), another small black fly commonly found on turfgrass, also has a triangle on its head, but it is smaller than that on the frit fly.

Pest Status. The frit fly is a sporadic pest of golf course and home lawn turfgrasses. Damage to grass by larvae is usually limited to golf course greens, aprons, and collars. Adults are considered a nuisance pest because of their habit of landing on white clothing, golf carts, and golf balls.

Injury. Individual turfgrass plants are injured by larvae rasping at plant tissue. Larvae may injure the crown, central stem, stems of tillers, and, on rare occasion, will also mine leaves. Larvae feeding at the crown or on stems produce a general yellowing of central parts of the plant. As injury becomes more severe, the central leaf of one or more shoots becomes yellow and eventually dies, while surrounding shoots and leaves remain green. On golf course greens, damage often first appears on collars and aprons. Common cool-season turfgrasses, such as bluegrass and bentgrass, are most susceptible to attack, especially when these grasses are mowed short and irrigated regularly. These conditions produce a proliferation of new shoots and tillers that adults find attractive as oviposition sites.

Life History. The number of generations per year differs across the continent. In northern latitudes (mid to southern Canada), two to three generations may occur; in middle latitudes (mid to northern United States), three and one-half to four generations may occur; and in southern latitudes (southern United States), at least four generations occur (five generations are probable). In

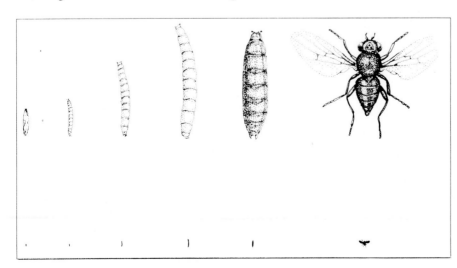

Egg, 1st, 2nd, and 3rd larval instar, pupa, and adult of the frit fly. Silhouettes show actual size of each stage.

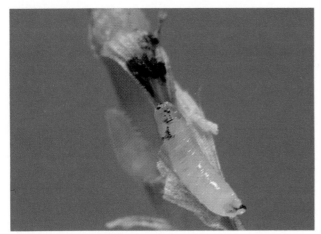
Frit fly larva (courtesy M. Tolley)

Ohio, peak adult densities occur during mid-May, late June, late July–early August, and mid-September. The occurrence of these peak densities may vary by 1–2 weeks depending on temperature. Natural enemies of frit fly life stages include various species of parasitic nematodes within three genera, one species of parasitic mite, at least 17 arthropod predators, and at least 39 parasitic wasps. None is believed to cause high mortality in the field. The frit fly mates during the warm part of the day, between 9:30 a.m. and sunset. After eclosion, males mate within 6 hours, and females are receptive after 2 days. Females usually are able to lay eggs within 5 days. After a 4- to 5-day period before oviposition, females fly to grasses to lay eggs. Egg laying is frequent at 64–86°F (18–30°C) and does not occur below 54°F (12°C). Eggs are laid in the axial of the leaf sheath and stem and, to a lesser extent, on leaves and the outside of stems. The frit fly has been reported to lay eggs on ryegrass, bentgrass, bluegrass, and fescue. Egg mortality caused by rain, wind, and predators can reach 45%. Depending on the temperature, the incubation period for eggs in the field is 3–7 days. After hatching, larvae immediately move down to the base of the grass, between the leaf sheath and stem, to begin feeding. On rare occasions, larvae also may be located within the stem or may mine leaves. The key mortality factor for larvae is desiccation of the first instar under hot and dry weather conditions. Larvae feed by rasping at plant tissue. Larvae are thought to release *Pseudomonas* bacteria onto plant tissue as they feed, which helps to break down proteins for ingestion. Larvae pupate after passing through three instars. Pupation most often occurs between the leaf sheath and stem at the base of the plant. No pupae are formed at temperatures less than 39°F (4°C). Adult flies emerge after 1–2 weeks of pupation, depending on the

temperature. Eclosion occurs about one-half hour after sunrise and is finished by about 10:00 a.m. After eclosion, adults climb from between the sheath and stem, move to the tips of leaves and face skyward. Flight activity begins and ends in the morning and evening, respectively, with maximum flight occurring during warmer parts of the day. Flight is arrested at 48°F (9°C) and is delayed by wind, rain, and overcast skies. Adults are collected in most abundance when sampled during periods of high temperature. Flies can live up to 1 week in the field. Developmental threshold studies of life stages reared on perennial ryegrass leaves under various temperature regimes indicate the lower developmental threshold for eggs, larvae, and pupae to be about 48°F (10°C). The upper developmental and lethal thresholds are 84°F (29°C) and 93°F (34°C), respectively. Celsius degree-day (CDD) accumulations of 49, 293, and 110 were required for completion of the egg, larval, and pupal stages, respectively. In total, 451 CDD were required for development from egg to adult in the laboratory.

Management. Adult populations have been sampled using a sweep net, D-vac machine, Berlese funnels, and water traps with a wetting agent. A blue or violet water trap will produce higher catches and a more balanced sex

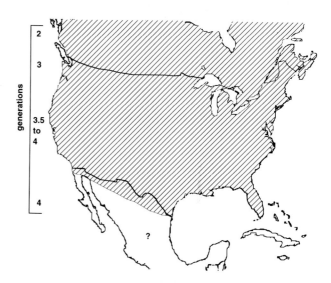

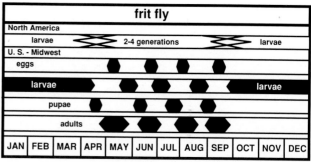

ratio than other colors. No injury or treatment thresholds have been determined for the frit fly on turfgrass. Currently, control of the frit fly is based on application of residual contact insecticides to turfgrass. No cultural control practices on turfgrass have been evaluated. Systemic insecticides, carbamates, pyrethroids, and organophosphates have provided acceptable control of the frit fly on grass crops and turfgrass. Insecticide applications are timed to control adults before oviposition and larval host penetration. An insecticide application timed to 40% adult occurrence (just before peak densities) is thought to be appropriate to control adults before substantial oviposition occurs. A repeat application of insecticide 14 days later may be required to control adults, depending on the residual activity of the product used. Research conducted in the midwestern United States has yielded degree-day models for predicting 40% adult occurrence for each of the generations present. Validation studies indicated predictions were off by no more than 9 days using models that were calculated with a base temperature of 32°F (0°C) and a 1 March starting date. Predictions based on calendar/Julian dates erred by 17 days from actual occurrence.

Selected References

Aldrich, J.M. 1920. European frit fly in North America. J. Agric. Res. 18: 451–473.

Tashiro, H. 1987. Turfgrass insects of the United States and Canada. Cornell University Press, Ithaca, NY.

Tolley, M. P. & H. D. Niemczyk. 1988. Seasonal abundance, oviposition activity, and degree-day prediction of adult frit fly (Diptera: Chloropidae) occurrence on turfgrass in Ohio. Environ. Entomol. 17 : 855–862.

1988. Upper and lower threshold temperatures and degree-day estimates for development of the frit fly (Diptera: Chloropidae) at eight constant temperatures. J. Econ. Entomol. 81: 1346–1351.

—Mike P. Tolley

Green June Beetle

Green June beetle adult (courtesy P. Cobb)

Scientific Classification. *Cotinis nitida* (L.) (Coleoptera: Scarabaeidae).

Origin and Distribution. This species is native to the eastern half of the United States and overlaps in distribution with *Cotinis mutablis* Gory & Perchron (formerly *Cotinis texana* Casey) in Texas and the southwestern states. However, because of interstate transit of nursery stock and grass sod, this species could become established in almost any urban landscape that provides a minimum of 20 in (50.8 cm) of irrigation per year, light-textured soils, and sources of organic matter such as grass clippings, wood mulches, and organic soil amendments.

Description. The adult beetle is 0.75–1 in (1.9–2.5 cm) long and 0.5 in (1.3 cm) wide and prefers warm, sunny days for mating flights. Its large size, forest green top surface (with or without two lateral, lengthwise tan wing stripes), and bright metallic green or gold underside distinguishes this species from other closely related species. Grubs have three instars (forms between molts) and all are similar in appearance. Body lengths of each instar reach 0.25, 0.75, and 2 in (0.64, 1.9, and 5.1 cm), respectively. See p. 18 for rastral pattern on last abdominal segment to distinguish from other scarab species. The grub is unique. It has stiff dorsal abdominal bristles; short, stubby legs; a wide, parallel-sided body form; and a habit of crawling on its back, constructing a vertical tunnel in the soil. These tunnels provide both protection during the day and pupation sites in late spring. Unlike other white grub species, mature green June beetle grubs often migrate at night by undulating and by utilizing the abdominal bristles for traction. Migrations can occur

Green June beetle 3rd instar grub crawling on back (courtesy NYSAES [H. Tashiro])

over long distances (40–65 ft [12.2–19.8 m] per night) and are often detected by trails in sand traps, loose soil, or dislodged morning dew on golf course greens.

Pest Status. Adults generally do not feed on turf, preferring overripe fruit and other sugary foods. However, they can present a serious nuisance problem in public areas when large numbers of adults emerge and concentrate around newly emerged females resting in isolated trees or in turf areas.

Injury. Small, early instar grubs tunnel horizontally in the top 4 in (10.2 cm) of the soil, loosening soil, severing roots, and thinning thatch. This activity may cause the grass to wilt or die under dry conditions, late July to mid-August in the Middle Atlantic states and year-round in southern areas. As grubs mature, tunnels become vertical and deeper, and turf damage becomes more severe. Grubs keep tunnels to the surface open by pushing little mounds of loose soil to the surface. The resulting mounds look like earthworm castings. In addition to direct turf damage, these grubs cause some indirect problems. The mounds and holes disfigure the turf, and tunneling dislodges the grass. Drought-stressed turf that is mowed short succumbs easily to this damage. As grass dies, spaces open up, allowing weed encroachment. The tunneling and excavation of subsoil brings acidic soil to the surface, and this changes the microhabitat in favor of grass and broadleaved weed species. Turf managers using reel mowers have complained that loose soil and grit from the mounds accumulate on machinery and dull cutter blades, especially when dew is still on the grass. In addition, predators, such as small mammals and birds, damage turf as they dig for grubs.

Life History. The green June beetle has one generation per year. Adults begin flying in June and may continue sporadically into late July. The peak occurrence of adults is during a 2 week period in mid-July in Maryland and Virginia, but may occur 2–3 weeks earlier in southern populations and 1–2 weeks later in the northern part of their range. On warm, sunny days, adults may swarm over open grassy areas. This flight behavior produces beelike buzzing sounds that frequently cause an unfounded fear of attack by the adults. At night, they rest in trees or beneath the thatch. In the Middle Atlantic states, most eggs hatch in late July. The first two grub instars feed at the soil/thatch interface. By the end of August, most are third-instar grubs, and these tunnel into the thatch layer and construct vertical burrows. Grubs may remain active into November in the Middle Atlantic region. In the more southern states, grubs may become active on warm nights throughout the winter. In

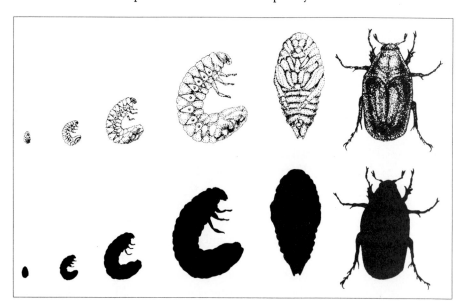

Egg, 1st, 2nd, and 3rd larval instar, pupa, and adult of the green June beetle. Silhouettes show actual size of each stage.

green June beetle											
larvae			pupae	adults							
					eggs		larvae				
JAN	FEB	MAR	APR	MAY	JUN	JUL	AUG	SEP	OCT	NOV	DEC

colder areas, they overwinter in burrows 8–30 in (20.3 –76.2 cm) deep. Grubs resume feeding after the ground warms in the spring and pupate in late May or early June. Adults begin emerging about 3 weeks later.

Management. Currently, no thresholds are available for landscape turf or lawns. Treatments are recommended on perennial ryegrass/bentgrass golf course fairways when grub counts exceed five per square foot (0.09 m²). Damage thresholds for Kentucky bluegrass and 'K31' tall fescue, based on field observation, are slightly higher, at six to seven grubs per square foot (0.09 m²). Tall fescue varieties with broadleaved blades tend to hide damage better than do turfgrass species with thin leaf blades. Kentucky bluegrass recovers quickly with new growth from underground stems. To prevent damage to turf, apply controls to grub sites in late summer before many mounds become evident. Historically, damage cycles run for 3 -6 years and then subside. During these outbreaks, damage may be expected if high populations of grubs were present the previous year or if there is an increase in the number of adults over the number observed in previous years. The most common parasite of the green June beetle is a type of digger wasp, *Scolia dubia* Say. This beneficial wasp enters the grub tunnel, stings the grub, and then lays an egg on the paralyzed grub. The resulting parasitic larva feeds on the grub, eventually killing it. Decline of June beetle problems has been

correlated with rapid increases in *Scolia* populations and with increases of several insect fungal diseases. To date, there are no effective commercial bacterial biological control agents available to control this grub. Grubs are effectively controlled by most insecticides labeled for grub control and by pyrethroids labeled for foliage-feeding insects in turfgrass. A word of caution is appropriate when an insecticide treatment is applied. After treatment, the grubs come to the surface within 12 hours and die, causing a foul odor as they decay. Some turfgrasses recover from damage after stress factors are removed. For example, grass species having stolons and rhizomes may repair themselves after the grub population is controlled. Also, the damage resulting from grub tunneling is less severe when the turf receives sufficient moisture, fertilizer, and lime. Overseeding in the fall is critical in preventing weed encroachment in the following season.

Selected References

Chittenden, F. H. & D. E. Fink. 1922. The green June beetle. U.S. Dept. Agric. Bull. 891.

Davis, J. J. & P. Luganbill. 1921. The green June beetle, or fig eater. N. C. Agric. Exp. Stn. Bull. 242.

Koehler, C. S. & W. S. Moore. 1983. Resistance of several members of the Cupressaceae to the cypress tip miner, *Argyresthia cupresella*. J. Environ. Hortic. 1(4): 87–88.

McKinney, K. B. & J. Milan. 1926. The green June beetle in tobacco beds. U.S. Dept. Agric. Farmers' Bull. 1489.

Tashiro, H. 1987. Turfgrass insects of the United States and Canada. Cornell University Press, Ithaca, NY.

—Lee Hellman

Greenbug

Greenbug [wingless] (courtesy NYSAES [H. Tashiro])

Scientific Classification. *Schizaphis graminum* (Rondani) (Homoptera: Aphididae).

Origin and Distribution. The greenbug has long been an agronomic pest of small grains throughout the United States and Canada. However, reports of damage to turfgrass have increased over the last 30 years (Metcalf et al. 1962). The seasonal cycle of the greenbug is dependent upon temperatures and thus distinct latitudinal differences exist. South of about 35° N latitude, the greenbug is present all year long and may reproduce in winter warm spells as well as during the summer months. Winged forms are often produced in the spring and fall or during periods of low food supply. Although winged forms of the greenbug are not especially strong fliers, they do become transported in abundance on southerly air currents from the southern states to the northern ones each spring. North of 35° latitude, the greenbug depends on the egg stage for overwintering survival. As a result, populations from late winter or ear-

ly spring hatches are augmented by the annual migration of winged forms from the south.

Description. Adult greenbugs are about 0.08–0.12 in (2–3 mm) long and have soft, somewhat pear-shaped bodies. Coloration varies from pale yellow to bright green with a dark green stripe running down the back. The tips of the antennae, all three pairs of legs, and the pair of cornicles (sometimes referred to as tail pipes) that poke out posteriorly are all tipped in black. Nymphs resemble wingless adults although they are reduced in size. Both nymphs and adults may be found feeding together on plants.

Pest Status. Overall, the greenbug may be considered a minor pest of turfgrass throughout the United States; however, in localized areas severe destruction of turfgrass has been experienced because of this pest.

Injury. The greenbug has a wide range of potential host plants, including bluegrasses, fescues, and perennial ryegrasses. Damage is caused when the aphid pierces a grass blade with its needlelike mouthparts and feeds on the phloem tissue. This feeding alone weakens the plants, but the greenbug also injects salivary toxins while feeding, which results in death of the tissues surrounding the puncture. The leaf area immediately surrounding the feeding site turns yellow with a necrotic center spot and, ultimately, becomes burnt orange in color. Translocation of this salivary toxin weakens the entire plant and may further contribute to its death. On a larger scale, areas of intense greenbug infestation appear to turn brown in small, irregular patches surrounded by narrow bands of chlorotic yellow and rust-colored turf. If feeding continues, patches of brown dead turf increase in size to more than 35 ft² (3.3 m²) and may sometimes be confused with early dormancy. Closer inspection of the perimeter of the damaged area may reveal as many as 100 feeding greenbugs per plant.

Life History. The greenbug is peculiar among insects

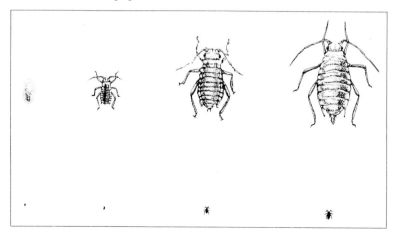

Egg, first stage nymph, final stage nymph, and adult of the greenbug. Silhouettes show actual size of each stage.

in that the predominant life form may be either winged or nonwinged females. The greenbug also has the ability to produce young parthogenetically (without fertilization) and viviparously as well as normally (can produce live young as well as eggs). These unique characteristics, together with its extremely high reproductive rate, give the greenbug a distinct survival advantage. Under optimal conditions, the young develop through several nymphal instars in about 7 days while feeding alongside the adults. A cast skin is shed after each nymphal growth period and is often found attached to infested leaves and stems. Adults may live up to a month and bear many young. With their short reproductive generations, as many as 20 generations of aphids can occur each summer even in the northern states.

Management. Local abundance and damage potential of the greenbug are largely dependent upon weather conditions. Because of the unpredictability of weather patterns, it is difficult to predict the severity of greenbug problems in turfgrass. When aphids are present and damage begins, most commonly used turfgrass insecticides seem to provide adequate control. However, because the greenbug has been the target of agricultural insecticides over many years, it has developed some resistance to several of the insecticides generally used on field crops and on turfgrasses. This resistance com-

Greenbug [winged] (courtesy NYSAES [H. Tashiro])

pounds the potential problems associated with the control of this pest based on insecticide use alone. Development of resistant plant varieties has been shown to be effective in eliminating greenbug damage. Preservation of natural parasites and predators also helps to reduce the need for chemical insecticides.

Selected References

Jackson, D. W., K. J. Vessels & D. A. Potter. 1981. Resistance of selected cool and warm season turfgrasses to the greenbug (*Schizaphis graminum*). Hortic. Sci. 16(4): 558–559.

Metcalf, C. L., W. P. Flint & R. L. Metcalf. 1962. Destructive and useful insects: their habits and control, 4th ed. McGraw-Hill, New York.

Tashiro, H. 1987. Turfgrass insects of the United States and Canada. Cornell University Press, Ithaca, NY.

—Timothy J. Gibb

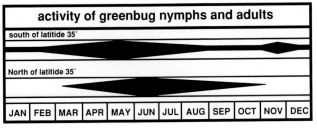

activity of greenbug nymphs and adults											
south of latitide 35˚											
North of latitide 35˚											
JAN	FEB	MAR	APR	MAY	JUN	JUL	AUG	SEP	OCT	NOV	DEC

Ground Pearls

Mature female Ground pearls (courtesy D. J. Shetlar)

Scientific Classification. Ground pearl is the common name for several species of scale insects. Two species are most common in turf, *Margarodes meridionalis* Morrill and *Eumargarodes laingi* Jakubski (Homoptera: Coccidae).

Origin and Distribution. *E. laingi* was first reported in Australia, and *M. meridionalis* was first reported in Florida and Georgia in 1927. Their precise origin is unclear. Ground pearls are found on warm-season grasses from North Carolina to southern California. These pests are quite sporadic in occurrence, but, in some areas, are responsible for widespread damage. Increasing awareness of their damage may be a reflection of increased use of susceptible host grasses throughout the South (e.g., centipedegrass).

Description. These insects are subterranean in nature, and the female spends most if its life in the soil.

The pinkish white eggs are laid in clusters and enveloped in a white waxy sac. The first-instar nymph is called a crawler and is about 0.008 in (0.2 mm) long. The crawler attaches itself to a root and covers itself with a hard, yellowish to purple, globular shell. This is the ground pearl stage. These "pearls" range in size from 0.02 to 0.08 in (0.5 to 2 mm). The adult female is a pinkish scale insect with well-developed forelegs and claws. Short second and third legs are also present. They have a saclike form and are about 0.06 in (1.6 mm) long. The adult males are quite rare, are gnatlike in appearance, and vary from 0.04 to 0.31 in (1 to 8 mm) long.

Pest Status. Ground pearls most frequently attack the roots of bermudagrass, St. Augustinegrass, zoysiagrass, and centipedegrass. Their occurrence is quite sporadic throughout the Southeast and the Southwest, but, in some localized areas, they can be quite common. Because the grass usually dies when infested with ground pearls and because there are no control strategies, an infestation of ground pearls, regardless of how localized and how small, is considered quite serious.

Injury. Ground pearl nymphs feed on the roots of various warm-season grasses. The nymphs extract juices from the plant. The damage to the turf initially appears as irregular unthrifty areas. During the summer, especially in hot, dry weather, the grass yellows, browns, and then usually dies. The rapid death of the plant may indicate that a toxin is present when ground pearls feed. The grass rarely grows back into the damaged area; only weeds will grow in these irregular or circular areas. Damaged areas may vary from 1 to 2 in (2.5 –5.0 cm) across to more than 3.3 yd (3 m) in diameter.

Life History. Because of its subterranean nature, the life cycle of ground pearls is not well understood. Overwintering usually occurs in the nymphal ground pearl

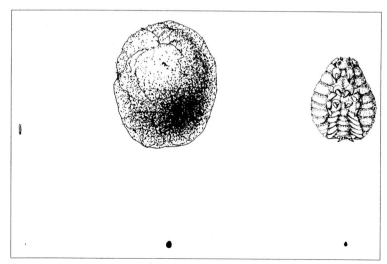

Egg, nymphal cyst, and adult female ground pearl. Silhouettes show actual size of each stage.

stage. Females reach maturity sometime in late spring and emerge from their cysts or pearls. During late May, June, and even early July, depending upon location, the adult females may be seen moving about on the soil surface. After this brief period of mobility (usually about 9 days), they move about 0.2–0.3 in (5–7.5 mm) down into the soil and secrete the waxy coat in which the eggs are laid. Five days after the waxy coat begins to form, egg laying usually begins. The females reproduce parthenogenically (without mating) and lay about 100 eggs early in the summer. The egg laying continues for about 7–12 days, and eggs begin to hatch about 9–15 days after the first eggs were laid. Egg hatch continues into August. The young crawlers move to roots, begin feeding, and develop the globular cystlike appearance. The nymphs continue to develop inside the cyst, attached to the root. Ground pearls have been found as deep as 9.8 in (25 cm) in the soil. There is probably only one generation per year; however, under unfavorable conditions, several years may be required to complete a generation. Little information is available on natural enemies or on conditions that favor these pests. Ants may play a role in predation, and a fungal disease of ground pearls has been reported.

Management. Ground pearls are not uniformly distributed in the soil. Sampling is difficult and can only be

Ground pearls in centipede grass (courtesy D. J. Shetlar)

accomplished by digging up the soil in suspicious areas to a depth of at least 5 in (12 cm). Ground pearls are often most common on the interface between dying and healthy turf, but their numbers can vary dramatically in just a few inches. No relationship has been established between ground pearl numbers per unit of soil and the extent of damage. No practical management strategies are currently available for ground pearls. Most management programs simply attempt to reduce other stresses upon the turfgrass to enhance the vigor of the grass and possibly reduce the amount of damage. Good fertility and watering programs may slow the spread of the damage but do not appear to stop it altogether. The ability of ground pearls to survive several years of adverse conditions in the soil creates special problems for management. Killing the turfgrass with a herbicide and reseeding, sodding, or sprigging at a later date does not eliminate the problem. Turf reestablished in areas where grass has been killed by ground pearls is attacked almost immediately and most likely will die. The depth to which ground pearls can be found in the soil makes fumigation impractical. Chemical treatments applied to the adult females in late spring and early summer, when they are present on the soil surface, have shown only limited success.

Selected References

Neeb, C. 1980. Ground pearls in home lawns. Tex. Agric. Ext. Serv. Bull. L-1740.

Tashiro, H. 1987. Turfgrass insects of the United States and Canada. Cornell University Press, Ithaca, NY.

—Rick L. Brandenburg

ground pearls											
				eggs							
			nymphs ("pearls")								
				adults							
JAN	FEB	MAR	APR	MAY	JUN	JUL	AUG	SEP	OCT	NOV	DEC

Harvester Ants

Harvester ant eating crushed snail (courtesy D. J. Shetlar)

Scientific Classification. "Harvester ant" and "harvesting ant" are terms generally applied to those ants (Hymenoptera: Formicidae) in the subfamilies Ponerinae, Myrmicinae, and Formicinae whose diet depends heavily on plant seeds that they harvest or collect. The following information pertains to the most important group of North American harvester ants, those that constitute the myrmicine genus *Pogonomyrmex*.

Origin and Distribution. Twenty-two of the approximately 60 known species in genus *Pogonomyrmex* occur in North America. The 37 other species are found in Central and South America; one species is endemic to Haiti. The four most important harvester ants in North America are the western harvester ant (*P. occidentalis* [Cresson]), the red harvester ant (*P. barbatus* [F. Smith]), the California harvester ant (*P. californicus* [Buckley]), and the Florida harvester ant (*P. badius* [Latreille]).

Description. *Pogonomyrmex* harvester ants have two enlargements (nodes) on the slender connection (petiole) between the leg- and wing-bearing part of the body (alitrunk) and the main part of the abdomen (gaster). They also differ from many other ants in having workers of only one size, as opposed to having large and small workers. The only exceptions to this are the Florida harvester ant and a species in Argentina. The Florida harvester ant has normal-looking minor workers, major workers with enormous heads and powerful jaws for cracking seeds, and intermediate workers of various sizes. Depending on the species, harvester ant workers range in length from about 0.02 to 0.04 in (0.5–0.9 mm) and vary in color from red to black. The key character for separating this genus from other similar ants is the presence on the underside of the head of a psammophore, which is a special fringe of long hairs used to help carry food, water, and soil.

Pest Status. Concern about harvester ants in turfgrass is primarily caused by the potential danger of their sting. Although some species of harvester ants are inoffensive and retiring, others are quite aggressive and will inflict painful stings if their nest is disturbed. In fact, harvester ant venom is reported to be among the most toxic of insect poisons to mammals. Symptoms of their sting include the rapid development of localized swelling and inflammation followed by a throbbing pain that may persist for several hours. The area around the sting may become moist. Multiple stings can produce excruciating pain, cause vomiting, and induce systemic disturbances of considerable severity. Hypersensitive victims may collapse from anaphylactic shock and may be in danger if not given prompt medical attention. The California harvester ant is unusual among ants in that its stinger, like that of the honey bee, is left in the wound.

Injury. Harvester ants can cause direct damage to turf by their nest-building activities. Nests are constructed in

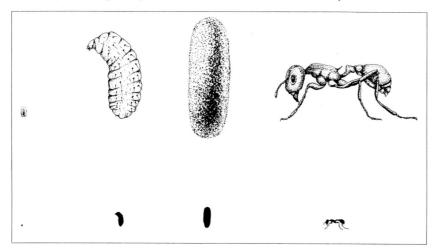

Egg, final larval instar, pupal case, and adult of the harvester ant. Silhouettes show actual size of each stage.

the soil, usually in areas receiving full sun. Although some species hide their nests beneath stones, others place them in the open. Nests may be topped by a soil crater or may be covered by small to huge mounds that may be decorated with gravel. Workers of the western harvester ant and several other species use their powerful mandibles (jaws) to denude the area around the nest of vegetation. This habitat modification can detract considerably from the appearance of carefully maintained turf. In cases where seed production is important, harvester ants can be a further problem because of the sheer quantity of seeds they consume.

Life History. Harvester ants are so called because they harvest seeds that they carry to their nest for husking, storage, and, later, for consumption. In some cases, the seeds are taken directly from the plant and in others they are collected from the ground. Harvester ants are different in this regard from certain other ants that utilize the myrmecochores (nutritious caps or sheaths of seeds) and discard the seed itself. They are also distinguished from leaf-cutter ants that grow fungi in their nests on a substrate formed from chewed-up pieces of leaves. In the case of leaf-cutter ants, the fungi, not the leaves themselves, are the ants' food. In addition to feeding on seeds, harvester ants also function as predators of other insects and as scavengers; they can frequently be seen transporting dead arthropods and a wide variety of other foods to

Harvester ant mound (courtesy D. J. Shetlar)

their nests. After wet weather, stored seeds may be taken outside to dry and then returned to the nest; seeds that sprout are removed from the nest and discarded. *Pogonomyrmex* are very opportunistic and provision their nests with a wide range of seeds. Foraging trails may extend 76.6 yd (70 m) from the nest. The ants give off chemical attractants (pheromones) to recruit other individuals to a new food source, but do not lay down a scent trail for other ants to follow back to the nest; instead, they apparently depend on conspicuous visual landmarks. When it is time for mating, males congregate at specific sites (the same ones year after year) and give off a chemical that attracts females. Some species mate on characteristic species of plants and others do so on the ground. Harvester ants generally prefer some of the more xeric habitats in the United States, and their nests (described above) are typical components of deserts and drier grasslands in the Americas. The only species of *Pogonomyrmex* found east of the Mississippi River is the Florida harvester ant, which occurs in the Coastal Plain states from Louisiana to North Carolina. Colony and nest size vary considerably depending on the species. Colonies of many species are quite small, containing only a few dozen ants. In contrast, red harvester ant colonies can include more than 12,000 individuals; nests of this species can extend tunnels laterally over an area 6.6 ft (2 m) in diameter, go to depths of 16.4 ft (5 m), and contain well over 400 chambers. Florida harvester ant colonies range in size from about 4,000 to 6,000 individuals and occupy a nest that may extend 6.6 ft (2 m) down. Western harvester ant colonies can exceed 10,000 insects. California harvester ant colonies apparently average around 4,500 ants, but some nests contain at least 6,300 individuals. Some species forage only during the day and block the entrance to the nest with a pebble at night,

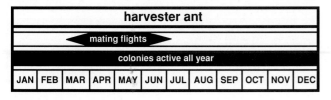

harvester ant											
◄ mating flights ►											
colonies active all year											
JAN	FEB	MAR	APR	MAY	JUN	JUL	AUG	SEP	OCT	NOV	DEC

but, in some cases, temperature can be more important than light in controlling when foraging takes place. Various other ants exploit harvester ant colonies. The thief ant, *Solenopsis molesta* (Say), builds nests near those of harvester ants; it then constructs small tunnels into harvester ant brood chambers and devours the larvae of the larger ants . Another small ant, *Dorymyrmex pyramicus* (Roger), nests near harvester ants and steals food (especially dead insects) from harvesters returning to their nest. Other natural enemies include rodents that steal seeds from their nests. Predators of harvester ants include horned lizards, toads, and birds.

Management. Ant baits containing an insect growth regulator can be effective tools for controlling harvester ants. Generally, the bait should be spread around the entrance to the nest where foraging workers encounter it and carry it into the nest. A disadvantage of the use of baits is that it may take several days to eliminate the colony. Other treatment options include dusting a small amount of insecticide into each entrance to the nest, introducing a residual insecticide into the entrance holes by means of a compressed-air sprayer, and drenching a mound with an insecticide. The latter methods are generally less desirable than is the use of baits; drenching is the least effective method because the nest may extend deep into the soil.

Selected References

Cole, A. C., Jr. 1968. *Pogonomyrmex* harvester ants: a study of the genus in North America. University. of Tennessee Press, Knoxville.

Dumpert, K. 1978. The social biology of ants. Pitman Advanced Publishing. Program, Boston, MA.

Hedges, S. A. 1965. Field guide for the management of structure-infesting ants. Franzak & Foster, Cleveland, OH.

Holldobler, B. & E. O. Wilson. 1990. The ants. The Belknap Press of Harvard University Press, Cambridge, MA.

Sudd, J. H. & N. R. Franks. 1987. The behavioral ecology of ants. Chapman & Hall, New York.

—Robert L. Crocker, Rosa M. Marengo-Lozada, James A. Reinert, and W. H. Whitcomb

Japanese Beetle

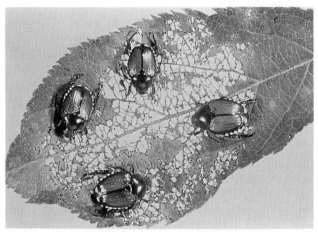

Japanese beetle adults feeding on apple leaf (courtesy NYSAES [G. Catlin])

Scientific Classification. *Popillia japonica* Newman (Coleoptera: Scarabaeidae).

Origin and Distribution. The Japanese beetle is native to the main islands of Japan, notably Kyushu, Shikoku, and southern Honshu. It was first observed in the United States in southern New Jersey in 1916 and spread gradually, over the next 40 years, until it was well established in much of the northeastern and Middle At-

Japanese beetle											
Northeast (New York, New England)											
third instar					pupa egg first second adults				third instar		
Mid Atlantic (Pennsylvania, Maryland, New Jersey)											
third instar				pupa egg first second adults				third instar			
Central Carolina, central Virginia											
third instar			pupa egg first second adults				third instar				
JAN	FEB	MAR	APR	MAY	JUN	JUL	AUG	SEP	OCT	NOV	DEC

lantic states. Populations are now well established in most states east of the Mississippi River except Florida, Mississippi, and Minnesota. Distribution appears to be closely related to the amount of annual rainfall and to soil temperatures. The Japanese beetle is best adapted to areas where the mean summer soil temperature is between 63 and 81°F (17.2–27.2°C), the mean winter soil temperature is above 15°F (9.4°C), and precipitation is spread relatively uniformly throughout the year with at least 10 in (25 cm) of rainfall during the summer. Thus, populations are not likely to become well established in the plains or deserts west of the Mississippi River except, perhaps, in well-irrigated locations. The Pacific coast appears to provide ideal conditions for the Japanese beetle, but, so far, quarantine and eradication programs have prevented establishment.

Description. Adult beetles have a metallic green thorax and head and coppery brown elytra that do not quite cover the abdomen. On each side of the abdomen is a row of five "brushes" or tufts of white hairs, with an additional pair of brushes on the dorsal surface of the last abdominal segment. Beetles are usually 0.3–0.5 in (7.6–12.7 mm) long and 0.25 in (6.3 mm) wide, with females usually slightly larger than males. Females have an enlarged and rounded first tarsal segment on the front leg, and while males have a smaller, more pointed first tarsal segment. Adults can fly as much as a half mile (0.8 km) and are usually active during the day. They feed on over 300 species of plants and can cause considerable damage to the foliage of these plants. Eggs are laid in the soil, usually in the top 2–3 in (5.1–7.6 cm). Young eggs are elliptical but they become more spherical as they absorb water and mature. Eggs are shiny and milky white during most of their development. Larvae are similar in shape to other scarab grubs, with a distinct C-shaped

contour, brown head capsule, three pairs of legs, and relatively distinct spiracles on the prothoracic segment and the first eight abdominal segments. They spend their entire development in the soil or lower thatch, moving laterally and vertically in response to temperature and moisture conditions. Newly hatched larvae are less than 0.1 in (0.3 cm) long and virtually translucent. After the larvae begin to feed, fecal matter accumulates in the hindgut, which takes on a gray or black appearance externally. The average length of a grub ranges from 0.4 in (1 cm) for first instars to 0.7 in (1.8 cm) for second instars to 1 in (2.5 cm) for third instars. Japanese beetle larvae are characterized by a rastral pattern consisting of two conspicuous rows of six or seven spines forming a distinct V and by a transverse anal opening (see p. 18 for rastral pattern on last abdominal segment to distinguish from other scarab species). The prepupa occurs within the soil and retains most of the characteristics of the larva (cream color, three pairs of legs, distinct sclerotized head capsule), but does not remain in a C-shaped contour. In addition, the prepupa voids most of the fecal matter in the gut system so that the posterior region loses its gray or black appearance and becomes cream-colored. The pupa forms within the thin, meshlike cast skin of the third instar and prepupa. This covering eventually splits along the central axis as the pupa matures and the adult nears emergence. The external features roughly resemble those of the adult, although the wings and legs are folded closely to the body. Pupae are about 0.6 in (1.5 cm) long and 0.3 in (0.8 cm) wide.

Pest Status. Japanese beetle grubs are generally considered to be the primary turf pest in much of New England as well as in parts of the Middle Atlantic states. In other regions of the eastern or midwestern United States, they may be one of several species of white grubs

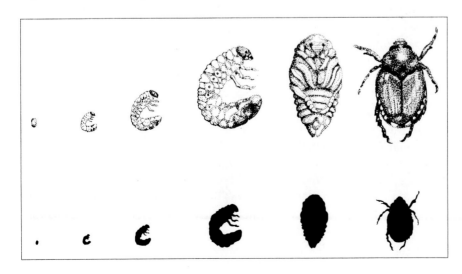

Egg, 1st, 2nd, and 3rd larval instar, pupa, and adult of the Japanese beetle. Silhouettes show actual size of each stage.

Japanese beetle pupa in earthen pupal cavity (courtesy NYSAES [H. Tashiro])

damaging turf in a given area.

Injury. Grubs feed on the roots of many different plants (including most grasses), destroying the roots and root hairs of those plants. In turf, the resultant symptoms include a general wilting appearance (yellowing, loss of turgidity in plants) and a gradual thinning of the turf stand. More severe infestations result in the outright death of turf. Heavily damaged turf can be lifted from the soil or rolled back because all of the connecting roots have been destroyed. Grubs also attack corn, beans, tomatoes, and assorted nursery stock. Secondary damage from foraging skunks, raccoons, crows, or other animals often causes more disruption to the turf surface than the initial feeding damage of the grubs.

Life History. The Japanese beetle has a 1-year life cycle throughout most of its range in the United States, but takes 2 years to complete a generation in the more northern latitudes (northern New England, the Adirondacks) or in unusually cool or wet years in southern New England. The date of emergence of adults and the subsequent timing of oviposition and larval hatch depends primarily on latitude, with as much as 6 weeks difference between the Carolinas and northern New England. Adult Japanese beetles in southern New Jersey begin to emerge in the last half of June, with beetles most abundant in late July. Individual beetles live about 4–6 weeks. Females are able to lay eggs within about 1 week of emergence. Oviposition begins in early July, and female beetles lay 40–60 eggs over a 2- to 3-week period. Eggs hatch in about 10–14 days, and the first instars feed for 2–3 weeks. These grubs then molt into second instars, which feed for 3–4 weeks. Thus, most grubs reach the third (last) instar by the middle of September. They continue feeding actively well into autumn and reach nearly full size before the onset of winter.

As temperatures begin to cool in the autumn, the grubs begin to move downward through the soil profile, typically remaining below the frost line. As soil temperatures warm in the spring, the grubs move upward again, returning to the soil/thatch interface in late March or early April. They feed for a few weeks in the spring before entering a prepupal stage, during which they no longer feed. This stage lasts about a week and usually occurs in late May. The pupa remains in the soil an additional 1–3 weeks before the new adults emerge in late June to complete the cycle.

Management. Virgin Japanese beetle females produce a powerful sex pheromone that makes them very attractive to males. A synthetic sex attractant that mimics this pheromone (R,Z-furanone) has been developed and is used in combination with an attractive floral scent type lure (phenethyl propionate) in commercial Japanese beetle traps. Although these traps can collect large numbers of beetles, they do not usually have a direct effect on population levels. The traps can, however, be used to monitor the activity of the beetle population. Grubs can be monitored by cutting three sides of a 6- to 12-in (15.2–30.5 cm) square of sod, turning back the sod, digging up the soil to a depth of about 4 in (10.2 cm), and using a hand trowel to dislodge loose soil in the upper soil profile and thatch. Grubs are readily discernible against the dark soil. An alternative approach is to cut a series of soil/thatch cores with a cup cutter (4.25 in [10.8 cm] diameter) to a depth of about 4 in (10.2 cm) and carefully break up the soil. Grubs should be removed from the sample and placed in a shallow pan so that they can be identified and counted accurately and observed for any unusual symptoms. The tolerance level for Japanese beetle grubs depends on many factors relating to the overall vigor of the turf. Cool-season turfgrass that is not under other stresses (water, mowing height, nutrition, traffic) usually can tolerate about 10 grubs per square foot (0.09 m²) and can often tolerate considerably higher numbers. However, skunk and raccoon damage can be severe when grub densities are lower than 10 grubs per square foot (0.09 m²), so many turf managers use six to eight grubs per square foot (0.09 m²) as a guideline. The traditional control strategy for Japanese beetle grubs is to apply a registered insecticide shortly after oviposition has ended, when the bulk of the population is still in the first or second instar. For most of the areas where the Japanese beetle occurs, this is some time in July or August, well before damage becomes apparent. For optimum results, the material should be watered in with at least 0.25 in (0.64 cm) of water. This enhances contact with the grubs by moving the material into the thatch and by drawing the grubs higher within the soil profile.

A second alternative for control is to apply an insecticide in the spring, shortly after the overwintering grubs have returned to the root zone. This spring application provides an alternative for turf managers who do not have access to adequate irrigation in the summer months, because the spring rain patterns usually provide adequate moisture to activate the material. However, this approach only provides control (or suppression) of the grubs present in the spring and will not carry over to reduce grub populations that result from summer oviposition.

Japanese beetle adults usually lay eggs in turf areas that receive adequate moisture throughout the summer months. In dry years, most eggs are laid in relatively moist areas (low spots, poor drainage); in unusually wet summers, most eggs are laid in drier areas (high spots, good drainage). In most turf settings, Japanese beetle grub distributions are relatively consistent, 8 years out of 10. If a turf manager can learn to recognize or identify those areas, spot treatments can often be done. Several insect parasites and predators can suppress grub populations naturally. Ground beetles (carabid beetles) can prey on substantial numbers of Japanese beetle eggs, and ants may be effective predators as well. Two species of tiphid wasps parasitize Japanese beetle grubs: *Tiphia vernalis* Rohw. attacks overwintered grubs in the spring, and *Tiphia popilliavora* Rohw. attacks young grubs in late summer. *Hyperecteina aldrichi* Mensil is a tachinid fly, sometimes called the "winsome fly," that parasitizes newly emerged Japanese beetle adults. Current field and laboratory research is centered on the use of various bacteria, nematodes, and fungi to control Japanese beetle grubs. *Bacillus popilliae* Dutky is a bacterium that is specific to Japanese beetle larvae and causes "milky disease," a septicemia of the target grub. The field efficacy has been difficult to prove in some parts of the country. However, two characteristics are certain: the bacterium works much more slowly than conventional materials and it usually remains detectable in the grub population for several growing seasons. Several species of nematodes have been investigated recently for control of Japanese beetle grubs. Species that currently appear to show promise include *Steinernema glaseri* and *Heterorhabditis bacteriophora* (Steiner). All of the entomopathogenic nematodes are sensitive to desiccation and to sunlight, so irrigation after application is especially important.

Laboratory studies and limited field trials are being conducted on some entomogenous fungi, such as *Metarhizium anisopliae* (Melchnikoff) and *Beauvaria bassiana* (Bals.).

Selected References

Fleming, W. E. 1968. Biological control of the Japanese beetle. U.S. Dep. Agric. Tech. Bull. 1383.

1972. Biology of the Japanese beetle. U.S. Dep. Agric. Tech. Bull. 1449.

Vittum, P. J. 1985. Effect of timing of application on effectiveness of isofenphos, isazophos, and diazinon on Japanese beetle (Coleoptera: Scarabaeidae) grubs in turf. J. Econ. Entomol. 78: 172-180.

1986. Biology of the Japanese beetle (Coleoptera: Scarabaeidae) in eastern Massachusetts. J. Econ. Entomol. 79: 387–391.

—Patricia J. Vittum

Masked Chafers

Northern masked chafer adult (courtesy NYSAES [G. Catlin])

Scientific Classification. The northern masked chafer, *Cyclocephala borealis* Arrow, and the southern masked chafer, *C. lurida* Bland (Coleoptera: Scarabaeidae). Former scientific names include *Ochrosidia villosa* Burm. for the northern masked chafer and *C. immaculata* (Olivier) for the southern masked chafer. A related species, *C. pasadenae* Casey, is common in parts of Texas west to California.

Origin and Distribution. Both the northern masked chafer and the southern masked chafer are native to the United States and are widely distributed east of the Rocky Mountains. The northern masked chafer occurs from New York and southern Ontario west to Illinois and south to Kentucky and Missouri; the southern masked chafer is especially abundant in Kentucky, Indiana, and Illinois, west to Nebraska and Kansas and south to Texas. The distributions of the two species overlap throughout much of the Ohio Valley.

Description. Larvae are typical, soil-inhabiting white grubs with C-shaped body contours. Newly hatched grubs are small, about 0.12 in (3 mm) long, and translucent white, becoming mostly gray after they feed. Mature, third-instar grubs are about 1 in (23–25 mm) long, have a 0.14- to 0.17- inch (3.6–4.2 mm) wide head, and are whitish, except for the gray posterior region. The head capsule of mature grubs is chestnut-colored, as compared with the more yellow-brown head of Japanese beetle grubs. Grubs of the northern masked chafer and the southern masked chafer are so similar morphologically that they cannot be separated. The raster of both species bears about 25–30 coarse, hooked setae (hairs) showing no distinct arrangement (see p. 18 for rastral pattern of the northern masked chafer). Pupae are reddish brown, about 0.67 in (17 mm) long, and found in earthen cells in the soil. Adults of the southern masked chafer are shiny, light red-brown beetles, 0.41−0.47 in (10.5−12 mm) long, 0.24 - 0.28 in (6−7 mm) wide, and have a chocolate brown head. Adults of the northern masked chafer are similar in size but are more yellow-brown. Males of the northern masked chafer can be distinguished from those of the southern masked chafer by the presence of a sparse covering of erect hairs on the elytra and much longer pygidial pubescence. Elytra of the southern masked chafer are bare of hairs except on the edges. Females of the northern masked chafer have dense hairs on the metasternum and a row of stout hairs on the outer edge of the elytra, characters lacking in females of the southern masked chafer. The sexes can be separated in both species by the distinctly longer lamellae of the antennal club in the male. Also, the prothoracic legs of males have heavier tarsi, with wider segments and much larger claws. Newly laid eggs are pearly white

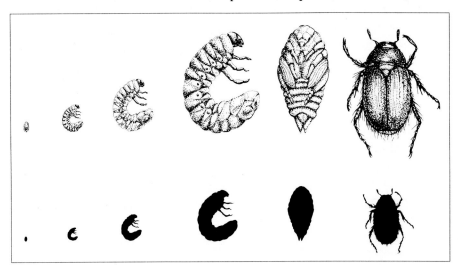

Egg, 1st, 2nd, and 3rd larval instar, pupa, and adult of the northern masked chafer. Silhouettes show actual size of each stage.

and ovoid (0.05 by 0.07 in [1.3 by 1.7 mm]), but become more spherical in a few days as they absorb water from the surrounding soil.

Pest Status. Grubs of both species inhabit the soil and feed on the roots of pasture grasses and turfgrasses. Masked chafer grubs are the most injurious root-feeding pests of turfgrasses throughout much of the Ohio Valley and the midwestern United States.

Injury. Grubs feed by chewing off and consuming grass roots just below the soil/thatch interface. The adults do not feed. Densities of 40 or more grubs per square foot (430 per square meter) are common. Damage to lawns and golf courses is most severe in late summer and early fall after the grubs have become third instars. Early symptoms of damage include wilting, gradual weakening, and thinning. Severely damaged stands develop irregular dead patches of turf that can be lifted or rolled back like a carpet to reveal the grubs. Damage from grubs is accentuated by heat and moisture stress. Damage is usually less severe in spring because of the shorter duration of the spring feeding period and the greater vigor of the turf. Predators such as birds, skunks, and moles cause further damage as they tear up the turf in search of grubs. Masked chafer grubs infest all common cool-season turfgrasses. They are also found under cattle droppings, in manure piles, under mulch in plant

Northern masked chafer 3rd instar grub (courtesy NYSAES [H. Tashiro])

beds, and in other sites with moist soil that is high in organic matter.

Life History. Both the northern and southern masked chafer have a 1-year life cycle, spending 14–21 days as eggs, 10–11 months as larvae, 4–5 days as prepupae, 11–16 days as pupae, and 5–25 days as adults. Third-instar grubs overwinter in earthen cells below the frost line, return to the root zone in late March, and feed until pupation in mid- to late May. Beetles are active during June and July; flights may be triggered by heavy rains. Males and unmated females of the southern masked chafer emerge from the soil about dusk and are active until about 11 p.m. Females remain on the ground or climb grass blades; males take flight and may be observed skimming over the turf in search of females. Mate location is aided by a female sex pheromone. Mating behavior of northern masked chafer adults is similar but occurs mainly after midnight. Mated females quickly burrow into the turf. Eggs of both species are deposited in the upper 2 in (5 cm) of soil. Females prefer to oviposit in moist, well-drained soils that are high in organic matter. Most of the eggs hatch by early August. Grubs grow quickly and reach nearly their full size by late August. Feeding continues until mid- to late October when cold temperatures force the grubs to move deeper in the soil for overwintering. Natural enemies include predators such as ground beetles and ants, parasitic wasps and flies, entomopathogenic nematodes, various fungi, and a specific strain of "milky disease"-causing bacteria.

Management. Damage thresholds for northern and southern masked chafer grubs vary with turf species and vigor. Tall fescue and creeping bentgrass are more tolerant than Kentucky bluegrass. Endophytes of perennial ryegrass or tall fescue do not provide notable resistance

northern and southern masked chafers											
northern range											
grubs			pupae	adults	eggs		grubs				
middle range											
grubs			pupae	adults	eggs		grubs				
southern range											
grubs			pupae	adults	eggs		grubs				
JAN	FEB	MAR	APR	MAY	JUN	JUL	AUG	SEP	OCT	NOV	DEC

71

to grubs. Vigorous turf may support 20 or more grubs per square foot (>200 per square meter) without visible damage; stressed turf can often withstand eight to 10 grubs per square foot (80–100 per square meter). Irrigation or rainfall during July favors survival of eggs and may increase grub populations. Adult females are attracted to irrigated sites for egglaying, especially during drought. Irrigation or rainfall in late summer after eggs have hatched help to mask symptoms of damage. Adults are attracted to lights and may be monitored with light traps. Severe infestations of white grubs are most often controlled with soil insecticides. When warranted, treatments are best applied in early August after the eggs have hatched but before the grubs have reached their full size. Irrigation or rainfall after treatment is necessary to help leach the residues into the thatch and soil. Formulations containing entomopathogenic nematodes have been effective in some tests, but commercial milky spore products are not effective against masked chafers.

Selected References

Johnson, J. P. 1941. *Cyclocephala (Ochrosidia) borealis* in Connecticut. J. Agric. Res. 62: 79–86.

Neiswander, C. R. 1938. The annual white grub, *Ochrosidia villosa* Burm., in Ohio lawns. J. Econ. Entomol. 31: 340–344.

Potter, D. A. 1980. Flight activity and sex attraction of northern and southern masked chafers in Kentucky turfgrass. Ann. Entomol. Soc. Am. 73: 414–417.

———. 1981. Seasonal emergence and flight of northern and southern masked chafers in relation to air and soil temperature and rainfall patterns. Environ. Entomol. 10: 793–797.

Potter, D. A. & F. C. Gordon. 1984. Susceptibility of *Cyclocephala immaculata* (Coleoptera: Scarabaeidae) eggs and immatures to heat and drought in turfgrass. Environ. Entomol. 13: 794–799.

—Daniel A. Potter

May and June Beetles

June beetle (*Phyllophaga latifrons*) adult (courtesy NYSAES [H. Tashiro])

Scientific Classification. The names May beetle, June beetle, and Junebug are commonly applied to adult scarab beetles in the genus *Phyllophaga* (Coleoptera: Scarabaeidae: Melolonthinae: Melolonthini). Larvae of all species are referred to simply as white grubs or grubworms. None of the *Phyllophaga* species has an approved common name. Species of *Phyllophaga* with spring reproductive flights are generally referred to as May beetles; those with summer reproductive flights tend to be lumped together as June beetles or Junebugs.

Origin and Distribution. Various species of *Phyllophaga* occur in most provinces of Canada, all of the contiguous United States, and into South America; more than 200 species of *Phyllophaga* occur in the United States alone.

Description. *Phyllophaga* adults of different species are similar in general appearance. However, careful examination shows that they come in various shades of brown, support differing amounts of body hair, range from about 0.3 to 1 in (7–25 mm) long, and vary in shape from parallel-sided to oval. In some species, the three-layered club (the terminal segment of the antenna) is longer in the male, and in many species the shapes of the segments of the lower surface of the abdomen differ between the sexes. Although a number of physical characters can be used to determine the species of an adult *Phyllophaga*, the internal genitalia (especially of the male) vary considerably between species and are usually of critical importance. The larvae of *Phyllophaga* can be readily separated from many other white grubs commonly encountered in turf by the shape of the anal slit. In this genus, it is vaguely V- or Y-shaped, as opposed to forming a simple straight line running transversely across the rear end of the abdomen. *Phyllophaga* larvae also differ from many other turf-inhabiting white grubs in that they possess palidia (a conspicuous longitudinally oriented pair of rows of sharp spines located just forward of the anal slit and near the midline of the lower surface of the abdomen). Depending on the species, the spines that make up the palidia may be organized into one or more rows or may appear to be randomly arranged. Spines in the palidia are noticeably different in shape from the numerous other spines that are loosely scattered across the raster of a larva (see p. 18 for rastral pattern). Identifying the species of a *Phyllophaga* white grub is difficult because it depends largely on microscopic examination of the palidia and mouthparts and because many species are poorly described in the literature.

Pest Status. Because of the superficial similarity of different species, most people fail to realize that on any particular night the stout brown beetles that they see swarming around outdoor lights may represent several different species with distinctive life cycles, habitat preferences, and host ranges. Not all species of *Phyllophaga* should be considered pests. Usually, only one, or only a few, species of *Phyllophaga* ever damage turf in any given locale. Even species that are common in black-light traps are often from other habitats and represent little threat to turf. Among the species of white grubs that are important turf pests in various parts of the United States are *P. anxia* (LeConte), *P. crinita* Burmeister, *P. ephilida* (Say), *P. fraterna* Harris, and *P. hirticula* (Knoch). In many parts of the country, it is not well known which *Phyllophaga* species are important turf pests.

Injury. Both the adult beetle and the larva are capable

Newly hatched June beetle (*Phyllophaga latifrons*) (courtesy NYSAES [H. Tashiro])

of causing damage. Adult *Phyllophaga* eat the leaves of certain grasses, herbs, shrubs, and trees. Feeding habits vary depending on the species of the beetle. Adults of some species feed little, if at all; others, at times, inflict serious damage on certain field crops, landscape trees, and shrubs. In turfgrass, adult *Phyllophaga* do not cause serious damage. However, larvae can cause severe damage and loss of stand in turf and other cultivated plants. The white grubs live in the soil where they consume roots and other subterranean parts of plants, especially of grasses. Much of the feeding occurs close to the soil surface where the impact of severing a root is more severe than it would be if the same amount of tissue had been consumed at a greater depth. In extreme cases, root loss becomes so severe that the plant has essentially no hold on the ground and can easily be lifted from the ground or rolled up like a carpet. Under some circumstances, white grubs actually pull seedling plants back

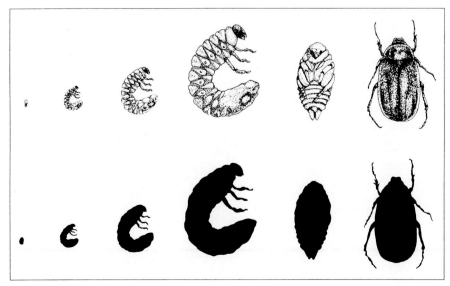

Egg, 1st, 2nd, and 3rd larval instar, pupa, and adult of the June beetle, *Phyllophaga anxia*. Silhouettes show actual size of each stage.

into the soil, consuming even the leaves. Grubs of northern species of *Phyllophaga* avoid freezing by overwintering below the frost line. In the spring, they ascend again to the upper part of the soil and resume their feeding. Early signs of white grub injury to a turf include reduced plant vigor, reduction in the turf's greenness, and unresponsiveness to fertilizer applications. Typically, heavily infested areas of a turf will take on an uneven appearance resulting from failure of leaves to attain cutting height and, frequently, will suffer invasion by broadleaved weeds. As the situation progresses, the turf tends to assume a droughty, brownish appearance as dead leaves become increasingly abundant in the canopy. Bare spots where the turf is completely lost may also begin to appear. In the final stage, all of the grass is dead in the most severely infested areas and all that may remain are various broadleaved weeds. Less severely damaged areas of turf may not die immediately, but their reduced vigor may prevent them from surviving the following winter. White grubs can also be an indirect cause of turf injury

because they are highly preferred foods of many nocturnal mammals such as skunks, opossums, raccoons, and armadillos. Foraging in the soil by these mammals can ruin areas of a turf even where the white grub population might otherwise be too low to be a practical concern.

Life History. All *Phyllophaga* species have a life cycle characterized by an egg, three instars, a pupa, and finally an adult. The generation time for different species of *Phyllophaga* ranges from 1 to 4 years. Among those species with functional wings, the life cycle begins with a reproductive flight triggered by the correct combination of environmental conditions. For many species, rainfall and temperature are of key importance in triggering the onset of reproductive flights. Conversely, dry weather may delay a reproductive flight by several weeks. Males often predominate in light trap samples, at least in part, because they are more active fliers. In some species, females are flightless. In many locations across the United States, there is a regular annual sequence of reproductive flights by different species of *Phyllophaga*. In parts of the South, some *Phyllophaga* flight activity may be encountered in any month of the year. Although a few species are active during the day, most *Phyllophaga* species do not appear before dusk. The feeding and reproductive activities of these nocturnal species may continue until near dawn. Even though *Phyllophaga* adults are strongly attracted to lights during the night, most species hide under litter or in the soil during the day. In many species, the male finds a receptive female by homing in on the odor of a species-specific volatile chemical (a sex pheromone) given off by the female. Mating may occur on a food plant, on the surface of the ground, or in the soil, depending on the species of beetle. A mating pair generally remains coupled for a prolonged period, and, in some species, the female feeds on foliage during copulation. After mating, the female lays her eggs singly in cells in the soil. The egg, the first two instars, and the pupa of the various species of *Phyllophaga* typically have relatively short duration. The majority of a *Phyllophaga*'s life is spent as a third-instar white grub. Some species appear to have multiyear life cycles in the northern parts of their range and single-year life cycles farther south. In the extreme southern parts of the United States, some species may even have two generations a year. Larvae of *Phyllophaga* feed primarily on live roots and other underground parts of a plant, although they may supplement that diet with organic matter. Before transforming into a pupa, a third-instar white grub ceases to feed and empties its gut. As a result, the rear end of its abdomen

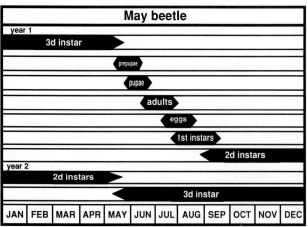

becomes shrunken. At that time it can be called a prepupa. As some species of *Phyllophaga* approach the end of larval development, they overwinter as mature third instars, pupating and transforming into adults only briefly before their reproductive flights. Other species pupate in the fall and pass the final winter before their reproductive flights as adults.

Management. Although recent progress in the development of biological controls for white grubs is encouraging, control of these pests is currently based on timely applications of soil insecticides. To minimize turf damage, chemical treatments generally should be applied as soon after eggs hatch as is practical. Black-light trapping of adults is a simple and reliable way to determine when oviposition takes place. Greater precision of treatment timing can be achieved by subsequently sampling the soil to check for the appearance of first and second instars. Spatial distributions of white grub populations tend to be irregular, with some areas being heavily infested and relatively similar locations nearby supporting few, if any, larvae. Thus, in large lawns and golf courses, much unnecessary application of pesticide can be avoided by sampling before treatment to determine which areas contain potentially damaging population densities of grubs. In the southern United States., it usually is considered that at least three or four *Phyllophaga* white grubs should be present per square foot (0.1 m^2) for insecticide application to be warranted. That criterion is not experimentally based and may vary according to local conditions. If the soil is dry, it may be advisable to irrigate a few days before insecticide application to aid penetration by the chemical and to encourage the larvae to move to more vulnerable locations close to the soil surface. Many chemical insecticides have great difficulty penetrating dense layers of accumulated organic thatch; thus, sometimes it is advisable to dethatch a lawn before applying a pesticide to control white grubs. A turf should be thoroughly irrigated as soon as possible after the application of a chemical to control white grubs, to wash the pesticide down into the layers of the soil where white grubs are found. Special attention should be given, however, to assure that the irrigation is applied slowly enough that no runoff is generated. Some insecticides are more susceptible to adverse environmental conditions than are others; thus, the choice of active ingredient and insecticide formulation can be especially important if thatch, soil moisture, the pH of the soil or water, or the timely availability of irrigation water is marginal. Any time pesticides are used, care must be taken to abide by label instructions. In many cases, poten-

tially damaging populations of white grubs subside without intervention, killed by other organisms that are their natural enemies. These antagonistic organisms include naturally occurring insect pathogens (microsporidia, rickettsia, bacteria, protozoans, and fungi), parasitic insects, and predators (birds, frogs, skunks, armadillos, raccoons, and predatory insects). Other white grubs die as a result of physical factors such as flooding, dry soil, or physical injury caused by soil cultivation. Among the most promising alternative approaches currently under scrutiny for biological control of white grubs is the use of certain nematodes in the genera *Steinernema* and *Heterorhabditis*. Although turf managers may be more familiar with pest species of nematodes, the species being developed for use in biological control of insects are incapable of damaging plant tissue and are harmless to higher animals and humans. Other biological control organisms also offer promise for the future, as does the development of varieties of turfgrass resistant to white grubs.

Selected References

Böving, A. G. 1942. A classification of larvae and adults of the genus *Phyllophaga*. Mem. Entomol. Soc. Wash. 2.

Luginbill, P., Sr., & H. R. Painter. 1953. May beetles of the United States and Canada. U.S. Dep. Agric. Tech. Bull. 1060.

Moràn, M. A. 1986. El genero *Phyllophaga* en Mexico. Instituto de Ecologea, Mexico, D.F.

Tashiro, H. 1 987. Turfgrass insects of the United States and Canada. Cornell University Press, Ithaca, NY.

Woodruff, R. E. & B. M. Beck. 1989. Arthropods of Florida and neighboring land areas. Vol. 13, The scarab beetles of Florida (Coleoptera: Scarabaeidae) Part II. The May or June beetles (genus *Phyllophaga*). Fla. Dep. Agric. Consum. Serv. Bur. of Entomol. Contrib. 716.

—Robert L. Crocker, William T. Nailon, Jr., and James A. Reinert

Mealybugs

Rhodesgrass mealybug adult females (courtesy NYSAES [H. Tashiro])

Common Names. Turfgrass mealybugs: Rhodesgrass mealybug, buffalograss mealybugs, etc.

Scientific Classification. (Homoptera: Pseudococcidae).

Origin and Distribution. Mealybugs occur worldwide and are widely distributed throughout the United States. In 1967, McKenzie recognized 46 genera of mealybugs in North America. Thirty-seven species within these genera were associated with grasses.

Description. Mealybugs are small, oval insects that are closely related to scale insects. Nymphs and adult females range in color from dark pink to light yellow and are usually covered with a white, waxy secretion. Some species have a series of short, waxy filaments projecting from the sides of the body. Individuals range in length from 0.008 in (0.2 mm) for early instar nymphs to over 0.20 in (5.0 mm) for adult females of certain species. Adult females are wingless and are similar in appearance to the nymphs, but adult males resemble tiny gnats and are characterized by a single pair of wings and three pairs of red, simple eyes. Because of the difficulty in obtaining males, mealybug identification is usually based on the adult female.

Pest Status. Mealybugs are sporadic, but occasionally serious, pests of many grasses including several important turfgrass species. Among the more important of the turfgrass-infesting mealybugs are the Rhodesgrass mealybug, *Antonina graminis* (Maskell) (formerly, Rhodesgrass scale), and the so-called buffalograss mealybugs, *Tridiscus sproboli* (Cockerell) and *Trionymus* sp. The Rhodesgrass mealybug has a very wide host range and has been found in over 100 grasses. Turfgrass species known to be seriously injured by this pest include bermudagrass, St. Augustinegrass, tall fescue, and centipedegrass. The two buffalograss-infesting mealybugs were first discovered infesting buffalograss turf in Nebraska. They subsequently have been found associated with seeded and vegetatively propagated buffalograss lawns, rights-of-way, cemeteries, golf courses, and natural buffalograss stands in pastures. However, serious injury to buffalograss by these mealybug species has been observed in only a few isolated situations. Other turfgrass-infesting mealybugs include the ryegrass mealybug, *Phenacoccus graminosus* McKenzie, an occasional pest of canarygrass and ryegrass; the bluegrass mealybug, *Heterococcus pulverarius* (Newstead), which has been found primarily in the Pacific Northwest on bluegrass grown for seed; and the bermudagrass mealybug, *Chorizococcus rostellum* (Hoke), an occasional pest of bermudagrass in the Gulf states.

Injury. Mealybugs typically feed under leaf sheaths, on nodes, or in the crown of the plant. Several mealybug species are root feeders. Mealybugs injure the turf by inserting piercing/sucking mouthparts into plant tissues and withdrawing plant sap. During the feeding process, the plant's vascular system is disrupted, which interferes with the translocation of water and nutrients and causes plant tissues to discolor and wilt. Early mealybug damage usually appears as minor discoloration and wilting of the turfgrass foliage. As feeding and injury continues, the turf begins to dry out and gradually turns from green

rhodesgrass mealybug											
5 generations											
JAN	FEB	MAR	APR	MAY	JUN	JUL	AUG	SEP	OCT	NOV	DEC

Rhodesgrass mealybug nymph (courtesy NYSAES [H. Tashiro])

to yellow to brown. At high infestation levels, mealybug feeding can result in stunting, thinning, or even death of the turf stand. Heavily infested plants often become covered with tiny masses of white, waxy secretions. Many mealybug species excrete honeydew, which promotes growth of black sooty mold. Mealybug damage is usually heaviest in sunny locations during hot, dry periods and is often mistaken for drought stress.

Life History. The life histories of most turf mealybug species are not well investigated. In general, adult females deposit up to 300–600 eggs in a cottony mass called an ovisac. Certain species, such as the Rhodesgrass mealybug, are parthenogenetic and give birth to living young. In either case, females typically die shortly after producing their eggs or nymphs. Eggs hatch in 1–3 weeks. The first-instar nymphs, referred to as crawlers, are highly motile and disperse to new feeding sites on the parent plant or nearby hosts. Females may remain mobile and undergo three nymphal instars which change little in appearance, except for increasing in size. Near the end of the second instar, immature males produce a white, waxy cocoon in which they transform into tiny, two-winged, flylike adults. Rhodesgrass mealybugs are all females. They settle at nodes and form sessile, saclike bodies. A wax tube arises from the anus that carries honeydew away from the insect. Depending on the mealybug species and geographic location, a generation may require from 30 to 70 days for completion, and there can be up to eight generations per season.

Management. Mealybugs can be detected by carefully inspecting the leaves, stems, crowns, and roots of plants in areas where mealybug infestations are suspected. Look for the presence of tiny white cottony masses attached to grass stems. Pull leaves away from stems and examine sheaths for the presence of mealybugs. The

presence of natural enemies, such as lady beetles, that feed on mealybugs or of ants that collect honeydew can also indicate an infestation. Effective cultural practices can substantially reduce the impact of mealybug injury. Selection of adapted turfgrass cultivars and proper fertilization and irrigation programs will minimize injury from minor mealybug infestations. In addition, certain turfgrass cultivars have natural resistance to mealybugs. A number of natural enemies, including lady beetles (especially the mealybug destroyer, *Cryptolaemus montrouzieri* Mulsant), bigeyed bugs, green lacewings, and parasitic wasps, often maintain mealybugs below damaging levels. When possible, adopt chemical, cultural, and other management practices that conserve natural enemy populations. There are no established treatment threshold levels for mealybugs on turfgrass. However, if large numbers of mealybugs are present and injury is increasing, an insecticide application may be warranted unless natural enemies are abundant. Apply a liquid insecticide to the mealybug infestation. Thorough coverage is important, and use of a surfactant should help improve the level of control. Do not irrigate for at least 24 hours after treatment. Closely mowing mealybug-infested areas and removing the clippings should help reduce mealybug numbers.

Selected References

Baxendale, F. P., J. M. Johnson-Cicalese & T. P. Riordan. 1994. *Tridiscus sporoboli* and *Trionymus* sp. (Homoptera: Pseudococcidae): potential new mealybug pests of buffalograss turf. J. Kans. Entomol. Soc. 67(2): 169–172.

Chada, H. L. & E. A. Wood. 1960. Biology and control of the rhodesgrass scale. U.S. Dep. Agric. Tech. Bull. 1221.

Ferris, G. F. 1950–1953. Atlas of the scale insects of North America. Series V-VI. The Pseudococcidae (Parts I-II). Stanford University Press, Stanford, CA.

McKenzie, H. L. 1967. Mealybugs of California. University of California Press, Los Angeles.

Schuster, M. F. & J. C. Boling. 1971. Biological control of rhodesgrass scale in Texas by *Neodusmetia sangwani* (Rao): effectiveness and colonization studies. Tex. Agric. Exp. Stn. Bull. 1105.

—Frederick P. Baxendale and David J. Shetlar

Mole Crickets

Southern mole cricket nymph (courtesy NYSAES [J. Ogrodnick])

Scientific Classification. The tawny mole cricket, *Scapteriscus vicinus* Scudder; the southern mole cricket, *S. borellii* Giglio-Tos (= *S. acletus* Rehn & Hebard); the short-winged mole cricket, *S. abbreviatus* Scudder; the northern mole cricket, *Neocurtilla hexadactyla* (Perty) (Orthoptera: Gryllotalpidae).

Origin and Distribution. All three *Scapteriscus* species were introduced into the southeastern United States from South America around 1900. They are widespread in northern Argentina, Uruguay, and Brazil. In the United States, the tawny mole cricket and the southern mole cricket are distributed throughout the Coastal Plain region of the Southeast, from southeastern North Carolina around to eastern Texas. The distribution of the short-winged mole cricket is localized around the ports of introduction and includes the southeastern coast of Florida, the Sarasota–Fort Myers and Tampa areas of southwestern Florida, and a few other isolated populations in that state. The northern mole cricket is native to the United States and ranges from southern New England south to Florida and west to the Central Plains. This cricket has been introduced into South America.

Description. Adults are cylindrical, 1.26–1.38 in (3.2–3.5 cm) long, and have spadelike front legs and a heavily sclerotized pronotum. The body is covered with a dense coat of fine hairs. The front wings are held folded on the back and do not quite reach the tip of the abdomen. The wings of the short-winged mole cricket cover only about one-third of the abdomen. Both long-winged and short-winged forms of the northern mole cricket are found. Nymphs are wingless but otherwise resemble small adults. The northern mole cricket is dark chestnut brown with long cerci. This cricket is easily separated from the introduced species by the front legs, which have four tibial dactyls in the genus *Neocurtilla* and only two in *Scapteriscus*. The tawny mole cricket and the short-winged mole cricket are golden brown with a mottled brown pronotum. The southern mole cricket is grayish brown with a bluish or greenish tinge to the underside of the abdomen and has four pale-colored dots on the pronotum. Mole crickets can be identified to species through an examination of tibial characteristics. For example, the two tibial dactyls are separated by a space narrower than the width of one dactyl in the tawny mole cricket or by a space about the width of a dactyl in the southern mole cricket.

Pest Status. The northern mole cricket prefers moist, low-lying areas and is seldom found in turf. Although its tunneling may cause some damage, it is rarely a pest. This is in marked contrast to the situation for the introduced *Scapteriscus* species. Where they occur, these mole crickets are the most serious insect pests of turf and pasture grasses. Their feeding and tunneling can also be destructive to seedlings of ornamentals, vegetables, and tobacco, both in seed beds and in recently transplanted fields or beds.

Injury. Mole crickets damage plants by feeding and by tunneling. They feed on both underground and

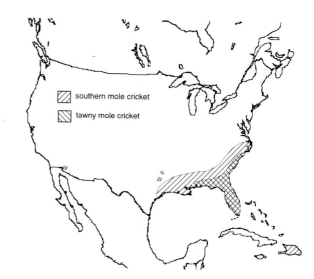

southern mole cricket

tawny mole cricket

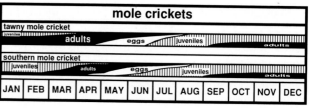

mole crickets											
tawny mole cricket											
JAN	FEB	MAR	APR	MAY	JUN	JUL	AUG	SEP	OCT	NOV	DEC

aboveground parts of the plants. Heavily infested turf has virtually no root system and is very susceptible to damage from foot traffic or golf carts. The green shoots are also consumed, and even the tough fibrous stems are eaten in extreme cases. Although all three *Scapteriscus* species cause damage in turf, their food preferences are quite different. The southern mole cricket is primarily a predator, feeding on a variety of small soil animals such as earthworms and insects, but it may also eat some plant material at times. Both the tawny mole cricket and the short-winged mole cricket are vegetarians. Food preferences are the same for nymphs and adults. Mechanical damage to turf is caused by the tunneling activity of mole crickets and is the principal detrimental effect of the southern mole cricket on turf. Tunneling is particularly damaging to newly sprigged or seeded areas and on sensitive locations such as golf greens. Rhizoctonia root rot also increases in seed beds infested with mole crickets.

Life History. The life cycle of the northern mole cricket reportedly takes one year to complete in Florida and 2 years from the Carolinas northward. Cycles of the short-winged mole cricket are poorly understood, but it apparently breeds continuously with all stages present in the field at all times. Both the tawny mole cricket and the southern mole cricket produce one generation per year, except in South Florida where the southern mole cricket has two generations per year. Different life stages behave differently, and knowledge of the timing of local population cycles is critical for designing management strategies for particular sites. Mating and dispersal

flights for mole crickets occur in the spring. Generally, flights of the tawny mole cricket start in February in Florida and peak in March. They taper off sharply after mid-April, although a few may fly on any given night through May. In contrast, flights of the southern mole cricket begin in March in Florida and peak in early May, with considerable flight activity through June. Flight periods for both species are delayed by about a month for the northern areas of the range in North Carolina. There is a much smaller flight in the fall for both species, primarily in November for the tawny mole cricket and in October for the southern mole cricket. For both species, flights begin about 15 minutes after sunset and last about 60–90 minutes. Local weather conditions determine whether crickets in a given area fly on a particular night. Cool (below about 65° F [18.3° C]), rainy, or windy conditions discourage flight activity. There have been few studies of individual flight behavior, but available data indicate a tendency for tawny mole cricket females to fly just once, generally before they begin egg laying. Females of the southern mole cricket tend to fly more than once, and to fly between egg clutches. Individual males have not been studied extensively, although males make up as much as 20% of the flying population. Flight typically ends in response to the calling song of a male mole cricket. However, mate finding is not the only, or even the main, reason for a female to land near a particular male. Only about 30% of the females attracted by a calling male enter the burrow of that male. Most have already mated and seem to be using the quality and intensity of the calling sound as an indicator of soil con-

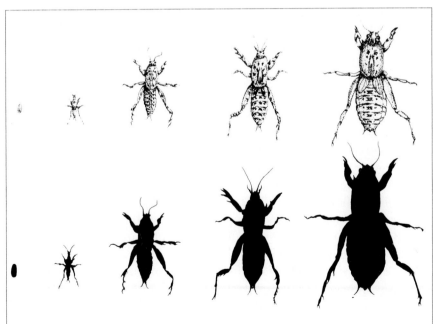

Egg, 1st, 3rd, and 5th larval instar, pupa, and adult of the Southern mole cricket. Silhouettes show actual size of each stage.

Pest Information

Tawny (l) and Southern (r) mole cricket dactyls (courtesy NYSAES [H. Tashiro])

ditions, particularly moisture levels, which strongly influence the intensity of the call. Both the crickets and their eggs are highly susceptible to desiccation, and adequate soil moisture is vital for successful oviposition.

After finding a suitable site, the female mole cricket spends about 2 weeks feeding and tunneling while her eggs mature. She then constructs a small chamber 4–12 in (10.2–30.5 cm) below the soil surface where she lays a clutch of 25–60 (average of about 40) eggs. After laying the eggs, she seals the entrance to the chamber and departs, leaving the eggs and young, which hatch in about 20–30 days (depending on temperature), to fend for themselves. Captive females of both species may lay as many as 10 clutches of eggs in a lifetime, although this is probably extremely rare in nature. In North Florida, egg laying for the tawny mole cricket begins as early as March, but most eggs are laid from April through early June. A few hatchlings may appear as early as April in some years, but most eggs hatch in May and June. By the first of July, virtually all tawny mole crickets that are going to hatch have already done so. Again, timing for egg laying and hatch are delayed by about a month in northern parts of the range. Some southern mole crickets begin laying eggs in April, but most oviposition occurs in May and June with some continuing through July. Hatchlings begin to appear in April, but most emerge in May and June. It is not unusual to see southern mole cricket hatchlings in the field as late as early September, although there are very few after late July. Both the tawny mole cricket and the southern mole cricket are highly variable in development; siblings reared to maturity in the laboratory under identical conditions pass through eight, nine, or 10 nymphal instars. Presumably, the variability in the field is even greater because food supply, environmental conditions, and ancestry are much less uniform. After spending the summer feeding and growing, tawny mole cricket nymphs begin to molt to the adult stage in mid-September. By December, adults make up about 85% of the population, and the rest are large nymphs. Adult southern mole crickets also begin to appear in September, but the population matures much more slowly and by December only about 25% of the population are adults, with the rest overwintering as nymphs. Although mole crickets of both species mature as adults in the fall, there is little mating and no eggs are laid until the following spring. Pitfall capture patterns suggest that fall adults of the tawny mole cricket do little tunneling. This is especially true for females, because pitfall captures are primarily males. Flying tawny mole crickets captured in sound traps in the fall include a higher proportion (>90%) of females than in spring flights. Apparently, female tawny mole crickets are sedentary unless they fly, but males are more likely to move about on or near the soil surface.

Management. Effective mole cricket control requires monitoring cricket activity and tailoring the management scheme to the condition of the grass, the demands on the turf, and the developmental stage of the crickets. Distinctly different strategies are appropriate for spring, summer, and fall treatments. Spring is the time of large, mostly adult, crickets. They are very active during warm periods and can do considerable damage. This is also the time of maximum flight activity. The crickets are sensitive to local weather activity and may retreat underground for extended periods if the weather turns cold or dry. Females are laying eggs and may spend several days at a time fairly deep in the ground constructing cells and depositing egg clutches. This combination of large crickets, unpredictable weather and pest activity, and large dispersal flights makes control difficult. As spring progresses, more and more eggs will have been laid that will not be affected by insecticidal treatments. The best strategy is to spot-treat those areas where the damage is extensive or critical, such as high-traffic areas or golf greens, and to keep a record or map of the areas where adult activity is detected for treatment later. After all the eggs have hatched, generally in mid-June to early July depending on location, the young nymphs are a much easier target for insecticidal control. This is the best time to treat, concentrating on those areas where adult activity was noted earlier. A treatment has its maximum effect if the soil is allowed to dry for several days and then watered thoroughly the night before application. This should bring the entire population to the surface where the insecticide can reach them. As summer goes on and the crickets grow, activity and damage increase and the crickets become harder to kill. In September, adults begin to appear, and dry weather and cool nights can again make activity difficult to predict. Considerable effort has been expended in developing biocontrol programs for mole crickets. In Florida, three natural enemies have been imported and established in the field. *Larra bicolor* F., a sphecid wasp parasitic on mole cricket nymphs and adults, has been established in the Fort Lauderdale area of South Florida; *Ormia depleta* (Weidemann), a tachinid fly, has been established throughout most of pennisular Florida south of Gainesville and released in Georgia and South Carolina; and *Steinernema scapterisci* Nguyen and Smart, a nematode parasite, has been released throughout the range and is currently under development as a commercial bioinsecticide.

Selected References

Cobb, P. P. & T. P. Mack. 1989. A rating system for evaluating tawny mole cricket, *Scapteriscus vicinus* Scudder, damage (Orthoptera: Gryllotalpidae). J. Entomol. Sci. 24: 142–144.

Forrest, T. G. 1986. Oviposition and maternal investment in mole crickets (Orthoptera: Gryllotalpidae). Fla Entomol. 70: 403–404.

Hayhip, N. C. 1943. Notes on biological studies of mole crickets at Plant City, Florida. Fla. Entomol. 26: 33–46.

Hudson, W. G. 1987. Variability in development of *Scapteriscus acletus* (Orthoptera: Gryllotalpidae). Fla. Entomol. 70: 403–404.

Hudson, W. G., J. H. Frank & J. L. Castner. 1988. Biocontrol of *Scapteriscus* spp. mole crickets (Orthoptera: Gryllotalpidae) in Florida. Bull. Entomol. Soc. Am. 34: 192–198.

Mathery, E. L., Jr., A. Tsedeke & B. J. Smittle. 1981. Feeding response of mole cricket nymphs (Orthoptera: Gyllotalpidae: *Scapteriscus*) to radio-labeled grasses with, or without, alternative food available. J. Ga. Entomol. Soc. 16: 492–495.

Nickle, D. A. & J. L. Castner. 1984. Introduced species of mole crickets in the United States, Puerto Rico, and the Virgin Islands (Orthoptera: Gryllotalpidae). Ann. Entomol. Soc. Am. 77: 450–465.

Parkman, J. P., W. G. Hudson & J. H. Frank. 1993. Establishment and persistence of *Steinernema scapterisci* (Rhabditida: Steinernematidae) in field populations of *Scapteriscus* spp. mole crickets (Orthoptera: Gryllotalpidae). J. Entomol. Sci. 28: 182–190.

Semlitsch, R. D. 1986. Life history of the northern mole cricket, *Neocurtilla hexadactyla* (Orthoptera: Gryllotalpidae), utilizing Carolina-bay habitats. Ann. Entomol. Soc. Am. 79: 256–261.

Walker, T. J. [ed.]. 1984. Mole crickets in Florida. Univ. Fla. Inst. Food Agric. Sci. Bull. 846.

Walker, T. J., J. A. Reinert & D. J. Schuster. 1983. Geographical variation in flights of mole crickets, *Scapteriscus* spp. (Orthoptera: Gryllotalpidae). Ann. Entomol. Soc. Am. 76: 507–517.

—William G. Hudson

Oriental Beetle

Oriental beetle adults (courtesy NYSAES [H. Tashiro])

Scientific Classification. *Exomala orientalis* (Waterhouse) (=*Anomala orientalis* in American literature and *Blitopertha orientalis* in Japanese literature, originally described as *Phyllopertha orientalis*) (Baraud 1991) (Coleoptera: Scarabaeidae).

Origin and Distribution. The oriental beetle is probably a native of the Philippine Islands and was introduced to the Hawaiian Island of Oahu sometime before 1908 (Tashiro 1987). On the mainland, it is thought to have reached New Haven, CT, in 1920 in balled nursery stock from Japan. It is currently known to be present in Connecticut, Hawaii, Maryland, Massachusetts, New Jersey, New York, North Carolina, Ohio, Pennsylvania, Rhode Island, and Virginia.

Description. Larvae are typical C-shaped white grubs of the family Scarabaeidae. They are nearly identical in size and shape to Japanese beetle larvae and can only be distinguished from them by the palidia, two parallel rows of 10–16 setae pointing toward the median line on the raster (see p. 18 for rastral pattern). The anal slit is transverse. First-instar grubs range from 0.16 to 0.31 in (4–8 mm) long, second instars attain a maximum length of 0.59 in (15 mm), and third instars are about 0.79 –0.98 in (20–25 mm) long. Head capsule widths are 0.05 in (1.2 mm), 0.07 in (1.9 mm), and 0.11 in (2.9 mm) for first to third instars, respectively (Tashiro 1987.). The prepupa is a quiescent, elongated third instar. The pupa develops within the prepupal exuvium. Adult beetles are very similar to Japanese beetle adults in size and shape, but show a wide variation in color from nearly all straw-colored to black.

Pest Status. Oriental beetle adults are rarely seen and

feed very little compared with Japanese beetle adults. Adults have been seen feeding on roses, hollyhock, phlox, dahlias, and petunias, but are not serious pests (Friend 1929). Grubs, however, are serious pests of turfgrasses (and sugarcane in Hawaii).

Injury. Larvae feed on grass roots within 1 in (2.5 cm) of the soil surface. As many as 60 grubs per square foot (0.09 m^2) have been found, causing complete destruction of turf. Larvae feeding on roots have also caused severe damage to strawberry beds and nursery stock.

Life History. Adults are present and females lay eggs from late June to August. The interval between mating and oviposition can be as short as 1 day, but is normally about 5 days. Oviposition occurs both during the day and during the night for up to 20 days after mating. Eggs are deposited singly at depths of 1–11 in (2.5–27.9 cm). Females lay an average of 25 eggs, but some may deposit as many as 63. The egg stage lasts about 17–25 days, depending upon temperature and moisture. First instars may feed up to 30 days before molting. By late September, most grubs are third instars, and, as soil temperatures drop to about 50°F (9.9°C) in October, larvae move downward for hibernation. They spend the winter at depths of 8–17 in (20.3–43.2 cm). In spring, as soil temperatures warm to 43°F (6.1°C) during late March or early April, grubs start to move upward. Grubs feed until the first part of June, when they move downward 3–9 in (7.6–22.9 cm) to pupate. The prepupal period lasts about 8 days (Friend 1929, Tashiro 1987).

Management. Because the life cycle is very similar to that of the Japanese beetle, both beetles are managed similarly. The very visible Japanese beetle adults, however, provide an indication that a grub problem may develop in turf. This is not the case with the oriental beetle, because adults are cryptically colored, hide during day-

Oriental beetle grubs feeding in thatch (courtesy NYSAES [H. Tashiro])

light hours, and do not feed in aggregations. A pheromone has been developed (Zhang et al. 1994) that should prove useful in monitoring and in the possible suppression of this pest. Preliminary data (Facundo et al. 1994) suggest that male beetle attraction to the pheromone is quite temperature-dependent and that peak beetle captures vary from late afternoon to evening depending upon temperature. Cultural control consists of adequate lime, fertilizer, and irrigation to maintain healthy turf. There are some data to indicate that tall fescue can withstand more grubs than the generally accepted threshold of eight per square foot (0.09 m^2) in other turfgrasses. Grubs are susceptible to "milky disease," but the exact causal organism is not known. Dunbar & Beard (1975) and Hanula & Andreadis (1988) reported a low incidence of "milky disease" in Connecticut white grub species. In 1992, a population of the oriental beetle in Norwich, CT. was found with nearly 50% milky grubs (S.R.A., unpublished data). Hanula & Andreadis (1988) also reported a protozoan (Gregarinidae) from *E.*

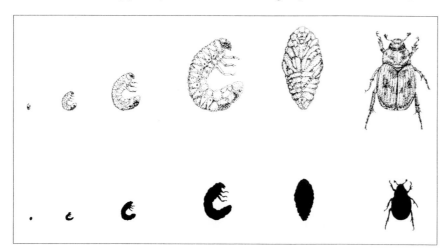

Egg, 1st, 2nd, and 3rd larval instar, pupa, and adult of the Oriental Beetle. Silhouettes show actual size of each stage.

orientalis in a survey of scarabs collected in Connecticut. Good control of grubs has been achieved with *Bacillus thuringiensis* serova *japonensis* (S.R.A., unpublished data). *Scolia manilae* Ashmead has been successfully introduced into Hawaii and has been so effective in parasitizing oriental beetle grubs that they are no longer a serious problem there. Entomopathogenic nematodes are being tested against the oriental beetle. S.R.A. (unpublished data) found substantial mortality of grubs with *Steinernema glaseri* (Steiner) at rates of 2 and 5 billion per acre (0.4 ha) with 0.5 in (1.3 cm) irrigation after treatment. Chemical control of adult beetles has not been adequately tested and may not be practical in most situations because there is a lack of information on where adults are at any given time. However, larval control should be considered if sampling reveals eight or more grubs per square foot (0.09 m²). Timing of larval control should be between 15 August and 15 September in the Connecticut and Rhode Island region. Egg hatch may occur as late as mid-September in that region, so continued monitoring throughout this period is necessary. Villani et al. (1988) found differential susceptibility

of oriental beetle, Japanese beetle, and European chafer larvae to five soil insecticides, indicating a need to develop species-specific insecticide recommendations for the white grub complex.

Selected References

Baraud, J. **1991.** Nouvelle classification proposee pour les especes du genre *Blitopertha* Reitter. Lambillionea 91: 46.

Dunbar, D. M. & R. L. Beard. **1975.** Present status of milky disease of Japanese and oriental beetles in Connecticut. J. Econ. Entomol. 68: 453–457.

Facundo, H. T., A. Zhang, P. S. Robbins, S. R. Alm, C. E. Linn, M. G. Villani & W. L. Roelofs. **1994.** Sex pheromone responses of the oriental beetle, (Coleoptera: Scarabaeidae). Environ. Entomol. 23: 1508–1515.

Friend, R. B. **1929.** The Asiatic (sic) beetle in Connecticut. Conn. Agric. Exp. Stn. Bull. 304: 585–664.

Hanula, J. L. & T. G. Andreadis. **1988.** Parasitic microorganisms of Japanese beetle (Coleoptera: Scarabaeidae) and associated scarab larvae in Connecticut soils. Environ. Entomol. 17: 709–714.

Leal, W. S. **1993.** (Z)- and (E)-Tetradec-7-en-2-one, a new type of sex pheromone from the oriental beetle. Naturwissenschaften 80: 86–87.

Tashiro, H. **1987.** Turfgrass insects of the United States and Canada. Cornell University Press Ithaca, NY.

Villani, M. G., R. J. Wright & P. B. Baker. **1988.** Differential susceptibility of Japanese beetle, oriental beetle, and European chafer (Coleoptera: Scarabaeidae) larvae to five soil insecticides. J. Econ. Entomol. 81: 785–788.

Zhang, A., H. T. Facundo, P. S. Robbins, R. Charleton, C. E. Linn, J. S. Hanula, M. G. Villani & W. L. Roelofs. **1994.** Identification and synthesis of the female sex pheromone of the oriental beetle *Anomala orientalis* (Coleoptera: Scarabaeidae). Chem. Ecol. 20: 2415–2427.

—Steven R. Alm, Michael G. Villani,
and Michael G. Klein

Hawaii

Oriental beetle											
3d instar											
					prepupae						
					pupae						
				adults							
					eggs						
					1st instars						
							2d instars				
								3d instar			
overwintering 2d (2 yr) instars											
JAN	FEB	MAR	APR	MAY	JUN	JUL	AUG	SEP	OCT	NOV	DEC

Red Imported Fire Ant

Red imported fire ant workers (courtesy NYSAES [H. Tashiro])

Scientific Classification. *Solenopsis invicta* Buren (Hymenoptera: Formicidae).

Origin and Distribution. The red imported fire ant, an introduced species from South America, entered the United States in Mobile, AL, around 1930. The species continues to spread into areas of the southern United States with mild climates and adequate moisture and food. The red imported fire ant currently infests all of Florida and Louisiana and portions of Georgia, South Carolina, North Carolina, Tennessee, Alabama, Mississippi, Arkansas, Texas, and Oklahoma.

Description. The red imported fire ant builds mounds in almost any type of soil, but prefers open, sunny areas such as pastures, parks, lawns, and cultivated fields. The size of the mound depends upon soil characteristics and the frequency with which the mound is disturbed. The above-ground portion of mounds is usu-

ally conical and can reach 10–12 in (25–30 cm) in height. The tops of mounds are less well developed in very sandy soils or where the land is frequently disturbed. Below ground, mounds are V-shaped and may penetrate 3–4 ft (0.9–1.2 m) deep in the soil. Mounds are occasionally located inside rotten logs, around stumps or trees, under structures, or inside electrical switch boxes. Red imported fire ant mounds contain the brood and three forms of adult ants: black reproductive males, red-brown reproductive females (queens), and worker ants. Egg-laying queens have no wings; unmated queens and males are winged. Worker ants are wingless, sterile females and vary greatly in size. The brood includes cream-colored, globular eggs, grublike larvae, and pupae.

Pest Status. The red imported fire ant is a predator as well as a scavenger and feeds on a wide variety of foods, including insects and closely related organisms, seeds, carrion, and processed foods. The biggest problem associated with these ants is their stinging and biting behavior. They can sting repeatedly and defensively and aggressively attack anything that disturbs their mounds or food sources.

Injury. Symptoms of a red imported fire ant sting include an intense burning and itching. Often, a white pustule forms at the site where the ant venom was injected into the skin. A few people are hypersensitive to red imported fire ant venom and may suffer chest pains or nausea, or lapse into a coma, from even one sting.

Life History. New red imported fire ant colonies are not conspicuous for several months after the young queen begins egg laying. After completion of the mating flight, the newly mated queen constructs a small chamber in the soil and lays a cluster of a dozen or so eggs. The eggs hatch 7–10 days later, and the immature ants

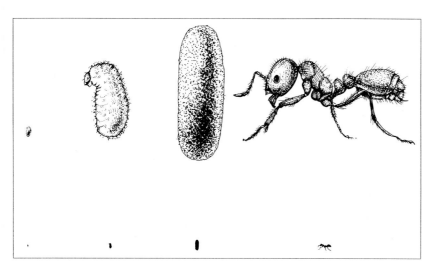

Egg, final larva instar, pupal case, and adult of the imported fire ant. Silhouettes show actual size of each stage.

Red imported fire ant mound (courtesy NYSAES [H. Tashiro])

are tended by the queen until they emerge from the pupae as adults, in 15–25 days. These worker ants care for the queen, and she begins to lay up to 200 eggs per day. Worker ants gather food, defend the colony, and care for the brood. The mature colony may contain 100,000–500,000 workers, the brood, and several hundred winged (reproductive) forms. Worker ants may live for 2 months, and queens can survive 5 years or more. Reproductive forms are most prevalent in the mound in spring and early summer. Mating flights can occur at any time

of year but are most common from April through June. Males die soon after the mating flight, and the newly mated queen falls to the ground, sheds her wings, and begins searching for a suitable site to start a new colony.

Management. In the 1960s and 1970s, attempts were made to eradicate the red imported these ant from the southeastern United States. These programs failed to eradicate the species and may actually have aided the spread of fire ants because chemicals used in the eradication program also affected populations of native ant species. In the absence of native ant species, the red imported fire ant becomes well established in an area and prevents other ants from reestablishing. Today we know that eradication of the red imported fire ant is not technically, economically, or environmentally feasible in fully infested areas. Chemicals provide temporary control of mounds and must be reapplied periodically for as long as control is desired. Reinfestation occurs if treatments are terminated, and new populations may be larger than populations before treatment began. The decision to control red imported fire ant populations must be accompanied by a long-term commitment to continue periodic treatments. Insecticides are currently the primary method of suppressing red imported fire ant populations in urban environments. The most effective control programs incorporate the use of bait products, treatment of individual ant mounds, and broadcast application(s) of contact insecticides.

Selected References

Drees, A. B., M. Bastiaan & S. B. Vinson. 1991. Fire ants and their management. Tex. Agric. Ext. Serv. Bull. B-1536.
Sparks, B. 1992. Controlling fire ants in urban areas. Univ. Ga. Coop. Ext. Bull. 1068.
Summerlin, J. W., A.C.F. Hung & S. B. Vinson. 1977. Residues in nontarget ants, species simplification and recovery of populations following aerial applications of mirex. Environ. Entomol. 6: 193–197.
Wilson, E. O. 1958. The fire ant. Sci. Am. March: 36–41.

—Beverly Sparks

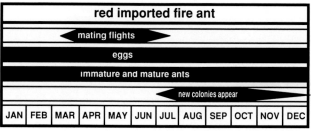

Sod Webworms

Lawn webworm moth (courtesy NYSAES [G. Catlin])

Scientific Classification. Formerly, most common sod webworms were listed as *Crambus* species. Some important species are as follows: the silverstriped webworm, *Crambus praefectellus* (Zincken); the bluegrass webworm, *Parapediasia teterrella* (Zincken); the larger sod webworm, *Pediasia trisecta* (Walker); the striped sod webworm, *Fissicrambus mutabilis* (Clemens); the tropical sod webworm, *Herpetogramma phaeopteralis* Guenée (Lepidoptera: Pyralidae).

Origin and Distribution. Most sod webworms are native to North America and are widely distributed within the continental United States. Except for the tropical sod webworm, the species mentioned above are found primarily in the eastern United States. The bluegrass sod webworm ranges over most of the eastern two-thirds of the country, from Massachusetts and Connecticut westward into Colorado and south through mid-Texas and eastward. It is most abundant in

Kentucky and Tennessee. The larger sod webworm is most abundant in an area including Ohio and Iowa, but ranges from southern Canada southward into North Carolina and westward into Tennessee, Texas, New Mexico, and Colorado. The striped sod webworm is most abundant in a central area of its range that includes Pennsylvania, Illinois, and Tennessee. This species also ranges westward into Texas and Colorado. Other sod webworm species such as *Crambus sperryellus* Klots are major pests along the Pacific coast and in areas west of the Rocky Mountains. The tropical sod webworm is distributed throughout the warmer areas of the southeastern United States and the Caribbean.

Description. Larvae vary from gray or light green to beige or brown. Most have dark spots scattered over their bodies. The tropical sod webworm is light green. Larval heads are light brown to black. Fully grown larvae generally range from 0.63 to 1.1 in (16–28 mm) long. Most larvae curl into a ball when disturbed; tropical sod webworm larvae can move rapidly forward or backward. Pupae of most species are usually enclosed in cocoons made from debris, soil particles, and fecal pellets. Cocoons are located in the soil or thatch. Pupae are reddish brown and 0.43–0.51 in (11–13 mm) long. Adults are moths, 0.51–0.75 in (13–19 mm) long, and have wingspans of about 0.59–1.38 in (15–35 mm). Most have a prominent snoutlike projection (formed by long labial palpi) on the head. Except for the tropical sod webworm, the wings of moths at rest are folded partially around the body, which gives a tubelike appearance. When disturbed, moths of most species fly short distances in a zigzag pattern. Most have front wings that are dull gray or brown with a light streak from the base to the margin; the back wings are light brown or tan. The tropical sod webworm moth has light tan or gray wings with darker lines running across them. It does not curl

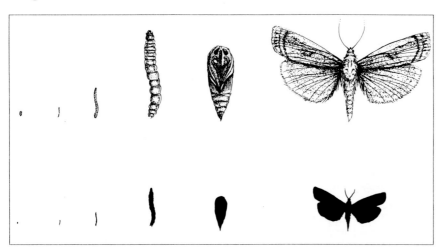

Egg, first, intermediate (third), and final larval instar, pupa and adult of the sod webworm.

Lawn webworm mature larva (courtesy NYSAES [G. Catlin])

its wings around the body when at rest. Sod webworm eggs are white to pale beige, aging to orange, oval with longitudinal ridges, and 0.01–0.28 in (0.3–0.7 mm) long. Eggs are deposited singly or in small clusters, depending upon the species.

Pest Status. Sod webworms feed primarily on turfgrasses, pasture and field grasses, and some small grain crops. New sod fields and newly established lawns often appear to be preferred sites. Serious damage may occur when drought conditions exist where sod webworms are feeding.

Injury. Young larvae feed by chewing the tender plant tissue of leaves and stems. Larger larvae may cut off grass blades and pull them into their tunnels to eat them. Sod webworm feeding may first be evident when small brown patches of closely cropped grass appear. These patches are often mistaken for disease damage. Tropical sod webworm larvae chew out notches in the leaves of bermudagrass, centipedegrass, zoysia, bahia, and St. Augustinegrasses, giving the turf a ragged appearance. Appearance of sod webworm damage on irrigated turf is likely during mid- to late summer when populations have increased.

Life History. Sod webworm moths deposit eggs indiscriminately over the turf at night. Eggs hatch in a week or 10 days. Larvae begin to feed and construct silken tubes. Young larvae feed on surface tissues of grass plants, but older larvae eat whole portions of leaves and stems. Feeding occurs at night and on cloudy days. There are usually six to eight instars. Most species overwinter in the soil as larvae. The tropical sod webworm overwinters in South Florida; south of Gainesville, all stages are present throughout the year. The tropical sod webworm larva is susceptible to cold temperatures and cannot survive in areas north of central Florida. Females

of most species live about a week. There are usually two or three generations a year for most species, and about 6 weeks are required between egg deposition and adult emergence.

Management. Most sod webworm problems on turf are associated with grass grown under high maintenance conditions. Thresholds for insecticidal treatment vary greatly from place to place, generally from six to 16 larvae per 4.65 in^2 (30 cm^2) area. Larvae can be flushed from infested sod with solutions of pyrethrins or liquid soap. Young larvae can be expected in infested turf about 2 weeks after peak moth flights. General turf vigor, maintenance practices, and use patterns may influence control strategies. Warm-season grasses may outgrow spring and early summer damage. Damage is most severe in late summer when populations have increased and grass growth has slowed. Biorational and insecticidal control applications should be applied late in the day, before larval feeding at night. Birds are important predators of sod webworm larvae, as are insect predators such as ground beetles, robber flies, and predator wasps. Larvae are susceptible to infection by such microorganisms as the fungus *Beauveria bassiana* (Balsamo), and the microsporidia *Nosema*. Parasitic nematodes (*Steinernema carpocapsae* [Weiser] and *Heterorhabditis heliothidis* [Khan, Brooke, and Hirschmann]) can infect sod web-

sod webworms*											
northern range											
larvae		pupae		1-2 generations					larvae		
middle range											
larvae		pupae		2-3 generations					larvae		
southern range											
larvae		pupae		3-4 generations					larvae		
JAN	FEB	MAR	APR	MAY	JUN	JUL	AUG	SEP	OCT	NOV	DEC

*General, and except tropical sod webworm

worms. Strains of *Bacillus thuringiensis* (bacteria) are used for control of young sod webworm larvae.

Selected References

Baker, J. R. 1982. Insects and other pests associated with turf: some important, common, and potential pests in the southeastern United States. N. C. Agric. Ext. Serv. AG-268.

Shetlar, D. J., P. R. Heller & P. D. Irish. 1988. Turfgrass insect and mite manual. Pennsylvania Turfgrass Council.

Tashiro, H. 1987. Turfgrass insects of the United States and Canada. Cornell University Press, Ithaca, NY.

Tolley, M. P. & W. H. Robinson. 1986. Seasonal abundance and degree-day prediction of sod webworm (Lepidoptera: Pyralidae) adult emergence in Virginia. J. Econ. Entomol. 79: 400–404.

—Patricia P. Cobb

Two-Lined Spittlebug

Two-lined spittlebug adult (courtesy of P. P. Cobb)

Scientific Classification. *Prosapia bicincta* (Say) (Homoptera: Cercopidae). Former scientific names include *Cercopis bicincta*, *Monecphora bifascia*, *M. angusta*, *M. basalis*, *M. neglecta*, *M. fraterna*, and *Tomaspis bicincta*.

Origin and Distribution. The two-lined spittlebug, a North American species, is widely distributed from Maine to Florida and west to Iowa, Kansas, and Oklahoma.

Description. Wedge-shaped adults are dark brown to black with red eyes and legs. Typically there are two prominent red or orange lines across the wings and a narrower band across the thorax. Occasionally unbanded specimens occur. The top side of the abdomen underneath the wings is bright red, and the bottom side appears dark red to black. Adults are about 0.38 in (9.5 mm) long. Nymphs are cream-colored with brown heads and red eyes. Nymphs are responsible for the name spittlebug because they produce the white, frothy mass that envelops them and that provides the high humidity and protective environment needed for development. Eggs are small (less than 0.06 in [1.6 mm] long), bright orange, and oblong.

Pest Status. The two-lined spittlebug has sporadically inflicted severe damage to coastal bermudagrass and other bermudagrass pastures in the Southeast since the early 1950s. In recent years, sporadic damage to warm-season turfgrasses has focused attention on the two-lined spittlebug as a serious pest of managed turfgrasses. Adults have been found resting or feeding on a wide variety of woody plants; hollies are especially prone to attack and injury. Nymphs are usually confined to low herbaceous situations and have been found to feed on

Two-lined spittlebug nymph in spittle mass (courtesy of P. P. Cobb)

many species of grasses, especially centipedegrass and St. Augustinegrass. The largest two-lined spittlebug populations and resultant damage occur in years with high spring and summer rainfall.

Injury. Nymphs and adults injure grasses when they insert their needlelike mouthparts into tissue and extract plant juices. Adults also inject a toxin, which results in a streaking or chlorotic stippling of the leaves. The vascular tissues transport the toxin up and down the stems and into the leaves from the initial feeding site. Only adults have been shown to produce these symptoms. Neither age nor sex is a factor in inducing the phytotoxemia. Areas subsequently coalesce and turn brown. Nymphs feed deep within the turf at the crown of the plant, near the soil. When large numbers of the two-lined spittlebug are present, the turf develops a "squishy" feel because of spittle masses, which are unpleasant underfoot.

Life History. Two generations of the two-lined spittlebug have been shown to occur in Georgia and Florida, with a possible partial third generation present in some

areas. Eggs overwinter in hollow stems, under leaf sheaths, and at the base of plants in moist litter and debris. Eggs are produced singly, but many eggs may be found at one location. Most eggs hatch at night. Upon hatching, first-instar nymphs seek suitable feeding sites. After the mouthparts are inserted, the spittlemass is produced. Nymphs are not confined to one site and sometimes move after molting. Nymphs have been recorded on over 40 different plants, predominantly grasses. Nymphs grow through five instars before becoming adults. The molt to the adult stage takes place within the spittlemass of the fifth instar. Nymphs that are ready to molt to the adult stage often crawl higher on the plant and feed long enough to produce the protective mass of spittle. Depending on temperature and precipitation, most overwintering eggs hatch in March and April. Adults of the first generation are active in June. Another peak in adult activity occurs in August and September, corresponding to the second generation, which deposits the overwintering eggs. Adults, especially males, are active at night and are attracted to light traps. Little is known of the biology of this species. Temperature influences the length of the life cycle. At 72–76°F (22.2 –24.4°C), eggs hatch in about 19 days. Under varying conditions, the nymphal period is about 30–50 days. Adults live 23–24 days at 80°F (26.7°C). Oviposition begins 6–10 days after adult emergence. Females oviposit an average of 45.1 eggs.

Management. Spittlebug problems are often associated with an overdeveloped thatch layer, which provides the high moisture environment that spittlebugs require. Therefore, cultural management of the two-lined spittlebug includes dethatching and topdressing at appropriate times. Susceptible grasses should be monitored closely for the appearance of small, cream-colored nymphs in spittlemasses deep in the turf. Treatment for adults, although they are the most visible stage, is rarely

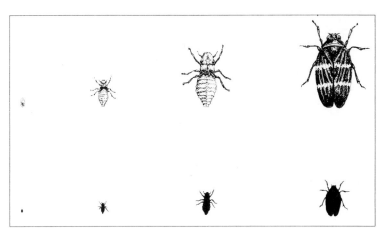

Egg, first stage nymph, final stage nymph, and adult of the two-lined spittlebug. Silhouettes show actual size of each stage.

twolined spittlebug											
eggs		2 generations							eggs		
JAN	FEB	MAR	APR	MAY	JUN	JUL	AUG	SEP	OCT	NOV	DEC

justified. Often, serious damage is associated more with the second generation than with the first. Application of an insecticide in July may be appropriate in heavily infested areas. Success is enhanced if turf is mown and irrigated several hours before treatment late in the day. Avoiding a combination of susceptible landscape plants will reduce the need to treat for the two-lined spittlebug. The combination of Japanese hollies, which serve as feeding sites for adults, and susceptible centipedegrass, for example, should be avoided. Few natural enemies of the two-lined spittlebug are known. No parasites or predators of the eggs or nymphs have been recorded. A fungus, *Entomophthora grylli* Fresenius, attacks the adults. The remains of adult spittlebugs have been found in the stomachs of several southern meadowlarks and red-winged blackbirds. Adults have been observed trapped in the webs of the yellow garden spider, *Argiope aurantia* Lucas, and the golden silk spider, *Nephila clavipes* (L.). An assassin bug, *Zelus bilobus* (Say), has also been recorded as a predator of the adult stage. Mites have been found attached to adult spittlebugs collected in light traps.

Selected References

Beck, E. W. 1963. Observations on the biology and cultural-insecticidal control of *Prosapia bicincta*, a spittlebug, on coastal bermudagrass. J. Econ. Entomol. 56: 747–752.

Byers, R. A. 1965. Biology and control of a spittlebug, *Prosapia bicincta* (Say), on coastal bermudagrass. Univ. Ga. Agric. Exp. Stn. Tech. Bull., n.s., 42.

Byers, R. A. & C. M. Taliaferro. 1967. Effects of age on the ability of the adult two-lined spittlebug, *Prosapia bicincta*, to produce phytotoxemia of coastal bermudagrass. J. Econ. Entomol. 60: 1760–1761.

Byers, R. A. & H. D. Wells. 1988. Phytotoxemia of coastal bermudagrass caused by the two-lined spittlebug, *Prosapia bicincta* (Homoptera: Cercopidae). Ann. Entomol. Soc. Am. 59: 1067–1071.

Fagan, E. B. & L. C. Kuitert. 1969. Biology of the two-lined spittlebug, *Prosapia bicincta*, on Florida pastures (Homoptera: Cercopidae). Fla. Entomol. 52: 199–206.

Pass, B. C. & J. K. Reed. 1965. Biology and control of the spittlebug *Prosapia bicincta*, in coastal bermudagrass. J. Econ. Entomol. 58: 275–278.

Stimmann, M. W. & C. M. Taliaferro. 1969. Resistance of selected accessions of bermudagrass to phytotoxemia caused by adult two-lined spittlebugs. J. Econ. Entomol. 62: 1189–1190.

Tashiro, H. 1987. Turfgrass insects of the United States and Canada. Cornell University Press, Ithaca, NY.

—S. Kristine Braman

Biting and Stinging Pests

One does not usually associate turfgrass with pests of medical importance. Biting and stinging arthropods can be a serious problem, however, along border areas of golf courses, parks, and lawns. Red imported fire ants, which are a particular nuisance in the southern United States, were discussed in a previous section. Human encounters with chiggers, fleas, ticks, and wasps can be annoying, painful, and, in some cases, even debilitating or life-threatening. Knowledge of these pests will help turf managers protect the health and well-being of their employees and customers.

Chiggers

Scientific Classification. *Trombicula* spp. (Acari: Trombiculidae).

Distribution. Chiggers are found throughout the continental United States. They are active all year in South Florida and Texas and from late spring through summer elsewhere. Chiggers are especially common in low, damp places where vegetation is rank and grass and weeds are overgrown. Some species also infest drier areas, however, making it difficult to predict where an infestation will occur.

Description. Chiggers are the larvae of a family of mites that are sometimes called red bugs. The adults are large, red mites often seen running over pavement and lawns. Chiggers are extremely small (0.02 in [0.5 mm]) and are difficult to see without magnification. The six-legged larvae are hairy and yellow-orange or light red. Chiggers are parasitic on humans and various animals. Nymphs and adults feed on insect eggs, small insects, and dead organic matter.

Medical Importance. Most people react to chigger bites by developing reddish welts within 24 hours. Intense itching accompanies the welts, which may persist for a week or longer if not treated. Bites commonly occur around the ankles, waistline, armpits, or other areas where clothing fits tightly against the skin. Besides causing intense itching, chigger bites that are scratched may result in infection and sometimes fever. Chiggers in North America are not known to transmit disease but, in other parts of the world they transmit scrub typhus.

Life History. Chiggers overwinter as adults in the soil, becoming active in the spring. Eggs are laid on the soil. After hatching, the larvae crawl about until they locate and attach to a suitable host. The larvae do not bur-

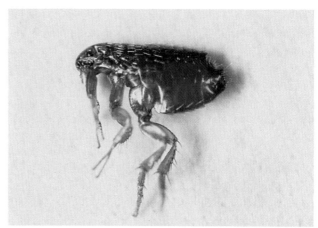
Dog flea adult (courtesy NYSAES [H. Tashiro])

row into the skin, but inject a salivary fluid that produces a hardened, raised area around them. Body fluids from the host are withdrawn through a feeding tube. Larvae feed for about 4 days and then drop off and molt into nonparasitic nymphs and adults. Chiggers feed on a variety of wild and domestic animals, as well as humans. The life cycle (from egg to egg) is completed in about 50 days.

Management. Regular mowing and removal of weeds and brush make areas less suitable for chiggers and their wild hosts. Mowing also enhances penetration and performance of miticides, should they be required. Persons working in chigger-infested areas can be protected by treating clothing (cuffs, socks, waistline, sleeves) or exposed skin with repellents. Some repellents should only be used on clothing, and it is important to follow label directions. People who suspect they may have been attacked by chiggers should take a soapy bath immediately and apply antiseptic to any welts. An anesthetic ointment will provide temporary relief from itching. Chigger populations can be reduced by treating infested areas with residual miticides. Applications should be thorough but restricted to areas frequented and suspected of being infested.

Fleas

Scientific Classification. (Siphonaptera: Pulicidae, Ceratophyllidae, Leptopsyllidae).

Distribution. Fleas are common throughout the United States and the rest of the world. More than 2,000 species have been described, most of which feed on mammals, especially rodents. The cat flea, *Ctenocephalides felis* (Bouché), is abundant in urban/suburban environments and is the species most often encountered by turf managers. The cat flea feeds on dogs and cats, as well as on several wild hosts. It also attacks and feeds on humans. Other species found in parks and recreational areas include the dog flea, *C. canis* (Curtis); the human flea, *Pulex irritans* (L.); the oriental rat flea, *Xenopsylla cheopis* (Rothschild): and chicken fleas, *Ceratophyllus* spp. These fleas feed on humans and various wild hosts, including rodents, rabbits, squirrels, skunks, and opossums.

Description. Adult fleas are small (0.04–0.16 in [1–4 mm] long), dark, reddish brown insects that are wingless and flattened from side to side. Their bodies are covered with backward-pointing bristles. Flea mouthparts are adapted for piercing and sucking blood. Fleas have powerful legs that enable them to jump about 7 in (18 cm) vertically and 16 in (40 cm) horizontally. Eggs are oval, pearly white, and about the size of a grain of sand (0.02 in [0.5mm]). Larvae are whitish, legless maggots (0.06 –0.20 in [1.5–5 mm] long) and live under grass, soil, and other organic matter. Pupae develop within silken cocoons that are usually covered with small bits of sand and organic debris. The adults are the only life stage likely to be seen, appearing as small, dark insects that jump.

Medical Importance. Flea bites usually produce pain, itching, and a small, red, hardened bump with a single puncture point in the center. Bites typically occur around the lower portions of the legs and ankles. Certain species, most notably the oriental rat flea, can transmit plague and murine typhus. Flea bites account for more than half of all dermatological conditions in pets, and may cause anemia.

Life History. Flea-host associations vary depending upon species. Some fleas remain on their hosts only long enough to feed; others, such as the cat flea, spend their entire life on the host. The cat flea lays all of its eggs on the host animal. Because the eggs are not attached, they fall off in areas frequented by the host animal. Development from egg to adult varies from a few weeks to several months. Cat flea larvae are very susceptible to heat and desiccation and generally do not survive in shade-free areas of turf.

Management. Outdoor flea infestations most often occur in yards and areas where pets are kept. One way to confirm that fleas are present is to walk the area wearing white athletic socks pulled to the knee. Fleas are attracted to and will be seen against the white background of the socks. Infestations are usually concentrated in moist, shaded areas where pets and wild hosts spend substantial amounts of time. If warranted, insecticide treatment should be focused around doghouse/kennel areas, porches, fence lines, gardens, and other favorable environments. It is seldom necessary to treat large expanses of turf in full sun. Control is enhanced by incorporating a light-stable insect growth regulator with a conventional residual insecticide. Mowing, raking and removing organic debris aid penetration of the insecticide and make areas less suitable for flea development. In most situations, indoor treatment of the home and pet are also required.

Ticks

Scientific Classification. (Acari: Ixodidae, Argasidae).

Distribution. Ticks are widely distributed throughout North America. About a dozen species, most of which are regional in occurrence, are of medical importance. Ticks feed exclusively on the blood of mammals, birds, reptiles, and amphibians and are found wherever these hosts are abundant. Consequently, they tend to congregate in tall grass, weeds, brush, and wooded areas rather than in open areas of mowed turf. Ticks are common along borders and paths because these areas are frequented by passing hosts.

Description. Ticks are more closely related to mites and spiders than to insects. Their bodies are oval, flattened, and have two body regions and no antennae. Adults and nymphs have eight legs, and the larval or "seed" ticks have six. Eggs are laid in a mass that may contain several thousand individuals. There are two broad groups of ticks: hard ticks (family Ixodidae) and soft ticks (family Argasidae). Hard ticks have a hard shield or plate covering part or all of their dorsum (back); soft ticks have a leathery, wrinkled appearance. Hard ticks are far more abundant and important in the transmission of disease. Common outdoor species include the American dog tick, *Dermacentor variabilis* (Say); the lone star tick, *Amblyomma americanum* (L.); the Rocky Mountain wood tick, *Dermacentor andersoni* Stiles, and the black legged tick, *Ixodes scapularis* Say (formerly reported as *Ixodes dammini*).

Medical Importance. Tick bites can cause itching, irritation, and infection. The likelihood of infection is increased if the tick is removed incorrectly, causing the mouthparts to remain in the wound. Ticks also transmit serious diseases, including Rocky Mountain spotted fever, Lyme disease, typhus, and tularemia, to humans, pets, and farm animals. People who develop a rash, fever, aches or other flulike symptoms in association with a tick bite should promptly see a physician. Some ticks can also produce a paralytic condition known as "tick paralysis," caused by a toxin injected during feeding.

Life History. Ticks have four life stages: egg, larva, nymph, and adult. Their life cycle varies depending upon the species. Some ticks feed exclusively on a single animal host; other species need two or more different hosts to complete development. Larvae and nymphs often feed on small animals such as rodents, but adults commonly feed on large animals. Mating usually occurs on the host, after which the engorged female drops to the ground to lay her eggs. Eggs hatch into tiny, six-legged larvae in 2 weeks to several months. After taking a blood meal, the larvae drop off the host, molt, and emerge as eight-legged nymphs. When not attached to a host, ticks remain on the ground or climb onto low vegetation to wait for another host to pass by. Most ticks are active from spring until fall and overwinter in the soil.

Management. Ticks are seldom a problem in well-maintained lawns, but often infest edges bordered by tall weeds and brush. Presence of ticks can be confirmed by dragging a 3-ft^2 (0.28-m^2) white flannel sheet through suspected areas. Clearing brush and mowing weeds and grass discourages ticks and their animal hosts. Persons working in tick-infested areas should walk in the center of mowed trails to avoid brushing against vegetation. Long pants should be worn, tucked into socks or boots. Repellents are effective when applied to clothing or exposed skin. Workers should inspect themselves often and promptly remove any ticks that are found. Attached ticks should be removed with a fine-point tweezers by grasping just behind the point of attachment and pulling slowly and steadily until the tick is dislodged. Residual insecticides are most effective when applied along borders, brushy areas, and footpaths that are routinely traveled.

Yellowjackets

Scientific Classification. *Vespula* spp. (Hymenoptera: Vespidae).

Distribution. Yellowjackets are worldwide in distribution with about 16 species occurring in the United States. Frequently encountered species include the German and the common yellowjackets (*V. germanica* [F.] and *V. vulgaris* L.), occurring throughout most of the United States; the eastern and the western yellowjackets (*V. maculifrons* [Buysson] and *V. pensylvanica* [Saussure]), occurring east and west of the Great Plains, respectively; and the southern yellowjacket (*V. squamosa* Drury), common throughout the southern states.

Description. Workers are yellow and black or white and black, and about 0.51 in (13 mm) long. Queens resemble workers, but are larger. The wings are folded lengthwise when at rest. Many species build their nests underground in abandoned animal burrows, or beneath rocks or logs. Some species also nest above ground in buildings, bushes, or trees. Nests are constructed of a paperlike material consisting of wood fibers and salivary secretions. Mature nests contain several tiers of cells surrounded by a continuous paper envelope. Within the cells are the developing eggs, larvae, and pupae. A mature yellowjacket colony may contain several thousand individuals.

Medical Importance. Yellowjackets are often considered the most dangerous stinging insects in the United States. The wasps tend to be unpredictable and usually sting if the nest is disturbed. Yellowjackets are seldom aggressive away from the nest, but people often are stung when a wasp accidentally becomes trapped in clothing or crawls inside a beverage container. Most stings produce pain and localized swelling. However, some people are hypersensitive to the venom, and a single sting can be life-threatening. Persons who develop hives, dizziness, or have difficulty breathing or swallowing should seek medical attention immediately.

Life History. Yellowjackets form annual colonies in all areas of the United States except southern Florida and portions of California. Inseminated queens overwinter under bark and in other sheltered locations. In the spring, the queens emerge and construct a small paper nest in which they lay their eggs. Larvae are fed by the queen and, in about a month, emerge as sterile adult females called workers. The newly emerged workers assume all nest activities except egg laying. Thereafter, the colony grows rapidly, containing up to 4,000 workers by the end of the summer. New males and queens are produced in late summer to early fall. After mating, the colony dies off and the newly fertilized queens seek out sheltered sites for overwintering. Abandoned nests are not reused and soon disintegrate.

Management. Yellowjackets are considered beneficial because they prey upon other insects. Control is warranted, however, when nests are located near areas of human activity. Nests can be eliminated by carefully applying an appropriately labeled dust or aerosol insecticide into and around the nest opening. Treatment should be performed at night when most of the wasps are in the nest. Pinpointing the nest entrance during the daytime aids in directing treatments made after dark. A protective bee suit is also recommended, particularly if

Cicada killer wasp (courtesy NYSAES [H. Tashiro])

work schedules necessitate treatment during the day. Foraging activity of yellowjackets in late summer can be reduced by maintaining high levels of sanitation throughout the season. Picnic and concession areas should be kept free of spilled food. Trash cans should be emptied and cleaned regularly and equipped with tight-fitting (preferably self-closing) lids. Although only of marginal benefit, baited traps can be used around the perimeter of an area to help reduce numbers of foraging workers.

Cicada Killers

Scientific Classification. *Sphecius speciosus* (Drury) (Hymenoptera: Sphecidae).

Distribution. Cicada killers occur in all states east of the Rocky Mountains and south into Mexico. Nests are located in the ground in areas that are well drained and in full sun.

Description. Cicada killers are very large wasps (greater than 1.2 in [30 mm] long) that resemble over-size hornets or yellowjackets. The body is black with pale yellow markings on the last three abdominal segments. The head and thorax are rust-colored, and wings are amber yellow. Female wasps excavate a burrow about 0.5 in (12 mm) in diameter, and in the process form a small mound of earth at the entrance.

Medical Importance. Cicada killers are menacing in appearance, but generally do not sting unless provoked. Females are able to inflict a painful sting. Males do not sting, but are aggressive and territorial during mating.

Life History. Wasps overwinter as mature larvae in cocoons in the soil. Pupation occurs in the spring, and adults emerge in late spring or summer. Cicada killers are solitary wasps and therefore do not nest together. Af-

ter mating, each female digs a burrow containing a series of cells for egg laying. After the burrow is completed, she provisions each cell with an insect (usually a cicada) paralyzed by her sting. An egg is then laid on the paralyzed prey, and the cell is sealed. Newly emerged larvae feed on the body fluids of the paralyzed (but still living) host, completing development in a few weeks. Mature larvae then form a cocoon for overwintering.

Management. Cicada killers may infest lawns in great numbers. Besides their threatening appearance, turf managers and customers may not wish to tolerate the unsightly mounds made as the wasps excavate their burrows. Control can be achieved by spraying or dusting the nest entrances and burrows with an appropriately labeled residual insecticide. A bee suit should be worn if female wasps become aggressive during treatment.

Selected References

Bennett, G. W., J. M. Owens & R. M. Corrigan. 1988. Truman's scientific guide to pest control operations. Edgell Communications, Duluth, MN.

Ebeling, W. 1978. Urban entomology. Division of Agricultural Science, University of California, Berkley.

James, M. T. & R. F. Harwood. 1969. Herms's medical entomology. Macmillan, New York.

Mallis, A. 1990. Handbook of pest control. Franzak & Foster, Cleveland, OH.

—Michael F. Potter

Microbial Control of Turfgrass Insects

By Michael G. Klein

There are few microorganisms commercially available for use against turf insects. Recent reviews indicate that only a handful of microorganisms are now in use or undergoing testing in the United States. Of these, only one bacterium, *Bacillus thuringiensis,* has had substantial commercial production. Although *B thuringiensis* products compose at least 90% of the bioinsecticides on the market, they make up less than 1% of the total pesticide market. In most cases, where microbial products are used, there has been large government input into the development and/or registration of the pathogens.

Several groups of microorganisms, including nematodes, bacteria, fungi, rickettsias, viruses, and protozoans, cause widespread natural mortality of turf insects. This mortality is seen as conspicuous epizootics or crashes in insect populations, or in more subtle infections that weaken insects, causing them to be more susceptible to other factors that lead to their death. Microorganisms have the potential to be used in one or more of the approaches to biological control. Classical biological control involves introduction of the microbe from the native home of an insect pest to a new location. In addition, it is possible to augment, or add to, the microorganisms naturally occurring in turf sites. This augmentation can be done on an inundative or inoculative basis. Inundative treatments utilize microorganisms much like conventional insecticides. For this approach to be successful, microorganisms do not need to reproduce or spread. *B thuringiensis* for example, is used in this manner. Repeated applications are made, with little or no persistence or replication. Inoculative treatments rely on the buildup and spread of the organism in the field. Use of *Bacillus popilliae* Dutky, which causes "milky disease" of grubs, is a classic example of this type of treatment. In these efforts, pathogens are colonized in a pest population and persist for many generations. The effects of microorganisms can also be enhanced by environmental manipulation or conservation.

Microorganisms offer several advantages over conventional insecticides. They are often specific for one species of insect or group of species and thus have little effect on beneficial insects. They have no serious effects on mammals, other vertebrates, and most invertebrates and have required no waiting time before humans can reenter treated areas. Furthermore, most microorganisms are utilized in a way that precludes buildup of resistance in their hosts.

However, use of these microorganisms is not without problems. The primary drawback with these living organisms revolves around production, storage, and distribution. Many of them require living hosts for their production. Most microbial control agents are relatively slow to act and are dependent on environmental factors for maximum activity. In general, microorganisms have been most successful in pest control in situations where relatively high injury levels can be tolerated. Nematodes and bacteria are the most prominent microorganisms available for biological suppression of turf insects. Protozoans and fungi can be important factors in regulating insect populations under natural conditions, but commercially viable products are not available currently.

Entomopathogenic Nematodes

Nematodes in the families Steinernematidae and Heterorhabditidae have recently received increased attention as alternatives to insecticides for turf insect control. They possess many qualities that are desirable in successful biological control agents. They have a broad host range, are easy to mass produce, can seek out their hosts

Nematode-infected (left) and normal (right) first instar Japanese beetle grub (courtesy NYSAES [J. Ogrodnick])

and kill them rapidly, and are environmentally benign. Their exemption from registration by the U.S. Environmental Protection Agency has allowed companies to bring these microorganisms to the marketplace quickly. These nematodes are harmless to plants because they are bacterial feeders and lack a stylet, or piercing mouthparts, characteristic of plant-parasitic nematodes. They carry their own strain of bacterium, which is released into an insect host. The bacteria kill the insect, and the nematodes grow and reproduce in the dead insect.

Several species and strains of nematodes from both families are currently available to turf managers. Overall, *Heterorhabditis* spp. are more effective against white grubs than *Steinernema carpocapsae* (Weiser), but not necessarily more effective than *S. glaseri* (Steiner). *Heterorhabditis* spp. may be effective against scarab larvae in the soil because they are more active than *S. carpocapsae* (Weiser), move down in the soil profile, and can directly penetrate the cuticle to overcome some of the grub's defense barriers.

Efforts to control mole crickets in the south have been enhanced by the discovery of a new and more efficacious nematode, *S. scapterisci* Nguyen and Smart, which appears to be specific to these pests. Releases of this nematode have resulted in reductions in mole cricket populations and in the distribution of the nematodes into untreated areas. A second species, *S. riobravis* n. sp., has also provided excellent control of mole crickets.

One species, *Steinernema carpocapsae* (Weiser), has been effective for control of billbugs and Lepidoptera larvae such as cutworms, webworms, and armyworms. However, control strategies may need to change from those used with conventional insecticides because the nematodes sometimes need to be applied before damage is seen. This may require early and repeated treatment of insect-prone areas to augment natural nematode populations.

The first effort to use nematodes against an insect pest involved *S. glaseri* (Steiner) against Japanese beetle, *Popillia japonica*, larvae in New Jersey. A large-scale colonization program initiated in the 1930s in New Jersey and Maryland was apparently unsuccessful because of the loss of the symbiotic bacteria during nematode production. However, those early field studies defined the desirable conditions for nematode establishment (soil temperatures higher than 61°F [16°C], soil moisture greater than 29% without flooding, the presence of turf or permanent cover, and dense host populations).

Some insects appear to have developed methods of avoiding nematode attacks. White grubs have low carbon dioxide output, special covers on their spiracles, frequently defecate, wipe their mouthparts to remove nematodes, and possess a gut lining that serves as a barrier after nematodes enter the insect gut. Species and life stage also affect host susceptibility. Certain grubs, such as the Japanese beetle, appear more sensitive to nematodes than do masked chafers, *Cyclocephala* spp., and the European chafer, *Rhizotrogus* (*Amphimallon*) *majalis* (Razoumowsky). It also appears that earlier instars may be more susceptible to nematodes than is the third instar.

Increased efficacy of nematode species against a particular host may be a result of the availability of different strains, the environmental parameters found in different habitats, the methods employed in rearing and applying the nematodes, or various combinations of these factors. In addition, the high application rates required for field efficacy, 3–6 billion nematodes per acre (1.2–2.5 billion nematodes per hectare), may reflect the lack of motility of many of the nematodes, be an indication of the success of grub defenses, or be caused by the action of biotic and abiotic factors on the nematodes in the soil.

Soil moisture is often the most critical factor in the survival and movement of entomopathogenic nematodes and in the subsequent control of turf pests. A requirement for watering nematodes into the soil and for keeping the soil moist over several weeks may restrict the utility of nematodes in many situations.

Entomopathogenic nematodes can be applied with standard insecticide application equipment, but screens smaller than 50 mesh should be avoided. In addition, care must be taken in mixing some chemicals with the nematodes. Subsurface injection of nematodes removes them from the exposed surface into the soil where they are protected from desiccation and ultraviolet inactivation and places the nematodes beyond the thatch barrier and into the zone of grub activity. However, use of subsurface application equipment to apply nematodes in the United States has, thus far, failed to improve on results obtained by applying nematodes to the surface.

The ability of nematodes to either persist or recycle in the soil environment is important if they are going to be used as inoculative agents similar to many parasitoids and the "milky disease" bacterium, rather than being used only as inundative agents or biological insecticides. Both abiotic and biotic factors influence the persistence of nematodes in the environment. Additional information is needed on the persistence of entomopathogenic nematodes in the field. *S. glaseri* was reported to have maintained itself in the field for 14 years in New Jersey with a Japanese beetle larval population of less than five per square foot (54 per square meter) and for 24 years when the grub population was augmented periodically. Other studies have shown that nematodes can exert control on more than a single generation of white grubs. However, such results may be the exception. Entomopathogenic nematodes may not be able to survive in the free-living stage in the soil for extended periods. Nematodes have been shown to replicate in insect larvae under field conditions, and it is likely that the nematodes recycle in the white grubs or other hosts, or that the cadavers offer some degree of protection to the nematodes. The role of adult insects in the persistence and dispersal of entomopathogenic nematodes through periods of time when larvae are not available is not clearly understood. Adult Japanese beetles and moths have both been suggested as factors in the persistence and movement of nematodes.

Bacteria

Bacillus thuringiensis. Although the preeminence of *B. thuringiensis* among the microbial insecticides was discussed earlier, *B. thuringiensis* products have not been used widely for controlling turf insects. Their primary use has been against forest pests, such as the spruce budworm and the gypsy moth, and in field crops. *B. thuringiensis* is a naturally occurring soil bacterium that possesses the ability to produce protein crystals that are toxic to many insects. Various strains have been identified with activity against caterpillars, fly larvae, and beetle larvae. The bacterium can easily be produced in artificial media and has typically been used as a microbial insecticide for short term-control. It acts as a stomach poison and must be eaten by pest insects to be effective. The bacteria do not normally reproduce in the insect host, persist in the environment, or spread from the treatment site. The turf/soil ecosystem is a very unsuitable environment for *B. thuringiensis* persistence because soil microorganisms quickly degrade the toxic protein crystal.

Bacillus thuringiensis products are registered for use against several turf-feeding Lepidoptera. However, because of their short residual, slow activity, and inability to kill larger larvae, these products have not been widely recommended or accepted in the turf industry. Several new *B. thuringiensis* varieties have been isolated in recent years, providing new strains for development against additional pests. *B. t.* var. *israelensis* and *B. sphericus* are used in the management of aquatic Diptera. Neither of these bacteria is registered for use against turf pests in the United States. However, the *israelensis* strain has shown activity against European crane fly larvae in The Netherlands and may be developed for use against that pest here. The *tenebrionis* strain of *B. thuringiensis* was originally developed for use against the Colorado potato beetle. Recent research has demonstrated that *B. t.* var. *japonesis* (*buibui* strain) has good activity against some species of scarab larvae (white grubs). Commercial development of this bacterium is under way in the United States and Japan. It is not clear just how these *B. thuringiensis* pathogens can best be used for scarab control because the toxins may degrade rapidly in the soil. It is possible that protective coatings could be developed to enable the toxins to remain active in the soil for longer periods of time. It is also possible that the toxic protein crystal from the bacterium can be moved by genetic engineering into desirable grass plants, thereby affording them a degree of protection.

"Milky Disease" Bacterium. *Bacillus popilliae* was the first microbial agent registered as an insecticide in the United States and has been used in suppressing Japanese beetle populations for over 50 years. During the infection process, spores of the bacteria are ingested and germinate in the gut. Bacteria move into the insect's blood, where they multiply and sporulate. Larvae die very slowly (taking 1 month or more), but the exact cause of death is still not understood. As spores and parasporal bodies build up in the blood, the larvae take on the characteristic milky appearance that gives the disease its name. The disease looks macroscopically similar in different grub species, but bacterial strains from various larvae differ in effectiveness. The only commercially available products are primarily active against Japanese beetle larvae.

In contrast to *B. thuringiensis*, the "milky disease" bacteria reproduce in the host and reinoculate the soil. The use of *B. popilliae* has been cited as a prime example of introducing an insect pathogen into the environment for permanent establishment (an inoculative release). Treatments have been designed to augment or supplement the natural occurrence of *B. popilliae* in the field. Through various state, federal, and now private efforts, "milky disease" bacteria were produced and distributed throughout the eastern states. Although the value of individual applications has often been questionable, the overall pattern of "milky disease" usage has been positive. Programs of community involvement and colonization have been stressed in the past. The primary value of "milky disease" has been its contribution to general population suppressions, not as a biological insecticide.

Although "milky disease" bacteria have a long history of use, there is little understanding of the factors causing the success or failure of the bacteria in reducing larval populations in the field. Little is known about movement of spores placed on the soil/thatch surface. Indications are that *B. popilliae* spores do not move very far in the undisturbed soil profile, but the importance of the thatch layer as a barrier to the downward movement of spores is not understood. Although "milky disease" bacteria can be recovered many years after application, the persistence of spores in the field has also been questioned.

Establishment and buildup of "milky disease" is dependent on several factors. One of the most important has been the length of time during the growing season when the temperature is above 70°F (21°C) and grubs are actively feeding at the thatch/soil interface. It has been suggested that these temperature limitations mean that "milky disease" bacteria are not highly effective north of latitude 40° in the United States where the soil temperatures do not exceed 70°F (21°C) when larvae are present.

Larval density is also an important factor in the development of "milky disease" in field populations. Rapid buildup of the disease has been noted with populations of 30 or more per square foot (0.09 m²). There are also indications that the potency of *B. popilliae* spores is favored by higher pH (near neutral). In addition, the nutritional state of larvae appears to be important in "milky disease" development. Although larval stress may be important in triggering the onset of the disease, the results of sublethal insecticide levels in the soil, or of starvation, may well have an adverse effect on field infections by *B. popilliae*. Recent tests in widely scattered locations have not produced levels of infection equal to historical standards.

The greatest deterrent to increased use of "milky disease" products is the inability to commercially produce highly infective *B. popilliae* spores on artificial media. It can only be produced commercially by finding naturally infected larvae or by collecting white grubs, infecting them, and extracting the spores. Recently reported breakthroughs in production have not provided large quantities of reliable *B. popilliae* spores. However, if spores could be grown on artificial media, attempts

could be made to overcome the temperature limitations in "milky disease" development by obtaining strains that are active at lower temperatures. It is also likely that strains with greater virulence could be produced and used as inundative agents for more rapid, but short-term, reductions of grub populations. An artificial medium would also allow for production of those strains and varieties of *B. popilliae* that are best suited for different scarab hosts.

The development of artificial production of bacterial spores as well as more information on the factors influencing "milky disease" development in its host are needed before we are able use *B. popilliae* products to their fullest potential. Until that time, "milky disease" bacteria will be in short supply and best thought of as agents that cause general population suppression, rather than relied upon to provide specific turf protection.

Amber Disease. Bacteria in the genus *Serratia* have long been associated with diseases of insects, but, until recently, no commercial utilization of this genus was achieved. Now, *Serratia* species, particularly *S. entomophila*, are available for use against a grass grub, *Costelytra zealandica* (White), in New Zealand pastures. The grubs become amber or honey in color when infected with these bacteria. Selected strains of *S. entomophila* Grimont *et al.* are able to colonize the insect gut and cause starvation of larvae, depletion of the fat bodies, and development of the amber color. The bacteria are being produced commercially for application to pastures with subsurface application equipment. These bacteria are used in an augmentative, inundative approach to speed up the natural buildup of the disease in the field.

Japanese beetle and masked chafer larvae with similar amber coloration have been found in the United States,

Tawny mole cricket infected with fungal pathogen *Metarhizium anisopliae* (courtesy NYSAES [J. Tashiro]).

and *Serratia* species have been isolated from them. Much work remains before commercial products are available in the United States. After the most active strains have been selected, methods for their production and application, as well as registration requirements, must be worked out. It seems likely that such a disease would work better against masked chafers than against Japanese beetles because chafers have a tendency to reinfect the same site for many years.

Fungi

There are currently no commercial fungal products available for management of turf pests. To compete in the turf market, producers of entomopathogenic fungi must develop formulations that survive and thrive in field conditions, are effective against the target insect, and can be mass-produced. In addition, safety and registration issues must be resolved. Soil is a suitable habitat for the development of fungal pathogens, and fungi are responsible for natural epizootics in turf settings when conditions are suitable. Fungi differ from most other microorganisms because they do not have to be ingested to be effective. Fungal spores or conidia adhere to the insect cuticle and penetrate through the body wall. Two genera of fungi (*Beauveria* and *Metarhizium*) used in pest management programs outside North America offer the most promise. *Beauveria bassiana* (Balsamo) has been used widely in both China and the former USSR, primarily against the Colorado potato beetle and the European corn borer. This fungus has been associated with the natural collapse of chinch bug populations in U.S. turf. The green muscardine fungus, *M. anisopliae* (Melchnikoff), is commercially available in Brazil for control of froghoppers and spittlebugs (Homoptera) on pasture turf.

Larvae of the cockchafer, *Melolontha melolontha* L., are being suppressed by the fungus *B. brongniartii* (Saccardo) Petch in Europe. Infections are initiated by application of conidia to soil or by treating adults of the cockchafer with fungal spores and allowing the infected females to start epizootics in larval breeding sites. It is possible that scarabs in the United States, such as the European chafer, with behavior similar to that of *M. melolontha*, could be treated in a similar manner. However, strains of the fungus with high pathogenicity need to be identified and registered. Additional effort is also being directed at the development of traps to infect adult beetles with fungi in an attempt to start epizootics in the field.

Experimental fungal products are now being tested against scarab larvae. However, problems in getting the material to the larvae, and concerns about movement of larvae away from the pathogen, have slowed progress toward an effective product. Both biotic and abiotic factors influence the survival of *B. bassiana* in soil. Many of the commonly used insecticides, herbicides, and fungicides applied to turf have a detrimental effect on the insect pathogenic fungi. We need to know more about the interactions of fungi and soil systems so that we can take greater advantage of the natural mortality caused by these organisms. We have much to learn about using fungi to their fullest potential to aid in the suppression of turf insects.

Rickettsias and Viruses

Rickettsias are microorganisms that possess characteristics of both bacteria and viruses. They are similar to viruses in that they are obligate pathogens, not being able to grow outside of living cells. Many scarab larvae are attacked by various strains of *Rickettsiella popilliae* (Dutky and Gooden) Philip. This disease (blue disease) develops slowly, and the larvae often take on a characteristic blue color. Although there is a need to recognize the role that rickettsias play in the natural control of scarab larvae, there seems to be little hope for commercial development of these organisms. A lack of artificial media for their production severely limits their availability. Probably of greater importance, concerns about the mammalian pathogenicity of *R. popilliae* preclude its registration and sale.

There are currently no commercial viral preparations available for use against turf pests. This is partly a result of low efficacy, production problems caused by the necessity of living hosts or tissue culture, and virus diseases being slow to act. Most viruses are active against Lepidoptera and have been used in forest situations. Commercial preparations of *Heliothis* nuclear polyhedrosis virus (NPV) have been marketed in the past, but were unable to compete in the marketplace. New efforts are being made to improve the production of virus products utilizing fermentation techniques. If successful, new products for cutworms, armyworms, or webworms may be developed in the future.

Scarab beetles are also infected by naturally occurring viruses. The most successful use of a scarab virus is the control of coconut beetles, *Oryctes* spp., by a baculovirus in the South Pacific. The virus has been spread by introducing virus-infected larvae to larval breeding sites and virus-infected adults into virus-free areas. This program is an example of a successful inoculative release of a pathogen. Virus particles can persist for extended periods of time in the soil. If the labor-intensive production process for scarab viruses can be overcome, it is possible that they may someday be used by managers as part of a turf integrated pest management program.

Protozoans

Protozoans can be important in the natural suppression of many insects, but have not been utilized as microbial pathogens against turf pests. Protozoans, like many microbial insecticides, are slow acting and would be useful only where economic injury levels are high. In addition, no artificial medium is currently available for production of protozoans, so they must be produced in living hosts. Only the grasshopper pathogen, a microsporidian, *Nosema locustae* Canning, has been developed commercially. It is a component of IPM programs for grasshopper control on rangelands in the United States and, more recently, in Africa.

Other microsporidian parasites have been found in several scarabs and sod webworms. Microsporidians are important in the natural mortality of white grubs, par-

ticularly when populations are stressed by managerial or chemical methods. Many scarabs are also infected by coccididan parasites, *Adelina* spp. *Adelina*-infected adults have lower fat levels than uninfected adults, and most infected females die before oviposition. Very little is known about the true effects of protozoans on insect populations, and they are often overlooked. Turf managers should be aware of these microorganisms, and increased emphasis should be placed on identifying signs of infection and on establishing the role protozoans play in reducing pest populations.

Selected References

Cranshaw, W. S. & M. G. Klein. 1994. Microbial control of insect pests of landscape plants, pp. 503–520. *In* A. R. Leslie [ed.], Integrated pest management for turfgrass and ornamentals. Lewis Publishers, Chelsea, MI.

Gaugler, R. & H. K. Kaya. 1990. Entomopathogenic nematodes in biological control. CRC, Boca Raton, FL.

Hanula, J. L. & T. G. Andreadis. 1988. Parasitic microorganisms of Japanese beetle (Coleoptera: Scarabaeidae) and associated scarab larvae in Connecticut soils. Environ. Entomol. 17: 709–714.

Jackson, T. A. & T. R. Glare. 1992. Use of pathogens in scarab pest management. Intercept, Andover, Hampshire, England.

Tanada, Y. & H. K. Kaya. 1993. Insect pathology Academic,. San Diego, CA.

Tashiro. H. 1987. Turfgrass insects of the United States and Canada. Cornell University Press, Ithaca, NY.

Beneficial and Innocuous Invertebrates in Turf

By Daniel A. Potter

Most turfgrass managers are familiar with white grubs, cutworms, and other pests, but it is doubtful that they often give much thought to the many other kinds of insects and related small creatures that inhabit turf. Some, such as springtails and millipedes, are relatively innocuous, feeding upon plant debris or fungi. Others, especially earthworms, can be a nuisance when their burrows disrupt smoothness and uniformity, but nonetheless play an important role by aerating and enriching the soil, enhancing water infiltration, and breaking down thatch. Still others are voracious predators or parasites, roaming through the grass or burrowing in the soil and thatch in search of victims, which often include the eggs or damaging stages of pest insects such as sod webworms, chinch bugs, or white grubs. This section concerns the role and importance of natural enemies and earthworms in the turfgrass system, how these beneficial organisms are affected by pesticides, and why preserving their populations may be essential to the health and long-term stability of turfgrass. Other innocuous invertebrates often seen by the casual observer are also discussed in this section.

Role of Predators and Parasites in Turf. The reproductive powers of many insects are enormous. Female sod webworms and armyworms lay hundreds of eggs, and the Japanese beetle or masked chafers can produce 60 or more offspring in their lifetime. Others, such as the greenbug and the winter grain mite, have rapid development and multiple generations during the growing season and can reach outbreak densities almost overnight. Why, then, are lawns and golf courses not uniformly and regularly overwhelmed by pest insects? Predatory insects can also be very abundant in turf. Surveys conducted in New Jersey, Florida, and Kentucky revealed dozens of species of ants (Formicidae), ground beetles (Carabidae), spiders, rove beetles (Staphylin-

idae), hister beetles (Histeridae), and other groups. Many of these groups feed mainly on the eggs or active stages of plant-eating insects and readily consume large numbers of eggs and larvae of sod webworms, armyworms, the Japanese beetle, and other pests in laboratory trials. One common species, aptly called a tiger beetle, was observed to kill as many as 20 fall armyworms in a single hour. Naturally occurring parasitic insects, including tiphiid, braconid, and ichneumonid wasps, tachinid flies, and other groups may also be abundant in turf.

The fact that outbreaks of pests are uncommon in low-maintenance turf suggests that most pests are normally held in check by natural buffers. Environmental stresses such as drought take their toll, especially on the immature stages, as do bacteria, fungi, and entomopathogenic nematodes. Predators and parasites also contribute to reduce pest populations. Much of the evidence for this comes from accounts of pest outbreaks at turf sites where natural enemies had been inadvertently eliminated by broad-spectrum insecticides. For example, outbreaks of the winter grain mite occurred on lawns in New Jersey that had been treated with carbaryl, evidently because the insecticide killed the predatory mites that normally held the pest mites in check. Similar outbreaks of the southern chinch bug were documented on heavily treated home lawns in Florida. Such phenomena are called "pest resurgence" if the outbreak pest was the target of the original treatment or "secondary pest outbreaks" if another pest was the original target. Practically every turfgrass pest has one or more predators or parasites associated with it. Although manipulation of natural enemies for the purpose of mass rearing and release by individuals has generally not proven to be practical or effective, conservation of beneficial insects should be a concern of turf managers.

Evidence for Importance of Predators. Only a few studies have attempted to measure rates of predation on pest insects in turf. In one such study, sod webworm eggs were placed in small dishes that were implanted on the surface of Kentucky bluegrass turf. Rates of predation on eggs were compared between untreated plots and plots that had been treated once with an insecticide. Predators, especially ants, consumed or carried off as many as 75% of the eggs in the untreated plots within 48 hours. Predators were less abundant in the treated plots, and consumption of the eggs was much lower for at least 3 weeks after treatment. Sixteen of 21 species of predators collected from the study site were found to feed readily upon sod webworm eggs. High rates of predation on the eggs may be one reason that outbreaks of sod webworms are uncommon in most turf sites.

In another experiment, Kentucky bluegrass was treated with insecticides in mid-June. Japanese beetle eggs and fall armyworm pupae were then implanted into the soil, and rates of predation were compared between the treated and untreated turf. As expected, abundance of many species of predators was reduced in the treated plots. Predators killed and consumed 30–60% of the pupae in just 48 hours, but, curiously, predation on pupae was not reduced by the insecticides. Rates of predation on Japanese beetle eggs, however, were much lower in plots treated with certain insecticides than in untreated plots, apparently because numbers of predators were reduced. Most notably, plots that had been treated with certain insecticides in June developed higher grub populations later in the summer than did untreated plots. This suggests that short-residual insecticides applied in June or early July have the potential to induce higher grub populations by interfering with predation on the eggs.

Spiders (Arachnida: Araneae) are often abundant in turfgrass. All species are predatory, feed mainly on insects, and kill their prey by injecting venom into it by biting. Some kinds of spiders make small webs in the grass; others are free-living, relying on ambush or speed to capture their prey. Spiders have two body regions and four pairs of legs. Most spiders are highly beneficial. Only two species, the black widow spider and the brown recluse spider, are potentially dangerous to humans, and neither of these is likely to be encountered in turf.

Ground beetles (Coleoptera: Carabidae) are fast-moving, beneficial insects that are abundant in turf. Both the adults and the soil-inhabiting larvae prey upon eggs or larvae of insects, and some species may be important in reducing populations of sod webworms, white grubs, or other pests. Most ground beetles are shiny and dark-colored, with long legs and forward-pointing mouthparts. Upper surfaces of the elytra are typically marked by longitudinal grooves or striations.

Rove beetles (Coleoptera: Staphylinidae) are fast-moving, slender, elongate, dark-colored insects that can usually be recognized by the very short elytra that leave much of the abdomen exposed beyond their apices. Their size varies from 0.1 to 0.5 in (2 to 12 mm) or more. Most species are predaceous and beneficial.

Ants are mostly beneficial because they prey upon the eggs and active immature stages of pest insects. They may play an important role in helping to buffer turfgrass against pest outbreaks. Ants are sometimes troublesome,

especially on and around golf greens, because they build mounds as they form subterranean homes for their colonies. A few species of ants have painful bites and stings, the red imported fire ant being the most important.

Wasps (Hymenoptera) of several families that are sometimes observed hovering over turfgrass in the spring or fall are parasitic upon pest insects. The Scoliidae are relatively large, hairy, dark-colored wasps with yellow or orange (or both) markings on the abdomen. Larvae of these wasps are external parasites of white grubs; the adults are often found on flowers. Tiphiidae are somewhat smaller black and yellow wasps that parasitize the larvae of Japanese beetles, masked chafers, and other scarabs. Females of both groups search out a grub in the soil, sting it to paralyze the grub temporarily, and then deposit an egg on the host. Upon hatching, the maggotlike larva attaches itself externally to the white grub, pierces the host's cuticle with its mouthparts, and feeds upon the body fluids, ultimately killing the grub. Rates of parasitism of 80% or more have been observed at some sites.

Centipedes (Chilopoda) are fast-moving predators that feed upon insects and spiders. They have a distinct head with relatively long antennae (14 or more segments) and a flattened, multisegmented body bearing one pair of legs per segment. Most species are reddish brown. Species found in the north are harmless to humans, but some southern species can inflict a painful bite if handled.

Effects of Insecticides on Predators. Broad-spectrum insecticides are toxic to beneficial insects as well as to pests. In one study in Kentucky, certain insecticides applied in June reduced populations of spiders and rove beetles by as much as 60%, with effects lasting for at least 6 weeks. Use of isofenphos on home lawns in Ohio reduced populations of some predators for more than 40 weeks. Different species are affected to various degrees by different insecticides, but unfortunately there have been few comparative studies from which to draw generalizations. Most studies have suggested that predators will repopulate relatively small areas within 1–3 months after treatment. Recovery of larger areas such as golf courses would probably take much longer. Surveys in Kentucky showed that predators were generally less abundant in turf receiving commercial lawn care than in low-maintenance lawns.

Role of Earthworms in Turf. Earthworms (Oligochaeta: Lumbricidae) feed mainly at night on organic matter on or in the soil. Earthworms are sometimes regarded as a nuisance by golf superintendents or landscape managers because their habit of depositing soil on the turf surface as "castings" can disrupt the smoothness and uniformity of greens or other fine turf. This minor nuisance is generally more than balanced by the importance of earthworms in enhancing soil aeration, water infiltration, and decomposition of thatch.

The Greek philosopher and scientist Aristotle called earthworms the "intestines of the earth." The importance of earthworms in breaking down plant litter and nutrient recycling is well documented in forest and pasture soils. Earthworms mix organic matter into the soil and fragment and condition plant debris in the gut before it is further broken down by bacteria and fungi. Decomposition of plant litter is usually much faster when earthworms are abundant. Burrowing activity of earthworms enhances soil structure and is critical for air and water infiltration. Two-thirds of the total pore space in soils may consist of earthworm tunnels. Earthworms also mix the soil and enrich it with their castings (excreta). Charles Darwin, better known for his work on evolution, conducted painstaking research on earthworms. Darwin showed that as much as 18 tons of earthworm casts could be brought to the surface per acre per year, about equivalent to a uniform, 1/4-inch layer of enriched soil being deposited annually. Presence of earthworms has been shown to enhance growth and yield of grass in pastures.

Thatch is a tightly intermingled layer of living and dead roots, stolons, and other undecomposed plant material that accumulates at the interface between the grass and soil. Thatch accumulations result from an imbalance between production and decomposition of organic matter. Excessive thatch causes long-term problems with reduced water infiltration, restricted penetration of insecticides and fertilizers, shallow rooting, and greater vulnerability to heat and drought stress. Thatch is often a problem in cultivated Kentucky bluegrass and creeping bentgrass when a high rate of nitrogen fertilization is applied for several years.

Thatch is rarely excessive where earthworms are abundant. In a study conducted in Kentucky bluegrass, pieces of thatch were buried in mesh bags that either admitted or excluded earthworms. Rates of decomposition of the thatch were measured over a period of 2 years. Another experiment compared rates of breakdown of thatch in untreated plots and in plots in which earthworms were deliberately eliminated with insecticides.

Dramatic differences were evident in both experiments after only 3 months. In the presence of earthworms the pieces of thatch were broken apart and dispersed. Rates of microbial decomposition were more than twice as high in the presence of earthworms. The worms incorporated large amounts of soil into the thatch, so that by the end of the tests the thatch that had been "worked" by earthworms contained about 80% mineral soil by weight, as compared with 35% mineral soil without earthworm activity. The effects of this natural process are very similar to those achieved by coring or topdressing. These experiments confirmed that earthworms play an important role in breaking apart and decomposing thatch and in improving its physical and chemical properties for growth of turfgrass. Preservation of earthworms is important where thatch is a concern.

Earthworms and Fertilizers. Excessive fertilization can encourage thatch accumulation both by increasing production of organic matter and by inhibiting the decomposition processes. Some fertilizers (e.g., ammonium nitrate) when applied at high rates cause the soil to become more acidic, which may in turn inhibit microbial activity. Earthworms are intolerant of low soil pH and tend to be sparse in acidic soils. Application of 5 lb of nitrogen per 1,000 ft^2 (244 kg of N per ha) per year for 7 years resulted in decreased soil pH (6.2–4.8), a 50% decrease in earthworm populations, and an increase in thatch accumulation of 0.24–0.67 in (0.6–1.7 cm).

Earthworms and Pesticides. Pesticides used on turf differ markedly in their toxicity to earthworms. Some products can cause severe and long-lasting reductions in earthworm populations, even when applied at labeled rates (Table 2). Earthworms are sometimes viewed as a nuisance on golf courses because their burrows and surface casts disrupt the uniformity and smoothness of fine turf. Moreover, because earthworms and white grubs are a preferred food for moles, pesticides are sometimes applied in the hope of reducing the food supply and causing the moles to go elsewhere. There is, however, no scientific evidence that elimination of earthworms will alleviate a problem with moles. There are no pesticides registered for use against earthworms in turf. Considering the importance of earthworms in aerating and enriching the soil, enhancing water infiltration, and breaking down thatch, turfgrass managers would be advised to conserve worm populations whenever possible.

Other Decomposers. Numerous species of mites (Arachnida: Acari) inhabit soils under turfgrass. Like spiders, mites have eight legs and two main body regions. Oribatids (Cryptostigmata) are often the most abundant group; these tiny (<0.02 in [0.2–0.5 mm]), rounded or pear-shaped, dark-colored creatures feed upon fungi and decaying organic matter and contribute

Table 2. Relative toxicity of turfgrass pesticides to earthworms based upon mean reduction in population density in two independent field tests (treatments were applied to Kentucky bluegrass in April and watered in, and earthworms were sampled using formalin drenches after 7–9 days)

Toxicity	Common	Formulation	Rate (kg [AI]/ha	Class[a]
Low				
(0–25% reduction)	2,4-D	Dacamine 4 D	2.24	H
	Trichlopyr	Garlon 3 A	0.56	H
	Dicamba	Banvel 4 E	0.56	H
	Pendimethalin	Pre-M 60 WDG	3.36	H
	Triodimefon	Bayleton 25 WDG	3.02	F
	Fenarimol	Rubigan 50 WP	3.02	F
	Propiconazole	Banner 1.1 EC	3.36	F
	Chlorothalonil	Daconil 2787	12.66	F
	Isofenphos	Oftanol 5 G	2.24	I-OP
Moderate				
(26–50% reduction)	Trichlorfon	Proxol 80 WP	8.96	I-OP
	Chlorpyrifos	Dursban 4 E	4.48	I-OP
	Isazophos	Triumph 4 E	2.24	I-OP
Severe				
(51–75% reduction)	Benomyl	Benlate 50 WP	12.21	F
	Diazinon	Diazinon 14 G	4.48	I-OP
Very severe				
(76–99% reduction)	Carbaryl	Sevin SL	8.96	I-C
	Bendiocarb	Turcam 2.5 G	4.48	I-C
	Ethoprop	Mocap 10 G	5.60	I-OP

[a]H, Herbicide; F, fungicide; I-OP, organophosphate; I-C, carbamate insecticide. Adapted from Potter et al. (1990).

to decomposition of plant litter and nutrient recycling in turf. Long-legged predatory mites help to reduce populations of plant-feeding mites (e.g., the winter grain mite) and may also prey upon eggs of pest insects such as sod webworms.

Springtails (Collembola) are minute (0.04 - 0.16 in [1 - 4 mm]), whitish, purple, or grayish insects that are often abundant in thatch and soil. There may be thousands in a single cubic foot (0.03 m^3) of surface soil. Most species have a forked structure on the abdomen with which they jump. Collembola feed upon decaying organic matter, fungi, and bacteria and may be important in decomposition of plant litter.

Millipedes (Diplopoda) are found in damp places where they feed on decaying vegetation and occasionally upon living roots. Millipedes are characterized by a distinct head with short antennae, a cylindrical or slightly flattened body, and two pairs of legs per body segment. They are slow-moving and typically curl up tightly when disturbed. They do no notable damage to turf, but can become a nuisance when they wander into buildings.

Pillbugs or sowbugs (Crustacea: Isopoda) are common in damp places and are often found under stones, logs, boards, or mulch. They feed mainly on decaying organic matter such as grass clippings or manure, but occasionally feed upon living roots of plants, especially in greenhouses. They do no substantial damage to turf.

Snails and slugs (Mollusca: Gastropoda) prefer damp locations, hiding under vegetation or debris during the day and venturing forth at night to feed. They sometimes damage bedding plants or vegetables by scraping the leaf tissues or leaving trails of slime, but they do no damage to turfgrasses.

Selected References

Potter, D. A. 1994. Effects of pesticides on beneficial invertebrates in turf, p 59–70. In A. R. Leslie [ed.], Integrated pest management for turfgrass and ornamentals. Lewis Publishers, Chelsea, MI.

Potter, D. A., Buxton, M. C., Redmond, C. T., and Smith, A. J. 1990. Toxicity of pesticides to earthworms (Oligochaeta: Lumbricidae) and effect on thatch degradation in Kentucky bluegrass turf. J. Econ. Entomol., 83: 2362–2368.

Principles and History of Turfgrass Pest Management

By Frederick P. Baxendale and Jennifer A. Grant

The importance of developing efficient and environmentally sound methods for managing turfgrass pests has been reemphasized by recent concerns over environmental safety, the loss of long-term residual insecticides, and a growing awareness of the problems associated with the overuse of pesticides. Integrated pest management (IPM) addresses these concerns while maintaining the aesthetic and utilitarian qualities of the turf. IPM is an approach that utilizes all suitable methods and techniques in a compatible manner to maintain pest densities below levels causing unacceptable damage. Although insects and mites are discussed in this handbook, the same management principles apply to other turf problems such as diseases and weeds.

Inherent in the IPM philosophy is the recognition that, for most pests, population levels exist that can be tolerated without substantial plant injury. Eradication of pests is not attempted because moderate pest levels help maintain natural enemies, and chemical overuse can lead to pesticide resistance. The overall objective of IPM is to optimize and diversify, rather than maximize pest control. The selection of optimal management strategies will vary depending on site requirements and will change as new practices and products become available.

An important aspect of the IPM approach involves planning ahead to avoid or minimize future pest problems. Decisions made during the establishment and maintenance of a turf area can substantially influence pest development. Among these key decisions are selection of turfgrass species and cultivar, weed and disease control strategies, irrigation, fertilization, thatch management, and other cultural practices that affect the health and vigor of the turfgrass. As a general rule, stressed or poorly maintained turf exhibits pest damage sooner than healthy turf and is slower to recover after insect or mite injury.

Despite appropriate measures to avoid or reduce insect problems, pest populations may increase under certain conditions. When using an IPM approach, control measures including conventional pesticides are employed only when pest numbers reach or threaten to reach predetermined levels (treatment thresholds). These thresholds are flexible guidelines that are usually defined in terms of the level of insect abundance or damage that can be tolerated before taking action. They are typically based on a number of variables including pest species, abundance, and life stage; variety, vigor, and value of the turfgrass; relative effectiveness and cost of control measures; and time of year. Treatment thresholds are not hard rules that apply to every situation, but when used conscientiously they should help turfgrass managers make effective pest management decisions.

Implementing an IPM Program for Turfgrass Insects

Establishing a pest management program requires a sound understanding of the growth habits and cultural requirements of the turfgrass; knowledge of the biology, behavior, life history, and type of damage caused by potential pests; and information regarding the time of year, growth stage of the turfgrass, and environmental conditions under which pest damage is most likely to occur. Accurate pest identification is also essential. In addition, turfgrass managers must integrate insect control with disease, weed, and cultural management strategies.

Pest Identification. All turfgrasses are inhabited by a diverse array of organisms, including insects, spiders, mites, nematodes, and many other small animals. Most of these cause little or no damage and are generally considered nonpests. Others serve important beneficial roles as a food source for wildlife, in the breakdown of thatch, in aeration of the soil, or as natural enemies of various insect and mite pests. Only a few of the species present are actually plant-feeding pests. Because of the many similarities between pests and nonpests, it is essential that the turf manager be able to accurately distinguish incidental and beneficial species from target pests.

Pest Monitoring. Successful management of most turf insects depends on the early detection of pests before they reach damaging levels. This can best be accomplished through frequent turf inspections to detect early signs of insects and their damage. Monitoring (scouting) is a systematic method of inspecting turf for pests and cultural problems and should be the backbone of any pest management program. Its primary goal is to detect, identify, delineate, and rank pest infestations and turfgrass abnormalities. All turf areas should be monitored on a regular basis during the growing season. The scouting interval may vary from 1 to 2 days to several months, depending on whether the turf is associated with a golf course, institution, home lawn, sod farm, or other area.

Among the more common symptoms of insect-damaged turf are a general thinning of the grass, spongy areas, irregular brown patches, or plants that easily break away at soil level. Substantiating the insect origin of the problem may be difficult, however, because many of the symptoms described above could also be caused by non-insect factors such as heat or drought stress, nutritional deficiencies, turf diseases, soil compaction, chemical burns from gasoline, fertilizers, herbicides or insecticides, scalping during mowing operations, or even excrement spots left by pets. If the problem is insect related, a close visual inspection of the damaged area should reveal either the presence of the pest or indirect evidence that an insect infestation has been present.

Bird and animal feeding activity often indicates potential insect problems. Starlings, robins, moles, skunks, and raccoons are well-known insectivores. However, confirmation of the insect origin of a problem requires close examination of the injured area. Look for signs of skeletonized leaves, clipped grass blades, fecal pellets, sawdustlike debris, stem tunneling, silken tubes, or webbing. Then, refer to individual sections of this handbook for a description of damage symptoms caused by specific insects. If no evidence of insects or their feeding is found, the condition is probably due to another cause, and use of insecticides or other insect control measures would be ineffective.

Insect Sampling Techniques. Insect sampling techniques provide an important complement to visual monitoring of turf. Sampling should be initiated when an insect infestation is suspected, at appropriate times in a pest's life cycle, in historically infested areas, or when a post-treatment analysis of pesticide efficacy or other control measures is desired. Because insect and mite pests rarely distribute themselves evenly throughout the turf, it is essential that the entire turfgrass area be sampled in a consistent, uniform pattern. Enough samples must be taken to assure a reasonably accurate estimate of pest numbers in the sampled area.

If turf damage is evident but no pests are detected, examine the turf for other causes of injury such as disease, excessive thatch, improper mowing, or heat or moisture stress. When examining turf, be on the lookout for beneficial natural enemies that may be reducing pest populations such as lady beetles, bigeyed bugs, lacewings, ground beetles, spiders, and parasitic wasps. Sampling techniques for detecting surface- and soil-inhabiting insects are described below.

Disclosing (Irritant) Solution. Surface-active insects can be flushed from the turf with a disclosing solution. Mix two to four tablespoons (30–60 ml) of liquid dishwashing soap, or 1 tablespoon (15 ml) of 1% pyrethrins, into 2 gal (7.6 liters) of water and pour the mixture over a 1.2-yd^2 (1-m^2) area of turf. Insects such as webworms, cutworms, armyworms, mole crickets, billbug adults, as well as earthworms, will come to the surface within 5–10 minutes. There they can easily be collected, identified, and counted. Treatment thresholds based on this sampling method are available for some insects and are described in their respective sections. Because detergents vary in their concentrations and components, they should always be tested to determine the soap-to-water ratio that will irritate the target insects, yet not be phytotoxic to the turfgrass.

Flotation. Many insects float to the surface when submerged in water. This phenomenon can be exploited by inserting a metal cylinder (preferably 8–9 in [20–23 cm] in diameter) about an inch (2.5 cm) into the ground. A large coffee can with both ends removed is suitable. Fill the can with water and replace any water that escapes until the turf has been underwater for 3–5 minutes. Insects will float to the water surface where they can be collected, identified, and counted. An alternative method is to remove a large soil core with a golf course cup cutter and place it in a bucket of water for the same amount of time. These techniques are ideal for detecting chinch bugs and many of their natural enemies. See the section on chinch bugs for further details regarding when to sample and threshold levels.

Soil Examination (Cup Cutting and Soil Diggings). Most soil-inhabiting insects, such as scarab grubs, cannot be sampled by the methods previously discussed. These insects must be sought in the root and thatch zones where they feed. One sampling method involves cutting three sides of a square turf area (0.25–1 ft^2 [0.02–0.09 m^2]) with a shovel or knife and peeling back the sod layer to expose white grubs, billbug larvae, and other soil dwellers. It is important to examine the entire root zone, including both the sod cap and the upper 1–3 in (2.5–7.6 cm) of soil. Several samples should be taken to determine population levels throughout the area.

A second method for sampling soil-inhabiting insects utilizes a standard golf course cup-cutter, which removes soil cores with diameters of 4.25 in (11 cm). Cores can be rapidly inspected for insects as the soil is discarded back into the original hole. If the sod cap is then replaced and the area irrigated, damage to the turf is minimal. Record the numbers of each insect species found and its predominant life stage (egg, larva [instar], nymph, adult), on a data sheet or map. Inspecting soil samples in a grid pattern across any turf area helps to delineate areas with insect infestations. Minimum intervals of 22–33 yd (20–30 m) between samples in large turf areas should be sufficient. Ultimately, the number of samples taken depends on the time and labor available. Studies in New York have shown that 20 samples can be examined per person per hour. Sampling time will also vary depending on insect density, soil type, thatch thickness, and other factors.

Traps. Insect activity can be monitored using a variety of trapping methods. Most traps utilize an attractant (lights, pheromones, food scents) that lures insects to the trap. Upon reaching the trap, insects are captured by mechanical means, such as sticky surfaces, or killed with insecticides. Typically, these traps are hung from trees or stakes in or near the turf area. Light traps collect a wide variety of flying insects, including scarab beetles and cutworm, webworm, and armyworm moths. The sheer abundance and diversity of insects collected can be a disadvantage to this approach because of the extensive sorting and identification time required. Pheromone traps are highly selective and usually capture only one sex (usually males) of a single species of insect. Pitfall traps are placed in the ground so that the top is flush with the turf surface. These traps capture insects as they move along the ground. Arthropods such as mole crickets, billbug adults, ground beetles, and the winter grain mite can be monitored using pitfall traps.

Insect traps are useful monitoring devices that provide important information confirming the presence and timing of a particular pest in an area. For example, peaks in adult activity can be tracked and used to predict when damaging larval activity will occur later in the season. Traps should not be relied on to reduce or eliminate pest infestations. It is important to understand fully the capabilities and limitations of any trapping method before use. Also remember that to be effective, traps must be checked on a regular basis - sometimes daily! Insect monitoring traps can be obtained from most pest management supply companies.

Visual Inspection. Certain insects are most easily detected by visual inspections. Billbug adults, for example, can be monitored as they stroll on paved areas and sidewalks in hot weather, and a treatment threshold is associated with this activity. The annual bluegrass weevil can be detected by inspecting the clippings in mowing boxes from close-cut turf, and chinch bugs can sometimes be found by separating grass plants with the thumb and forefinger and examining the base of the plant. Visual inspection can be used to detect most insects, but it is rarely as efficient as other sampling techniques.

Other Detection Methods. Standard insect sweeping nets are useful for collecting flying insects in turf areas. Mole crickets in flight have been monitored using sound-trapping stations that broadcast recordings of males. Their damage can be assessed by placing a square frame 30 by 30 in (76 by 76 cm), divided into nine equal sections, over damaged turf. Turf is then rated from 0 to 9 by the number of sections containing mounds or tunnels.

Record Keeping and Evaluation. Accurate records are essential for the success of a turfgrass pest management program. During the growing season, day-to-day pest management decisions are based on scouting information. Effective record keeping greatly increases the long-term value of this information by providing the turf manager with historical, site-specific knowledge of pest activity. This information can be used to predict when certain pest problems are most likely to occur later in the season and in subsequent seasons. In addition, records call attention to patterns and associations that may be overlooked during a pest event. Examples include particular turf areas or cultivars that are chronically infested or insect activity coinciding with drought or disease stress. Pest histories should be reviewed several times each season so that potential pest problems can be anticipated and initial monitoring efforts focused on historical "hot spots."

Pest management records should be as complete as possible. Record the kinds and numbers of pests present, when and where they were found, and exact locations and extent of any turf damage or abnormalities observed. Information on the turf species and cultivar development, turf health, and current environmental conditions is also valuable. When recording scouting or other management information, be as quantitative as possible. Record the actual number of insects per unit area and assign damage ratings to injured turf (e.g., 1 = severe damage, 3 = moderate damage, 5 = no observable damage). Avoid vague designations such as high or low, or heavy or light. It is often useful to divide turf areas into pest management units (PMUs) that can be considered individually when making pest management decisions. For example, each tee, green, and fairway on a golf course constitutes a PMU. Likewise, the front and back lawns of residential properties can often be placed in separate PMUs because homeowners typically have different aesthetic standards for these areas. When recording pest management information, be sure to specify both the PMU and the location within the PMU where the data were collected.

Assessing the effectiveness of cultural and pest control practices is an important yet often overlooked component of a turfgrass pest management program. In most cases, the same sampling techniques used to detect the original pest infestation can be used to ascertain the success or failure of a control strategy. However, when evaluating the efficacy of a control measure, sampling can be limited to only a few previously infested areas. The turfgrass manger can use the evaluation process to determine management approaches that were effective and those that need to be modified. At the end of the season, this information can be reviewed to plan and prioritize scouting and management activities for the future.

Pest Management Options

As previously discussed, IPM uses a combination of complementary strategies to manage pest populations. This section describes some of the pest management options currently available to the turfgrass manager.

Cultural Methods. Cultural methods involve manipulation of the environment to make it less suitable for pest survival. These measures are usually preventive in nature and must be implemented before the insect reaches pest status.

Turfgrass Selection. Select turfgrass species or cultivars that are well adapted to local soil and environmental conditions. Adapted turfgrass cultivars are better able to tolerate stress and are less likely to be damaged by insects than unadapted grasses. Further, a blend of improved adapted grasses will usually outperform a single cultivar. Information on locally adapted turfgrasses is available from local seed dealers, Cooperative Extension offices, as well as most nurseries and garden centers.

Insect-resistant turfgrasses provide another valuable IPM tool. Plant resistance to insect pests has been found in many turfgrasses, although the degree of resistance may vary considerably from one species or cultivar to another. Several cultivars of billbug-resistant Kentucky bluegrass are available commercially.

Endophyte-Infected Grasses. Endophytes are organisms, typically bacteria or fungi, growing within a plant.

Turfgrasses infected with endophytic fungi in the genus *Acremonium* have shown enhanced resistance to 14 species of insects including aphids, leafhoppers, chinch bugs, armyworms, webworms, and billbugs. Among the turfgrasses containing endophytes are certain cultivars of perennial rye and tall and fine fescues. Useful endophytes have not been found in creeping bentgrass or Kentucky bluegrass.

Effective Maintenance. Many turfgrass insect pests are attracted to lush, overly maintained turf. Sound cultural practices that optimize plant health and vigor enable the turf to withstand higher pest infestation levels and recover more rapidly from insect and mite injury. Therefore, careful turfgrass management is one of the best insect prevention strategies available.

Biological Control. This important IPM strategy uses beneficial organisms including predators, parasites, or insect pathogens to reduce pest populations. Biological control can be implemented by releasing beneficial organisms into the turf area or by modifying cultural, chemical, and other control practices to conserve and enhance existing natural enemy populations. In general, effective use of this approach requires a detailed knowledge of the specific predator/prey or parasite/host relationship being manipulated. See the section on beneficial organisms for detailed information on various options for biological control of turfgrass insects.

Insecticides/Acaricides. Insecticides and acaricides are probably the most powerful tools available for insect and mite control in turf. In many cases, they afford the only practical method of reducing pest populations that have already reached damaging levels. Insecticides have rapid corrective action in preventing pest damage and offer a wide range of properties and methods of application. They are relatively low in cost, and their use often results in a substantial economic or aesthetic benefit. Some potential problems associated with insecticide use include the development of pest resistance; outbreaks of secondary pests; adverse effects on nontarget organisms including humans, pets, wildlife, and beneficial insects; hazardous residues in our food supply; and groundwater contamination.

Factors that can influence the effectiveness of an insecticide application include the insect species present, insecticide selection, timing of the application, irrigation before and after treatment, thatch and soil organic matter, water and soil pH, resistance of insects to pesticides, and soil microbial degradation. These factors should be considered carefully when making an insecticide treatment decision.

When insecticides are used in an IPM program, they should be carefully selected and their application timed with respect to the developmental stages of the target pest. Insect monitoring information can help pinpoint the optimal time for treatment. Proper selection and timing of pesticide applications are extremely important in obtaining the best possible control with the least adverse effect on the environment. Observe treatment threshold levels (i.e., treat only when necessary) and limit treatments to infested areas of the turf whenever possible. Ensure proper calibration of the application equipment and always read, understand, and follow all label directions.

Application Techniques. The following recommendations apply mainly to standard insecticide applications. Some biological control agents and new-chemistry insecticides require special handling and application techniques. Read the product label and discuss application procedures with the supplier before use.

For surface-active insects, the turf area should be mowed and the clippings removed before application to enhance insecticide penetration into the canopy. A thorough irrigation before application moves insects out of the thatch and soil and brings them to the surface. For night-feeding insects, apply the insecticide in the late afternoon or early evening. Light irrigation after spraying rinses the insecticide off grass blades and into turf where billbugs and other thatch-active insects reside. A heavier irrigation should follow granular applications to wash granules off grass blades and activate the insecticide. For blade-feeding insects such as aphids, spider mites, and armyworms, do not irrigate for 24–48 hours after application.

In the case of soil-inhabiting insects, it is important that the insecticide move through the thatch layer and down to the root zone of the turf where the insects are feeding. Thatch layers of 0.5 in (1.2 cm) or more can greatly reduce the effectiveness of an insecticide by intercepting and chemically binding the active ingredient. Reduction of the thatch layer or aeration of the turf before application increases insecticide efficacy. For optimum control of soil-active insects, apply 0.5 in (1.2 cm) of water 24–48 hours before the chemical application to encourage the insects to move closer to the surface and to decrease the absorbency of the thatch. Irrigation before treatment is especially important if conditions have been hot and dry and insects are deep in the soil. Immediately after the insecticide treatment, a heavier irrigation of 0.75–1 in (1.9–2.5 cm) should be applied to ensure effective thatch/soil penetration.

Always follow label directions for reentry periods. Never allow sprays to puddle, because honey bees and wildlife may be injured. Remember that it may take several days after treatment to achieve control of surface-active insects and longer for soil inhabitants. Further information on pesticide safety, application methodology, and listings of registered turfgrass pesticides can be obtained from local Cooperative Extension offices.

Turfgrass Insect Management and Unique Control Considerations

By S. Kristine Braman

Development and implementation of integrated pest management programs for the turfgrass system has roughly paralleled that for agricultural crops. Certain aspects of the turfgrass system, however, present unique challenges that must be addressed. Three considerations appear prominent in their influence on management decisions: (1) diversity of the turfgrass ecosystem, uses, and clientele; (2) high aesthetic standards for turfgrass; and (3) proximity of turf to people, pets, and permanent dwellings.

Managed turfgrasses support a rich diversity of insects and their close relatives. We are fortunate that relatively few of these organisms ever achieve pest status. In comparison with traditional agricultural crops, however, the diversity of grass and pest species, and associated beneficial organisms is noteworthy. More than 71 species of arthropods were mentioned by Tashiro (1987) as occasional-to-serious pests of one or more of the 20 most commonly used species of turfgrass. Pest management strategies will understandably differ according to the purpose for which the turf is used. Various conditions under which turf is grown include those found on airports, cemeteries, churches, commercial dwellings, home lawns, golf courses, institutions, parks, roadsides, schools, and sod farms.

Management decisions in agricultural systems are based on the quantifiable and predictable relationship between pest abundance and economic loss in terms of yield or quality. Similar decisions for turfgrass where pests cause aesthetic as well as economic damage become considerably more complex. They must incorporate turfgrass use, turfgrass species, pest species, and the variable and subjective public perception of what constitutes unacceptable levels of damage.

Often even minimal insect damage (mole cricket tunnels on golf course greens) is considered unacceptable.

Insect population levels tolerated on home lawns, commercial properties, athletic fields, parks, or sod farms vary with each setting. Pest suppression tactics suitable for sod farms would prove inappropriate for the playground in a day-care facility. The lack of situation-specific decision-making guidelines for pests causing aesthetic damage is limiting to the implementation of integrated pest management. Losses caused by insect injury are difficult to quantify. The monetary loss resulting from reductions in yield of an agricultural commodity may be readily determined. Economic impact of insect injury to turf involves more than the expense of pest control and turf renovation. It includes the less readily assigned cost of dissatisfied clients.

Simple, noninvasive, and reliable means of sampling populations and assessing risk are needed for turfgrass pests. The damaging stage of many turfgrass pests may be present in large numbers, yet go unnoticed until severe injury has occurred. This is particularly true for subterranean pests such as white grubs. Often the adult stage of a pest is more easily monitored with light or pheromone traps. However, the relationship between adult numbers in these traps and the corresponding population level of the damaging immatures is not well understood. The potential uses for adult trapping methods include detection of pest presence or peak oviposition activity and optimizing timing of control measures.

Problems of predicting location and severity of pest outbreaks are compounded by a lack of consistently effective, economic alternatives to conventional insecticides. Environmental concerns have not lessened the demand for high-quality landscapes. Economics, scheduling considerations, and the high expectations of a diverse group of end users dictate the choice of control products and the decision of whether to apply preventive treatments.

Managed turfgrasses also differ from agricultural settings because implicit in their intended use is a close proximity to people, pets, homes, and businesses. This creates a situation of some sensitivity with regard to the perceived potential for both environmental and human health risks associated with pesticide use. The implementation of integrated pest management programs in urban settings is favored by this growing societal concern relative to pesticide use in the landscape. The escalating level of concern in recent years is evident in the sharp increase in the number of jurisdictions within most states that now regulate pesticide use in landscape settings. Political and legal issues surrounding pesticide use in the urban environment will almost certainly dictate more limited and selective use of pesticides on turf-grasses.

Opportunities to offer plant care services based on monitoring and appropriately timed intervention exist as alternatives to traditional calendar applications of insecticides. As regulations and restrictions on traditional means of pest suppression increase, the demand for alternatives will also escalate. Ultimately, changes in public perception of acceptable levels of pest presence and subsequent injury will be required to effect the desired flexibility in decision making. We must recognize our responsibility to increase tolerance of limited insect presence through public education.

Selected Reference

Tashiro, H. 1987. Turfgrass insects of the United States and Canada. Cornell University Press, Ithaca, NY.

Insect/Plant Stress Interactions

By S. Kristine Braman

The ability of managed turfgrass to withstand insect pest pressure is often directly related to the vigor of the turf. Permanent turf damage caused by insect feeding or burrowing activities may often be avoided by maintaining a healthy, actively growing turf that is able to regenerate after injury. Supplemental irrigation and application of fertilizer at appropriate times can aid recovery from low to moderate insect damage. However, these same practices may actually render turf more susceptible to injury by other insect species or disease-causing organisms.

Prediction of pest presence, a key component of efficient pest management, is made difficult by our lack of understanding of how environmental stresses mutually affect host plants and their insect pests. Plants are often faced with one or more abiotic factors that affect turf vigor and appearance. These include water excess or deficit, nutrient imbalances, shade, scald, heat or cold stress, pollution, wear, and compaction. Biotic stresses caused by insects and disease also reduce turf vigor. Cultural management factors such as irrigation, fertilization, mowing, thatch management, and choice of adapted varieties can affect plant stress.

Plant stress may alter the suitability of a grass species as a host for insect pests and therefore influence the distribution of a pest or the severity of infestation. Experiments with plant/herbivore systems have shown that numerous aspects of an insect's biology can be affected by plant stress. Ability to locate the proper host plant, feeding and egg-laying behaviors, growth, survival, and number of offspring may all be affected by stress-induced changes in typical host plants. Furthermore, these responses to stress may differ depending on insect species; insect outbreak potential may increase, decrease, or remain the same.

Little data exist detailing the effects of routine cultural management practices, and associated changes in plant stress, on pest density and damage. Available information is largely anecdotal and primarily associated with water relations, fertilizer effects, and thatch management. Appropriate management tactics involve an appreciation for the response of the plant to stress as well as the variable responses of insects to that stress and to the stress-imposed changes in the plant.

Water Relations. Water content in a plant is the balance between absorption and transpiration (intake and loss). As long as absorption exceeds transpiration, the balance is favorable. Under conditions of moisture deficit, however, the plant responds with morphological and physiological changes. Morphological changes in response to moisture stress as summarized by Beard (1973) can include increased rooting depth and root/shoot ratio; decreased tillering and leaf number; reduced shoot elongation; decreased number, thickness, and area of leaves, smaller cells, and intercellular spaces; and thicker cuticles and cell walls. Plant function or physiological processes also change in response to water deficit. Changes may include decreased succulence, protein content, and photosynthetic rate and a general reduction in physiological activity.

Turfgrasses are able to survive periods of drought by entering a dormant state. This also tends to render detection of harmful populations of insects difficult. Two groups of surface-feeding insects, the chinch bugs and the sod webworms, inflict most of their damage during periods of drought and high temperatures. Early symptoms of damage may be masked by the dormant condition of grass under drought stress. Leaf yellowing and small brown patches that indicate an incipient pest problem in actively growing turf are not apparent in a turf under stress-induced dormancy.

The southern chinch bug is known to prefer open sunny areas (Reinert & Kerr 1973). Kerr (1966) noted that moisture had a "marked but paradoxical" effect on this species. Lush grass resulting from heavy rains or irrigation might be assumed to be attractive to the insects. However, not only did the rapidly growing grass withstand the effects of feeding, moisture somehow seemed related to actual suppression of the population. Subsequent reports of infection of chinch bugs with the pathogenic fungus *Beauveria bassiana* (Reinert 1978), which is encouraged in humid conditions, may at least partially explain this phenomenon. This points out yet another level in the complexity of interaction in the turfgrass community, the effect of abiotic stresses on natural enemies: parasites, predators, and pathogens.

Bohart (1947) mentioned a historical connection between drought and sod webworm injury to lawns or golf courses. Ainslee (1922) discussed sod webworms as occasional turf pests in "times of deficient rainfall." The first widespread reports of webworm injury to turf in North America occurred in 1929-1933 and coincided with widespread drought conditions. Noble (1932) theorized that concentrations of moths on irrigated lawns and golf courses contributed to injury experienced during the dry summers of 1930 and 1931.

Effects of soil moisture on insect behavior has also received attention in relation to white grub injury to turf. Villani & Wright (1988) reported that both soil moisture and temperature influence the position of grubs in the vertical soil profile. Thus, under drought conditions, white grubs move out of the soil/thatch interface and travel deeper into the soil becoming more difficult to reach and control with insecticides.

The influence of rainfall on adult masked chafer flight patterns and on numbers of grub-related service calls received by a Kentucky lawn care company was discussed by Potter (1981a, b). Although temperature-based degree-day accumulations adequately predict the first emergence of beetles from the soil, peak flights are more closely related to rainfall and soil moisture. The number of grub-related service calls was greatly increased during years with lower than average rainfall.

Potter (1982) studied damage thresholds in relation to soil moisture and determined that well-watered Kentucky bluegrass could tolerate 14–18 southern masked chafer grubs per square foot (0.09 m^2) before showing any damage. Moisture-stressed turf, on the other hand, expressed injury at infestation levels of eight to nine grubs per square foot (0.09 m^2). Irrigated 'Tifway' bermudagrass and 'Kentucky-31' tall fescue also showed no loss in above-ground plant quality with similarly high initial infestation levels of the southern masked chafer and the Japanese beetle (Braman & Pendley 1993).

Susceptibility to certain turfgrass diseases can increase or decrease under soil moisture stress (reviewed in Beard 1973). Examples of increased incidence of disease influenced by plant water deficits include dollar spot susceptibility of Kentucky bluegrass, *Pythium* blight susceptibility of 'Highland' colonial bentgrass, and crown and root rot phases of *Helminthosporium* diseases. On the other hand, 'Rainier' red fescue was more tolerant of red thread, and the leaf spot phase of *Helminthosporium sativum* Pammel, C. M. King, and Dakke on Kentucky bluegrass was less severe under soil moisture stress.

Excess soil moisture injures turf primarily by lack of aeration. The oxygen deficiency of saturated soil restricts root growth, leading to an overall decline in turfgrass quality, rooting depth, and vigor. Waterlogged soils also provide favorable conditions for growth of algae and anaerobic organisms. When given a choice of soil moisture conditions, the white grub *Phyllophaga crinita* (Burmeister) did not oviposit in wet soil or the eggs that were deposited did not survive (Gaylor & Frankie 1979). Previous mention was made of the apparent negative effect of high moisture on southern chinch bug biology. However, the two-lined spittlebug is favored by high-moisture environments.

Fertilizer Practices. Fertilizer is applied to supply plant nutrients that are deficient in the soil in order to maintain plant quality. Supplemental fertilizer applications after insect injury can encourage rapid turf recovery. Conversely, the biochemical, anatomical, and physiological characteristics of leaves and other plant parts as affected by fertilizer practices can influence the potential for pest population increase. Nitrogen nutrition affects turf shoot and root growth, shoot density, color, disease proneness, temperature and drought tolerance, regeneration potential, and the composition of the turfgrass community (Beard 1973).

Evidence in the literature links excessive application of nitrogen with increases in numbers of the southern chinch bug and spittlebugs. Horn (1962) demonstrated that chinch bug populations develop more rapidly and cause injury sooner on heavily fertilized grass using inorganic forms of nitrogen quickly available to the grass. Populations developed more slowly and caused less injury on the same grass receiving more moderate amounts of fertilizer or nitrogen from an organic source.

Observations on the biology of the two-lined spittlebug in relation to both cultural and insecticidal management in coastal bermudagrass pastures were made by Beck (1963). His data suggested that nymphal survival was dependent on "shade and a highly nutritious host." High-nitrogen plots were most severely damaged. Neither of the two previously mentioned studies, however, attempted to directly relate increased insect populations with nitrogen-induced changes in host plant quality or other possibilities such as a more favorable microclimate or reduction in natural enemies in fertilized plots.

Turf grown at high nitrogen levels is also more prone to injury by *Helminthosporium* leaf spot, brown patch, *Fusarium* patch, *Ophiobolus* patch, *Fusarium* blight, and gray leaf spot. Nitrogen deficiencies render turf more prone to facultative saprophytes (e.g., dollar spot, rust, and red thread).

Thatch Management. Thatch is the term describing the layer of dead and living stems and roots between the zone of green vegetation and the soil surface. When the accumulation of dead organic matter exceeds the rate of decomposition, thatch develops. Mowing infrequently or too high, excessive nitrogen nutrition, acidic conditions, and poor aeration may contribute to an over accumulation of thatch. Several problems are associated with excessive thatch accumulation, including increased disease and insect problems, localized dry spots, proneness to scalping, and decreased tolerance to extremes in temperature or moisture (Beard 1973). Thatched turf becomes hydrophobic, dries out, and prevents water from reaching the soil. Thatch conditions elevate crowns, rhizomes, and roots above the soil surface, increasing the potential for heat, drought, and cold stress. Thatch provides a microenvironment conducive to the development of several insect and disease-causing organisms. Thatch may also reduce the effectiveness of fungicides and insecticides.

Davis & Smitley (1990a) examined the relationship between hairy chinch bug infestation and parameters of the turfgrass environment. Thatch thickness was positively correlated with chinch bug presence and abundance in all 3 years of that study. Thatch was thicker in lawns with the hairy chinch bug than in lawns without it; the number of chinch bugs increased as thatch increased. Thatch thickness was not related to turfgrass species composition of the home lawns examined. In a related study, larger average populations of the hairy chinch bug occurred in plots where a thick thatch layer was induced by application of the fungicide mancozeb compared with untreated control plots (Davis & Smitley 1990b). These combined results indicated that hairy chinch bug abundance was closely linked with the thatch thickness of home lawns. Davis & Smitley (1990b) suggested four hypotheses that may explain the observed relationship: thatch helps the hairy chinch bug escape predation, thatch reduces mortality from environmental stress, feeding injury by the hairy chinch bug induces thatch, and pesticide applications cause thatch buildup and also suppress natural enemies of chinch bugs.

Additional research of this type will enhance our understanding of insect community/plant/environment interactions as mediated by management practices. Because turf is rarely exposed to a single stress, the dynamics of multiple stresses need also to be considered. Knowledge in these areas may indicate practical ways to modify the turfgrass system to reduce the probability of insect infestation and damage.

Selected References

Ainslee, G. G. 1922. Webworms injurious to cereal and forage crops and their control. U.S. Dept. Agric. Farmers' Bull. 1258: 1-16.

Beard, J. B. 1973. Turfgrass: science and culture. Prentice-Hall, Englewood Cliffs, NJ.

Beck, E. W. 1963. Observations on the biology and cultural-insecticidal control of *Prosapia bicincta,* a spittlebug, on coastal bermudagrass. J. Econ. Entomol. 56: 747-752.

Bohart, R. M. 1947. Sod webworms and other lawn pests in California. Hilgardia 17: 267-308.

Braman, S. K. & A. F. Pendley. 1993. Growth, survival and damage relationships of white grubs in bermudagrass vs. tall fescue. J. Int. Turf Sci. 7: 370 - 374.

Davis, M.G.K. & D. R. Smitley. 1990a. Relationship of hairy chinch bug (Hemiptera: Lygaeidae) presence and abundance to parameters of the turf environment. J. Econ. Entomol. 83: 2375-2379.

1990b. Association of thatch with populations of hairy chinch bug (Hemiptera: Lygaeidae) in turf. J. Econ. Entomol. 83: 2370-2374.

Gaylor, M. J. & G. W. Frankie. 1979. The relationship of rainfall to adult flight activity; and of soil moisture to oviposition behavior and egg and first instar survival of *Phyllophaga crinita.* Environ. Entomol. 8: 591-594.

Horn, G. C. 1962. Chinch bugs and fertilizer, is there a relationship? Fla. Turfgrass Assoc. Bull. 9(4): 3, 5.

Kerr, S. H. 1966. Biology of the lawn chinch bug, *Blissus insularis.* Fla. Entomol. 49: 9-18.

Noble, W. B. 1932. Sod webworms and their control in lawns and golf greens. U.S. Dep. Agric. Bull. 248: 1-4.

Potter, D. A. 1981a. Biology and management of masked chafers. Am. Lawn Appl. July/August: 2-6.

1981b. Seasonal emergence and flight of northern and southern masked chafers in relation to air and soil temperature and rainfall patterns. Environ. Entomol. 10: 793-797.

1982. Influence of feeding by grubs of the southern masked chafer on quality and yield of Kentucky bluegrass. J. Econ. Entomol. 75: 21-24.

Reinert, J. A. 1978. Natural enemy complex of the southern chinch bug in Florida. Ann. Entomol. Soc. Am. 71: 728-731.

Reinert, J. A. & S. H. Kerr. 1973. Bionomics and control of lawn chinch bugs. Bull. Entomol. Soc. Am. 19: 91-92.

Villani, M. G. & R. J. Wright. 1988. Use of radiography in behavioral studies of turfgrass-infesting scarab grub species (Coleoptera: Scarabaeidae). Bull. Entomol. Soc. Am. 34: 132-144.

Turfgrass Diseases and Their Relationship to Insect Management

By Gail L. Schumann

Many kinds of plant-parasitic microorganisms have been identified in turfgrasses, including fungi, nematodes, bacteria, mycoplasmalike organisms, and viruses. Of these, fungi and nematodes are the most common and important causal agents of turfgrass diseases. The other types of pathogens are less frequently observed and cause only a few economically important diseases.

Bacteria, Mycoplasmalike Organisms (MLOs), and Viruses. Bacterial wilt, caused by various pathovars of *Xanthomonas campestris* (Pammel) Dowson, has been observed occasionally on a few species and cultivars of turfgrass. Because bacteria are easily dispersed to wounds created by routine mowing, management of this disease is extremely difficult and expensive. Therefore, infected turf should be replaced with resistant species or cultivars.

The aster yellows MLO has been identified in several turfgrass species. It is vectored by a leafhopper and causes stunting, yellowing, and witches'-brooms of turfgrass shoots. MLOs are not mechanically transmitted, so control of the insect vector may reduce infection of new plants.

A number of viruses have been detected in turfgrass species, however St. Augustine decline, caused by *Panicum* mosaic virus, is apparently the only virus disease of economic importance in turf. Aphids, beetles, leafhoppers, mites, and planthoppers have been identified as vectors of viruses that infect turfgrasses. In addition, a few soilborne fungi and some nematodes vector turfgrass viruses, and a few viruses, including *Panicum* mosaic virus, are mechanically transmitted in the mowing process. Because there is no treatment once virus infection has occurred, infected turf areas must be replaced. Mites, plantbugs, and thrips have been implicated in one inflorescence disease of turfgrass known as silvertop in North America. The silvertop symptom is caused in part by the puncture wounds made by these arthropods.

Nematodes. Nematodes are roundworms that are usually less than 0.04 in (1 mm) long. They are numerous in nearly all environments and are an important component of the soil microfauna. In turfgrass, populations of plant-parasitic nematodes may increase to levels that cause substantial injury. Nematode injury may result in distortion or inhibition of root growth, necrotic root lesions, and increased susceptibility to other pathogens, particularly fungi.

Determination of economic injury thresholds is difficult, especially for those nematodes species that do not actually enter the root tissue. The presence of several species of plant-parasitic nematodes is common in and around turfgrass roots and may further complicate threshold determinations. Temporal and spatial variations in nematode populations occur in most turfgrass areas. As a result, high nematode population densities or "hot spots" may be detected.

In general, nematode injury is more common in sandy soils, warm environments, and where other stresses, such as compaction, low mowing height, fungal root diseases, and root-feeding insects, injure roots or reduce root growth. Substantial injury caused by plant parasitic nematodes in northern regions is more likely to occur on putting greens and other turf maintained at very low mowing heights.

Fungi and Environmental Conditions That Enhance Fungal Disease Development. Fungi cause the most common and economically important turfgrass diseases. Fungi are eukaryotic organisms that exist as threadlike mycelium or hyphae. They produce spores that enhance their ability to disperse and survive. Water is essential for spore germination and for infection of turfgrass plants. Fungi infect all parts of turfgrass plants and can be divided into two groups: (1) species that infect the turfgrass blades and cause leaf spots, foliar blights, and, sometimes, crown and root rots, and (2) soilborne species that infect roots and crowns and cause cortical and vascular decay.

The fact that diseases occur intermittently and seasonally illustrates the extremely important role that environment plays in disease development and severity. Unless the turf area is being reestablished or overseeded with a new species or cultivar, disease management of turfgrasses must emphasize modification of the environment. The key environmental factors that affect the development of foliar diseases are water and temperature. Spore germination and fungal infection require free water and very high relative humidity. Many cultural practices seek to minimize the length of time leaf blades remain wet. The site of putting green establishment, pruning of tree branches and other landscape plants, whipping or pooling of dew and guttation fluid from leaf blades, and the timing and duration of irrigation all attempt to minimize the time the leaves are wet. Air movement is such a critical aspect of this type of disease management that some golf courses have installed fans near putting greens where landscaping or natural weather conditions preclude rapid drying.

Most turfgrass diseases may be categorized as either cool-, warm-, or hot-weather diseases. The role of temperature is complex because it affects many aspects of fungal biology including spore formation and germination, hyphal growth, and host colonization as well as plant growth. Minimum, maximum, and optimum temperatures can be determined for each of these factors that affect disease severity. A key factor in disease development is infection of the turfgrass by a pathogen. Various combinations of temperature and moisture levels may be used to define infection periods. Infection periods are the basis of most disease prediction systems for foliar diseases such as anthracnose, brown patch, dollar spot, and *Pythium* blight.

A third important environmental factor associated with foliar diseases of turfgrass is nitrogen fertility. Many diseases are more severe under "low nitrogen" or "high nitrogen" conditions. The succulent growth of turfgrass induced by nitrogen applications is more susceptible to brown patch, leaf spots, *Pythium* blight, and a number of other diseases. Conversely, slow-growing, nitrogen-deficient turfgrass is more susceptible to anthracnose, dollar spot, red thread, and rust.

Diseases caused by fungi that infect turfgrass roots are also affected by moisture and temperature, although variations in the soil environment are more buffered. Many diseases are caused by fungi that are able to thrive under extremely dry or extremely wet conditions. These conditions also contribute to turfgrass stress, increasing its susceptibility to disease. Soil pH is an important soil environmental factor that influences a number of diseases, most notably take-all patch. The soil environment, like the more variable environment surrounding the leaf blades, affects the interactions between turfgrass plants, potential pathogens, and other soilborne species in the turfgrass ecosystem.

Management Practices That Affect Disease Development. Most turfgrass management practices have both direct and indirect effects on turfgrasses and their ecosystems, particularly the microbial community. In re-

cent years, the increased importance of *Pythium* root diseases, patch diseases caused by root-infecting fungi, and nematode problems in both warm- and cool-season turfgrass species has been associated with the decreased organic matter in modern, sand-based putting greens and a concomitant decrease in microbial competition and antagonism. Severity of these root diseases has also been associated with lower mowing heights and compaction, which increase plant stress, reduce root growth, and modify disease susceptibility.

Mowing increases the incidence and severity of many turfgrass diseases. Mowers dislodge and disperse spores, mycelia, and sclerotia and create wounds that are entry sites for pathogens. Disease symptoms may be associated with mowing patterns, especially when grass is wet and pathogenic fungi are active. Improper mowing and low mowing heights contribute to stress and make turf more susceptible to some diseases. On the other hand, mowing of putting greens early in the morning can help remove water and nutrient-rich guttation liquid from leaf blades and help reduce infection in diseases such as dollar spot. Infected tissue may also be removed by mowing. If the cut blades are not removed from the mowed surface, however, they may serve as a source of inoculum for further infections.

Many management practices also focus on creating an optimal environment for root growth. Thick thatch and compacted soils should be corrected through proper aeration and topdressing to relieve stress and improve root development, water infiltration, and drainage.

Although pesticide and fertilizer recommendations for turfgrass areas are often designed to manage a primary target pest or to improve turfgrass growth, these chemicals may directly or indirectly affect many other components of the turfgrass ecosystem. For example, most of the insecticides used to control soil insect pests are also nematicidal, killing both plant parasites and beneficial nematodes. They may also be toxic to mycophagous arthropods and other beneficial predators and parasites of pathogenic fungi and nematodes. The fungicide benomyl is toxic to earthworms. The association of excess thatch accumulation with the overuse of some pesticides is at least partially related to these effects.

Many herbicides used on turfgrass function as growth regulators, which can increase plant stress and susceptibility to certain diseases. The demethylation-inhibiting (DMI) or sterol biosynthesis-inhibiting (SBI) fungicides are chemically related to some of the commercial plant growth regulators used to reduce turfgrass growth. Multiple applications of several of these chemically related compounds may result in phytotoxicity and increases in certain diseases.

Repeated use of a number of fungicides has also been associated with resurgence of target diseases and enhancement of nontarget diseases. These observations are probably related to a disruption of the ecological balance between plant pathogens and beneficial microorganisms and arthropods. Systemic fungicides that are applied for root disease control are typically irrigated into the thatch after application, which may further increase the adverse ecological effects of these compounds in the soil and thatch.

Diagnostic Challenges. An accurate diagnosis of a problem is necessary to make appropriate management choices. The symptoms of many foliar turfgrass diseases are relatively easy to identify, although disease symptoms of turfgrass maintained at low mowing heights may not always be easy to discern. Fungal diseases often occur in circular patterns that are associated with the radial growth of a fungus from a central point. This is reflected in the numerous turf disease names that include the words "patch" or "spot." With time, patches and spots may coalesce into large areas of blighted turf, obscuring the circular patterns. Turfgrass areas composed of several cultivars or species that vary in disease susceptibility may also disrupt the natural appearance of circular patterns. Injury from insect pests can obscure or mimic diagnostic disease symptoms. For example, bluegrass billbug injury produces symptoms very similar to summer patch in Kentucky bluegrass. Some diseases, such as anthracnose, typically produce irregular symptoms that may easily be confused with insect injury.

Turfgrass problems that involve the roots and other below-ground parts of the plants are often difficult to diagnose. Similar above-ground symptoms may be induced by many below-ground problems, including diseases, nematodes, insect pests, and various stress factors. Thus, turf that is stressed by low mowing height, low fertility, drought, poor drainage, or compacted soil is not only less able to tolerate pest and pathogen populations, but the resulting damage can produce confusing symptoms. Although it is clear that multiple stress factors and pest problems may influence each other and the turf quality, these interactions are complex, poorly understood, and rarely studied.

Integrating Management Strategies. Public pressure to reduce pesticide use combined with the serious nontarget effects of many pesticides has encouraged many turfgrass managers to utilize cultural practices, genetic resistance, and biocontrol for a more environmentally

sound approach to pest management. To be successful, however, the entire turfgrass ecosystem must be considered when strategies are developed. For example, a pesticide that disrupts natural populations of competitors and antagonists may reduce a target pest population, but may also allow unacceptable increases in nontarget pests.

A number of biocontrol options are now in development, and some are even available as commercial products for turfgrass insect pests. Bacteria, fungi, and nematodes are biocontrol options for some turfgrass insect pests. Bacteria, fungi, and insects are potential bioherbicides. Bacteria, fungi, and populations of antagonistic microbes in organic composts have been shown to provide biocontrol of turfgrass diseases such as brown patch, dollar spot, and gray snow mold. Because these potential biocontrol agents are living organisms, it may be necessary to modify the turf environment to enhance their survival and dispersal.

The cultural practices that enhance the success of these microbial biocontrol agents could possibly also enhance diseases caused by plant-parasitic species of bacteria, fungi, and nematodes. For example, several potential bioherbicides are pathogens of weed species. Biocontrol agents may also be sensitive to a number of the pesticides used in routine turf management. Little is known about the effects of repeated use of broad-spectrum pesticides on the successful application of biocontrol agents.

Turfgrass cultivars with fungal endophytes are becoming increasingly popular for the biocontrol of foliar insect pests. Studies have shown that fungicides used for disease control do not eliminate endophytic fungi from turfgrass plants when applied according to label recommendations. Some preliminary observations suggest, however, that the presence of an endophyte in a turfgrass cultivar may modify its disease resistance, either increasing or decreasing resistance depending on the particular disease and the turfgrass species and cultivar.

Modern pest management theory includes the concept of economic or aesthetic injury thresholds. The elimination of insect pests and pathogens is no longer the goal of ecologically based turfgrass management. Because insect pests, nematodes, and fungal parasites are always present in a turfgrass ecosystem, the focus of turfgrass management must shift from individual recommendations for target pests to an integrated approach. Turf management should focus on maintaining high-quality turfgrass that can withstand continual pressure from pest and pathogen populations. Cultural recommendations must reduce stress, improve root growth, and provide a balanced fertility without enhancing disease problems.

Selected References

Clarke, B. B. & A. B. Gould [eds.]. 1993. Turfgrass patch diseases caused by ectotrophic root-infecting fungi. APS Press, St. Paul, MN.

Smiley, R. W., P. H. Dernoeden & B. B. Clarke. 1992. Compendium of turfgrass diseases, 2nd ed. APS Press, St. Paul, MN.

Smith, J. D., N. Jackson & A. R. Woolhouse. 1989. Fungal diseases of amenity turf grasses. E. & F. N. Spon, London.

Vargas, J. M., Jr. 1994. Management of turfgrass diseases, 2nd ed. Lewis, Chelsea, MI.

Weed Management in Turf and Weed/Arthropod Interactions

By Joseph C. Neal

Weeds affect turfgrass quality and utility by competing with desirable species for space and resources and by producing a nonuniform surface. Because the first step in any pest management program is to properly identify and understand the pest, let us first consider what makes a plant a weed and why they are present. A weed is often defined as a plant out of place. In turf, this means any plant other than the desirable turf species, although we must understand that a weed to some may be a desirable wildflower to another. To most turfgrass maintenance professionals, white clover (*Trifolium repens* L.) is considered a weed; however, this "weed" was once included in most lawn seed mixtures and is still considered by many a desirable component of turf. In addition, the expected turf quality (and tolerable "weediness") will differ between sites and uses. Therefore, before developing a weed management program one must first understand the expectations of the owner, client, or user regarding what species they consider to be weeds and how severe an infestation they are willing to tolerate (the action threshold). High-maintenance and high-visibility areas, such as golf greens, obviously have a lower weed density threshold than low-maintenance, low-priority areas.

Turfgrass Weed Management. In general, a healthy and vigorous turf will outcompete most weeds, and any biotic, abiotic, or cultural factor that reduces turfgrass vigor will contribute to an increase in weeds. Consequently, weed species found in turf are either well adapted to the unique conditions under which we manage turfgrasses or are opportunistic and invade when other factors have weakened the turf. Therefore, the first line of defense against weeds is a healthy turf. To maintain optimum turfgrass vigor and limit weed encroachment, consider the following general guidelines.

Select the Best Turfgrass Species and Varieties for the Site. Turfgrass species and variety selection must consider many factors, including hardiness, soil type and native pH, resistance to important insect pests and diseases, the purpose for which the turf will be used, and the anticipated maintenance program.

Properly Prepare the Soil for Seeding, Sodding, or Sprigging. Site preparation includes eliminating weeds that are difficult to control and remediating any deficient soil physical or chemical properties, including, but not limited to, improving drainage, incorporating soil amendments, adjusting pH, and providing fertilizer amendments. These operations should be done at times that will allow seeding or sodding during the season of optimal turf growth and minimal weed seed germination. For cool-season turf, this is best done in the late summer or early fall. Warm-season turfgrass is best established in the spring.

Maintain Optimum Fertility and Irrigation Regimes. Too little or excessive fertilization or irrigation will lead to weakened turf and, consequently, to more weeds.

Maintain the Optimum Mowing Height and Frequency. Mowing too close stresses the turf and encourages the encroachment of certain weeds that are better adapted to close mowing. Mowing height should be at the higher end of the recommended range for the turf type and the intended use. Infrequent mowing scalps the turf, causing stress and allowing weeds to germinate and establish. Infrequent mowing may also produce a shift in the weed spectrum toward those species commonly seen along roadsides, such as common chicory (*Cichorium intybus* L.), teasel (*Dipsacus sylvestris* Huds.), and wild carrot (*Daucus carota* L.). Mow frequently enough to remove no more than one-third of the leaf area at a time.

Manage Disease and Insect Pests. Where diseases or arthropod pests have weakened or damaged the turf, the inevitable result is weed encroachment.

Some other factors that tend to promote weed germination or encroachment include damage to the turf from overuse, introduction of weed propagules, and compaction. Also, weed seed and tubers may lie dormant in the soil for many years just waiting for an opportunity to emerge and spread. Soil disturbances caused by use or by repair operations often stimulate weed germination. In athletic fields, little can be done about damage from use; however, rotating area use and overseeding can minimize the impact. Weed propagules are spread by wind, water, and birds and other animals; in topsoil, organic amendments, and mulch; and on equipment. In addition, weeds may encroach from adjacent properties or come from rootballs of infested trees and shrubs.

Sanitation, vigilance, and optimized turfgrass management can minimize the opportunities for weeds to become established; however, some weeds will inevitably encroach even under the best management conditions. When this occurs, first consider if control is warranted. This decision is based on the previously mentioned quality expectations. If herbicides are deemed to be necessary, select and apply them properly. Use the following criteria to select the best one for the job:

- target weed species
- turfgrass species and management (particularly mowing height)
- weed status (i.e., preemergent, size of seedlings, established, etc.)
- efficacy of herbicide on primary and secondary target weeds, longevity of control, and if repeat applications may be necessary
- available application equipment (i.e., are you restricted to granules or sprays?)
- economics, based on acre-treatment costs and efficacy considerations
- proximity of susceptible species such as trees and shrubs or crops
- potential environmental impact and toxicology (when a choice is available, use safer and more environmentally benign products)

There are many sources for information on herbicides and their use in turfgrass management including trade journals, texts, dealer/distributor representatives, consultants, your peers, and others, but the best and most up-to-date should be your local Cooperative Extension Service.

Interactions Between Weeds and Arthropods. *Weeds May Affect Arthropod Populations.* In agronomic and horticultural crops, the types of vegetation present have been shown to dramatically affect the type and populations of arthropod pests and beneficials. William (1981) reviewed these interactions and found that, in horticultural cropping systems, weed or weed control practices affected arthropod pest establishment by altering visual, olfactory/chemical, or microenvironmental cues. Unfortunately, little such information is available on the interactions between weeds and arthropods in the turfgrass ecosystem. However, it is reasonable to assume that as in horticultural crops, weeds may affect turfgrass arthropod pests by serving as alternative hosts, providing shelter, or harboring beneficial species.

An example of a weed providing an alternative host in the turfgrass ecosystem involves the annual bluegrass weevil, *Listronotus maculicollis* (Dietz). This insect is most commonly found on annual bluegrass (*Poa annua*); however, adult feeding has also been observed on more desirable turfgrass species. When high populations of the annual bluegrass weevil decimate the preferred host, damage to desirable turf is more likely.

In fruit crops, a ground cover dominated by dicot weeds including vetch (*Vicia spp.*), clover (*Trifolium* spp.), henbit (*Lamium amplexicaule* L.), lespedeza (*Lespedeza* spp.), common chickweed (*Stellaria media* [L.] Vill.), or pepperweed (*Lepidium* spp.) attracted stink bugs (Pentatomidae), the tarnished plant bug (*Lygus lineolaris* [Palisot de Beauvois]), and spider mites (*Tetranychus* spp.), which subsequently damaged the fruit (Killian & Meyer 1984, Meagher & Meyer 1990, Meyer et al. 1992). The same arthropods are often considered to be nuisance pests in recreational turfgrass areas. The presence of dicot weeds, such as those found in orchards, may contribute to increased populations of these arthropods. It is therefore reasonable to assume that by controlling dicot weeds we may reduce populations of these arthropod pests.

In other crops, weeds have been shown to serve as alternate hosts for plant pathogens (particularly viruses) or as vectors of crop pathogens. Common chickweed is an obligate alternate host for yellow witches'-broom of fir trees, and dandelion (*Taraxacum officinale* Weber) is an alternate host for the nematode that has been associated with peach tree decline and bacterial canker. Shurtleff et al. (1987) suggested that weeds may also harbor insects capable of transmitting turfgrass diseases. However, this association has not been demonstrated.

Clearly, the potential interactions between weeds and arthropod pests have not been adequately investigated. Perhaps because of the assumption that before weed populations get high enough to have a substantial effect on arthropod populations, they are removed for aesthetic reasons. As integrated pest management and action threshold concepts are applied to turfgrass weed management, we may need to reevaluate this assumption.

Arthropods May Affect Weeds. The presence of turfgrass arthropod pests at populations greater than damage thresholds will result in thin turf, creating opportunities for weeds to encroach. It is common to find a proliferation of weeds like nutsedge (*Cyperus* spp.), crabgrass (*Digitaria* spp.), spurge (*Euphorbia* spp.), wood-sorrel (*Oxalis* spp.), and black medick (*Medicago lupulina* L.) in areas heavily infested with chinch bugs. These weeds are suppressed by a vigorous, healthy turf, but are well adapted to the environmental conditions that worsen chinch bug feeding damage.

This general concept can be applied to almost any turf-grass arthropod pest. Whenever turf is thinned by arthropods, diseases, or other factors, weeds will encroach to fill the void. Therefore, one important step in turf-grass weed management is the effective management of other turfgrass pests.

Arthropods have been utilized for biological control of weeds in many crops; however, currently no biological control agents are available for turfgrass weeds. Three criteria for selecting biological control agents for testing include (1) specificity: the agent must have a limited host range lest it escape and injure desirable species; (2) efficacy: in turf the threshold for weeds approaches zero, therefore efficacy must be excellent; and (3) economics: turfgrass managers can afford to spend more than most farmers for weed control, but any control strategy must be cost-effective. Considerable research is being conducted worldwide on weed biocontrol. Julien (1992) published a catalog of weed biological control agents and their target weeds. Included in that text are examples of many insects that have been evaluated for the control of common turf weeds including purple nut-sedge (*Cyperus rotundus* L.), bindweed (*Convolvulus* spp.), alligator-weed (*Alternanthera philoxeroides* [Mart.] Griseb.), docks (*Rumex* spp.), and thistles (*Cirsium*

spp.). The insects evaluated were predominantly from three orders: Coleoptera, Diptera, and Lepidoptera. Although those insects have not been evaluated under turf-grass conditions, potential for utilization of arthropods for turfgrass weed management exists. Clearly, much more research is required to bring weed biocontrol agents into general use.

Selected References

Julien, M. H. [ed.]. 1992. Biological control of weeds; a world catalogue of agents and their target weeds, 3rd ed. CAB International, Wallington, UK.

Killian, J. C. & J. R. Meyer. 1984. Effect of orchard weed management on catfacing damage to peaches in North Carolina. J. Econ. Entomol. 77: 1596-1600.

Meagher, R. L., Jr., & J. R. Meyer. 1990. Influence of ground cover and herbicide treatments on *Tetranychus urticae* populations in peach orchards. Exp. Appl. Acarol. 9: 149-158.

Meyer, J. R., E. I. Zehr, R. L. Meagher, Jr., & S. K. Salvo. 1992. Survival and growth of peach trees and pest populations in orchard plots managed with experimental ground covers. Agric. Ecosyst. Environ. 41: 353-363.

Shurtleff, M. C., T. W. Fermanian & R. Randell. 1987. Controlling turf-grass pests. Prentice-Hall, Englewood Cliffs, NJ.

Tashiro, H. 1987. Turfgrass insects of the United States and Canada. Cornell University Press, Ithaca, NY.

William, R. D. 1981. Complementary interactions between weeds, weed control practices, and pests in horticultural cropping systems. Hort-Science 16(4): 508-513.

Glossary

abdomen. The third or most posterior of the three major body divisions of an insect.

aestivate. To spend the summer in a dormant condition; opposed to hibernate.

alate. Winged.

antennae. In larval and adult stages of an insect, paired segmented appendages, on each side of the head, functioning as sense organs.

anterior. Toward the front (head), as opposed to posterior.

antibiosis. Plant characteristics that affect insects in a negative manner (such as increased mortality or reduced fecundity); a type of plant resistance to insects.

apical. At, near, or pertaining to the tip or apex.

apices. At or near the apex or "top" of a structure.

arthropods. Invertebrate animals with jointed appendages; members of the phylum Arthropoda.

beneficial. A useful insect, often one that is a predator or parasitoid of a harmful insect.

biological control. Using any biological agent (often an insect) to control a pest.

bivoltine. Two generations per year.

brachypterous. Having short wings not covering the abdomen.

broods. A group or cohort of offspring produced by a parent or parent population at different times or in different places.

callow adult. A recently molted, soft-bodied, pale adult.

caterpillar. The larva of a moth, butterfly, skipper, or sawfly..

cephalothorax. The combined head and thorax of spiders and other arachnids.

cerci. A pair of appendages at the tip of the abdomen.

chitin. A colorless, nitrogenous polysaccharide secreted by the epidermis and applied to the hardened parts of an insect body.

chlorophyll. The green, light-sensitive pigment of plants that in sunlight is capable of combining carbon dioxide and water to make carbohydrates.

chlorosis. A yellowing or loss of color of plant leaves, caused by loss of chlorophyll.

chlorotic. Having a fading of green color in plant leaves to light green or yellow.

chorion. The outer covering of an insect egg.

cocoon. The silken or fibrous case spun by a larva for protection during its pupal period.

cool-season grass. A cold-tolerant grass with an optimum temperature range of 60 - 75° F. (15.5 - to 24° C.).

costal margin. The front edge of a wing.

crochets. Hooked spines on the underside of prolegs of caterpillars.

culm. The stem of a grass plant.

cultivar. Cultivated variety.

cultural control. Manipulation of a crop environment to reduce pest increase and damage.

cuticle. The outer covering of an insect formed by a layer of chitin.

cyst. A sac or vesicle.

degree-day. An accumulation of degrees above some threshold temperature for a 24-hour measure of physiological time for cold-blooded organisms, like insects. Degree-days can be expressed in Fahrenheit (FDD) or Celsius (CDD).

developmental threshold. The minimum temperature required for development.

diapause. Physiological state of arrested metabolism, growth, and development that may occur at any stage in the life cycle.

dormant. A state of reduced physiological activity.

dorsum. The upper surface, or back.

eclosion. Emergence of the adult insect from the pupa; act of hatching from the egg.

economic injury level (EIL). The number of insects (amount of injury) that will cause losses equal to insect management cost.

economic threshold (ET). The pest density at which management action should be taken to prevent an increasing pest population from reaching the economic injury level.

ecosystem. A living community and its nonliving environment.

elytra (sing., elytron). The two thickened, hardened forewings of beetles.

endoparasite. Parasitic organism living inside its host.

entomophagous. Insect-eating.

Glossary

exoskeleton. The outside skeleton of insects.

femur (pl., femora). The thigh; in insects, usually the largest segment of the leg articulated at the proximal end nearest the body to the trochanter and distally to the tibia.

frass. Solid larval excrement.

generation. A group of offspring of the same species that develop in approximately the same time frame.

gregarious. Occurring in aggregations.

grub. An insect larva; a term usually with specific reference to larvae of Coleoptera and Hymenoptera.

head capsule. The combined sclerites of the head, forming a hard, compact case.

hemimetabolous. Simple, incomplete metamorphosis where larval stages (nymphs) are often similar to adults in appearance and feeding behavior.

hibernate. To pass the winter in a dormant state.

hindgut. The posterior region of the digestive tract, between the midgut and anus.

holometabolous. Having a complete transformation, with egg, larval, pupal, and adult stages distinctly separated.

indigenous. Native to an area.

insectivorous. Feeding on insects.

instar. The stage between molts or shedding of the exoskeleton.

integrated pest management (IPM). A system of economically and environmentally sound practices to reduce the deleterious impact of pest activities; frequently associated with the use of multiple management tactics (e.g., pesticides, cultural control, host plant resistance, and biological control).

larva. A young insect; an immature form called a caterpillar, slug, maggot, or grub, depending on the kind of insect.

life cycle. The period between egg deposition and attainment of sexual maturity as shown by egg laying.

macropterous. Long- or large-winged.

maggot. The larval stage of a true fly (Diptera).

mandibles. An insect's jaws.

maxilla. The hind or second set of jaws behind the mandibles.

metamorphosis. The process of changes through which an insect passes during its growth from egg to adult.

microsporidium. Any of a group of protozoans some of which are pathogens to insects and other animals.

migrant. An insect that migrates. Commonly, migrations are usually one way (usually northward) and are dependent on wind currents and weather patterns.

molt. To cast off or shed the outer skin and so forth at certain intervals before replacement of the cast-off parts by new growth.

moth. An adult insect (Lepidoptera) with two pairs of scale-covered wings and variously shaped (but never clubbed) antennae.

multivoltine. Having more than one generation in a year or season.

nematode. Any of a class of phylum of elongated cylindrical worms that are parasitic in animals or plants or are free-living in soil or water.

nocturnal. Active at night.

nymph. An immature stage in insects with incomplete metamorphosis.

overwinter. To survive the winter.

oviposition. Egglaying.

palidia. A group of spines, usually in a line, found near the anus of scarab grubs.

palp. A segmented process on an arthropod's mouthpart.

parasite. Any animal that lives in, on, or at the expense of another.

parasitoid. An arthropod that parasitizes and kills an arthropod host; parasitic in the immature stages but free-living as an adult.

pathogen. A disease-causing organism.

peripheral. Relating to the outer margin.

phenology, phenological. Temporal and seasonal pattern of life history events in plants and animals.

pheromone. A substance secreted by an animal that influences the behavior of other individuals of the same species.

phytophagous. Feeding upon plants.

phytotoxic. Poisonous to plants.

polyphagous. Eating many kinds of foods.

posterior. Toward the rear, as opposed to anterior.

predator. An animal that preys on another.

prepupa. A transitional stage between the end of the larval period and the pupal period.

profile. An outline as seen from a side view.

prolegs. Fleshy, unsegmented abdominal walking appendages of some insect larvae.

pronotum. The upper or dorsal surface of the prothorax.

prothorax. The first, or anterior, of the three segments of the thorax.

pubescence. Fine hair or setae.

pupa. The resting, inactive stage between the larva and the adult in all insects that undergo complete metamorphosis.

raster. A complex of specifically arranged bare places, hairs, and spines on the ventral surface of the last abdominal segment, in front of the anus; found on scarabaeid larvae.

rhizome. A jointed underground stem that can produce roots and shoots at each node.

rostrum. A snoutlike projection on an insect's head.

sclerotized. Of an insect, hardened in definite areas by formation of substances other than chitin.

snout. The prolongation of the head of weevils at the end of which the mouthparts are located.

sod. Plugs, blocks, squares, or strips of turfgrass plus soil that are used for planting.

species. The smallest taxonomic group; a population that has a defined range and can exchange genes.

spiracle. A breathing pore through which air enters the trachea; in insects, located laterally on body segments.

spittle. A frothy fluid secreted by insects; saliva.

stage. An insect's developmental status (e.g., the egg stage).

stipe. A small stalk-like structure associated with the maxilla.

stolon. A jointed, aboveground, creeping stem that can produce roots and shoots at each node and may originate extravagantly from the main stem.

stylet. One of the piercing structures in piercing-sucking mouthparts.

subterranean. Existing under the surface of the earth.

tarsal claw. The claw, usually paired, found on the end of the last tarsal segment.

tarsus (pl., tarsi). The foot; the distal part of the insect's leg that consists of one to five segments.

teneral (callow) period. The time immediately after adult emergence; the adult is soft-bodied and pale.

thatch. The layer of plant litter from long-term accumulation of dead plant roots, crowns, rhizomes, and stolons between the zone of green vegetation and the soil surface.

thorax. The second or intermediate region of the insect's body, bearing two legs and wings and composed of three rings, the pro-, meso-, and metathorax.

threshold. A beginning point in physiology; the point at which a stimulus is just strong enough to produce a response.

tibia. In insects, the fourth division of the leg articulated at the proximal end nearest the body to the femur and at the distal end to the tarsus.

tolerance. The ability of a host to withstand injury by pests; a plant response to insect injury and a mechanism of plant resistance to insects.

topdressing. A light covering of soil spread over an established turfgrass.

toxin. A poisonous substance.

turgidity. The extent of being distended, swollen or bloated.

univoltine. Having one generation in a year or season.

vector. An organism that is the carrier of a disease-producing organism.

ventral. The underside.

warm-season grass. A cold-intolerant grass with an optimum temperature range of 80 - 95° F. (27 - 35°C.).

white grub. Whitish, C-shaped larva of insects belonging to the family Scarabaeidae.

wing pads. The undeveloped wings of nymphs of hemimetabolous insects (e.g., Hemiptera), which show behind the thorax as two lateral, flat structures.

witches'-broom. An abnormal brushlike growth of weak, tightly clustered plant shoots.

worker. Among social bees, ants, and wasps, a female either incapable of reproduction or capable of laying only unfertilized eggs from which males emerge.

xeric. Adapted to an extremely dry habitat.

Sources of Local Information

Extension Hall
Auburn University
Auburn University, AL 36849-5413
(205) 844-6392
FAX (205) 844-8002

Department of Entomology
University of Arizona
Tucson, AZ 85721
(602) 621-1153
FAX (602) 621-1150

Department of Entomology
321 Agriculture Building
University of Arkansas
Fayetteville, AR 72701
(501) 575-3376
FAX (501) 575-2452

Department of Entomology & Parasitology
201 Wellman Hall
University of California
Berkeley, CA 94720
(510) 642-3327
FAX (510) 642-7428

Department of Entomology
University of California
Davis, CA 95616-8584
(916) 752-0475
FAX (916) 752-1537

Department of Entomology
University of California
Riverside, CA 92521
(909) 787-3231
FAX (909) 787-3086

Department of Zoology & Entomology
Colorado State University
Fort Collins, CO 80523
(303) 491-6781
FAX (303) 491-0564

Department of Entomology
Connecticut Agricultural Experiment Station
123 Huntington Street, Box 1106
New Haven, CT 06504
(203) 789-7241
FAX (203) 789-7232

Department of Entomology & Applied Ecology
University of Delaware
Newark, DE 19717-1303
(302) 831-8883
FAX (302) 831-3651

Department of Entomology
NHB-105, Room W-308
National Museum of Natural History
Smithsonian Institution
Washington, DC 20560
(202) 357-2078
FAX (202) 786-2894

University of the District of Columbia
901 Newton Street, NE
Washington, DC 20017
(202) 274-6922
FAX (202) 274-6930

Center for Studies in Entomology
Florida A&M University
Tallahassee, FL 32307
(904) 599-3912
FAX (904) 561-2248

Department of Entomology & Nematology
P.O. Box 110620
University of Florida
Gainesville, FL 32611
(904) 392-1901
FAX (904) 392-5660

Department of Entomology/Extension
200 Barrow Hall
University of Georgia
Athens, GA 30602
(706) 542-1765
FAX (706) 542-3872

Department of Entomology
413 Biological Sciences Building
University of Georgia
Athens, GA 30602-2603
(706) 542-2816
FAX (706) 542-2279

Department of Entomology
Box 1209
University of Georgia
Tifton, GA 31793
(912) 386-3424
FAX (312) 386-7133

Department of Entomology
Georgia Experiment Station
College of Agriculture & Environmental Sciences
University of Georgia
Griffin, GA 30223
(404) 228-7288
FAX (404) 228-7270

Department of Entomology
3050 Maile Way, Gilmore 310
University of Hawaii at Manoa
Honolulu, HI 96822
(808) 956-7076
FAX (808) 956-2428

Plant, Soil & Entomological Sciences
University of Idaho
Moscow, ID 83843-2339
(208) 885-5972
FAX (208) 885-7760

Illinois Natural History Survey
607 East Peabody Drive
Champaign, IL 61820
(217) 244-2149

Office of Agricultural Entomology
University of Illinois
Center for Economic Entomology
Illinois Natural History Survey
607 East Peabody Drive
Champaign, IL 61820
(217) 333-6656
FAX (217) 333-4949

Center for Biodiversity
Illinois Natural History Survey
607 East Peabody Drive
Champaign, IL 61820
(217) 244-2149
FAX (217) 333-4949

Department of Entomology
320 Morrill Hall
505 South Goodwin Avenue
University of Illinois
Urbana, IL 61801
(217) 333-2910
FAX (217) 244-3499

Agricultural Experiment Station
Purdue University
1140 Agriculture Administration Building
West Lafayette, IN 47907-1140
(317) 494-8363
FAX (317) 494-0808

Department of Entomology
Purdue University
1158 Entomology Hall
West Lafayette, IN 47907-1158
(317) 494-4570
FAX (317) 494-2152

Department of Entomology
104 Insectary
Iowa State University
Ames, IA 50011-3140
(515) 294-1101
FAX (515) 294-8027

Department of Entomology
123 Waters Hall
Kansas State University
Manhattan, KS 66506-4004
(913) 532-5891
FAX (913) 532-6230

Department of Entomology
University of Kansas
Lawrence, KS 66045
(913) 864-4578

Department of Entomology
S225H Agricultural Science Central North
University of Kentucky
Lexington, KY 40546-0091
(606) 257-2398
FAX (606) 258-1120

Department of Entomology
Louisiana State University
P.O. Box 25100
Baton Rouge, LA 70803-1710
(504) 388-2180
FAX (504) 388-1643

Department of Entomology
University of Maine
Orono, ME 04469
(207) 581-2960
FAX (301) 504-6482

Department of Entomology
1300 Symons Hall
University of Maryland
College Park, MD 20742-5575
(301) 405-3920
FAX (301) 314-9290

Systematic Entomology Laboratory
Building 046, BARC-West
Agricultural Research Service, USDA
10300 Baltimore Avenue
Beltsville, MD 20705
(301) 504-5183
FAX (301) 504-6482

Department of Entomology
Fernald Hall
University of Massachusetts
Amherst, MA 01003
(413) 545-2283
FAX (413) 545-2115

College of Food & Natural Resources
University of Massachusetts
Amherst, MA 01002
(413) 545-2776

Department of Entomology
243 Natural Science Building
Michigan State University
East Lansing, MI 48824
(517) 353-3885
FAX (517) 353-4354

Department of Entomology
219 Hodson Hall
1980 Folwell Avenue
University of Minnesota
St. Paul, MN 55108-6125
(612) 624-3636
FAX (612) 625-5299

Department of Entomology
P.O. Box Drawer EM
Mississippi State University
Mississippi State, MS 39762-5667
(601) 325-2085
FAX (601) 325-8837

Department of Biology
Delta State University
Cleveland, MS 38732

Department of Biology
University of Mississippi
University, MS 38677

Department of Entomology
1-87 Agriculture Building
University of Missouri
Columbia, MO 65211
(314) 882-7894
FAX (314) 882-1469

Entomology Research Laboratory
Montana State University
Bozeman, MT 59717
(406) 994-3860
FAX (406) 994-6029

Department of Entomology
210 Plant Industry
University of Nebraska - East Campus
Lincoln, NE 68583-0816
(402) 472-2125
FAX (402) 472-4687

Division of Agriculture
350 Capitol Hill Avenue
University of Nevada
Reno, NV 89502

Department of Entomology
Nesmith Hall
University of New Hampshire
Durham, NH 03824-3597
(603) 862-1159
FAX (603) 862-4757

J. B. Smith Hall, Georges Road
Rutgers, The State University of New Jersey
Cook College, P.O. Box 231
New Brunswick, N J 08903-0231
(908) 932-9324
FAX (908) 932-7229

Department of Entomology, Plant Pathology
    & Weed Science
New Mexico State University
Box 30003, Dept. 3BE
Las Cruces, NM 88003-0003
(505) 646-3225
FAX (505) 646-5975

New Mexico State University
9301 Indian School Road NE, #201
Albuquerque, NM 87112

Department of Entomology
Comstock Hall
Cornell University
Ithaca, NY 14853
(607) 255-3253
FAX (503) 737-3643

Department of Entomology
NYS Agricultural Experiment Station
Barton Lab
Geneva, NY 14456
(315) 781-2323
FAX (315) 787-2326

Entomology Concentration Leader
133 Illick Hall
SUNY College of Environment Science & Forestry
Syracuse, NY 13210-2788
(315) 470-6742
FAX (315) 470-6934

Department of Entomology
North Carolina State University
Raleigh, NC 27695-7613
(919) 515-2703
(FAX) 515-7746

Department of Entomology
202 Hultz Hall
Box 5346, University Station
North Dakota State University
Fargo, ND 58105-5446
(701) 237-7582
FAX (701) 237-8557

Department of Entomology
Ohio State University
1991 Kenny Road
Columbus, OH 43210
(614) 292-5274
(614) 292-1687

Department of Entomology
OARDC
Wooster, OH 44691
(216) 263-3730

Department of Entomology
127 Noble Research Center
Oklahoma State University
Stillwater, OK 74078
(405) 774-5531
FAX (405) 744-6039

Department of Entomology
Cordley Hall, Room 2046
Oregon State University
Corvallis, OR 97331-2709
(503) 737-5499
FAX (503) 737-3643

Department of Entomology
Penn State University
501 Agric. Science & Industries Building
University Park, PA 16802
(814) 865-3008
FAX (814) 865-3048

Crop Protection Department
Box 5000
University of Puerto Rico
Mayaguez, PR 00681
(809) 265-3859
FAX (809) 265-0860

Department of Plant Sciences
University of Rhode Island
Kingston, RI 02881
(401) 792-5998
FAX (401) 792-4017

Entomology Section
Department of Plant Sciences
University of Rhode Island
Kingston, RI 02881-0804
(401) 792-2924
FAX (401) 792-4017

Department of Entomology
109 Long Hall
Clemson University
Clemson, SC 29634
(803) 656-5043
FAX (803) 656-5065

Department of Plant Science
South Dakota State University
Brookings, SD 57007
(605) 688-4601
FAX (605) 688-6065

Department of Entomology & Plant Pathology
University of Tennessee
Knoxville, TN 39701
(615) 947-7135

Department of Entomology
Texas A&M University
College Station, TX 77843
(409) 845-2516

Department of Agronomy, Horticulture &
  Entomology
Box 42122
Texas Tech University
Lubbock, TX 79409-2122
(806) 742-2838
FAX (806) 742-2836

Department of Biology
University of Utah
Salt Lake City, UT 84112
(801) 581-6517

Department of Biology
Utah State University
Logan, UT 84322-5305
(801) 750-2514
FAX (801) 750-1575

Insect Biology Division
Department of Biology
Utah State University
Logan, UT 84322-5305
(801) 750-2515
FAX (801) 750-1575

Department of Zoology
Brigham Young University
Provo, UT 84601
(801) 378-2006

Virgin Islands Cooperative Extension Service
R.R.2
Box 10,000 Kingshill
St. Croix, VI 00850
(809) 788-9491
FAX (809) 778-8866

Plant & Soil Science Department
Hills Building
University of Vermont
Burlington, VT 05401
(802) 656-3131

Department of Entomology
215 Price Hall
Virginia Polytechnic Institute & State University
Blacksburg, VA 24061-0319
(703) 231-4045
FAX (703) 982-6050

Department of Entomology
FSHN Building 166
Washington State University
Pullman, WA 99164-6382
(509) 335-5505
FAX (509) 335-1009

Division of Plant and Soil Sciences
West Virginia University
P.O. Box 6108
Morgantown, WV 26506-6108
(304) 293-4817 (Division)
(304) 293-6023 (Entomology)
FAX (304) 293-3740

Department of Entomology
University of Wisconsin
Madison, WI 53706
(608) 262-3227
FAX (608) 262-3322

Department of Plant, Soil & Insect Sciences
P.O. Box 3354 University Station
University of Wyoming
Laramie, WY 82071-3103
(307) 766-3103
FAX (307) 766-3379

Entomology Department
2-27 Earth Sciences Building
University of Alberta
Edmonton, AB
Canada T6G 2E3
(403) 492-4652
FAX (403) 492-1767

Department of Entomology
University of Manitoba
Winnipeg, MB
Canada R3T 2N2
(204) 474-9257
FAX (204) 275-0402

Department of Environmental Biology
University of Guelph
Guelph, ON
Canada N1G 2W1
(519) 824-4120
FAX (519) 837-0442

University Laval
Department of Biology
Sainte-Foy, QC
Canada G1K 7P4
(418) 656-3180

Department of Entomology
Faculty of Agricultural & Environmental Sciences
21,111 Lakeshore Road
McGill University (MacDonald Campus)
Sainte-Anne-De-Bellevue, QC
Canada H9X 3V9
(514) 398-7911
FAX (514) 398-7990

Department of Biology
York University
Willowdale, ON
Canada M3J 1P3
(416) 736-5243

Department of Zoology
University of British Columbia
Vancouver, BC
Canada V6T 1W5

Department of Biology
University of Saskatchewan
Saskatoon, SK
Canada S7N 0W0

Department of Biology
University of Ottawa
Ottawa, ON
Canada K1N 6N5

Department of Zoology
University of Western Ontario
London, ON
Canada N6A 5B7

Lyman Entomological Museum
MacDonald College
Sainte-Anne-de-Bellevue, QC
Canada H9X 1C0

Entomology Coordinator
Department of Biology
Carleton University
Ottawa, ON
Canada K1S 5B6

Department of Entomology
Royal Ontario Museum
100 Queen's Park
Toronto, ON
Canada M5S 2C6

Department of Biological Sciences
Simon Fraser University
Burnaby, BC
Canada V5A 1S6

Collections & Research
National Museum Natural Science
P.O. Box 3443, Stat. D
Ottawa, ON
Canada K1P 6P4

Department of Zoology
University of Toronto
Toronto, ON
Canada M5S 1A1

Department of Biology
Queen's University
Kingston, ON
Canada K7L 3N6

Biology Coordinator
Department of Biology
University of New Brunswick
St. John, NB
Canada E2L 4L5

Department of Biology
Memorial University
St. John's, NF
Canada A1C 5S7

Center for Land and Biological Resources
  Research-BRD
Agriculture Canada
Ottawa, ON
Canada K1A 0C6

Instituto de Biologia
Ciudad Universitaria
Pedregal de San Angel
Mexico, D.F., Mexico

Instituto de Ecologia
Km. 2.5 Antigua Carretera a Coatepec
Xalapa, Vestet, Mexico

Facultad de Ciencias
Ciudad Universitaria
Pedregal de San Angel
Mexico, D.F., Mexico

Graduados en Agricultura
ITESM, Suc. Correos "J"
Monterrey, N.L. 64849, Mexico

Facultad de Biologia
Universidad Autonoma de Nuevo León
Monterrey, N.L., Mexico

Escuela Nacional de Ciencias Biologicas
Instituto Politecnico Nacional
Apdo. Postal 42186
Mexico, D.F. 17, Mexico

Colegio de Graduados de la Facultad de Agron
Universidad Autonoma de Nuevo León
Apdo. Postal 358
San Nicolas de las Garza, N.L., Mexico
(83) 522139,524783

Facultad de Agonomia
Universidad Autonoma de Tamaulipas
Apdo. Postal 37
Ciudad Victoria, Tamaulipas, Mexico
(131) 21738,27065

Escuela Superior de Agricultura
Universidad Autonoma de Sinaloa
Apdo. Postal 726
Culiacán, Sinaloa, Mexico

Escuela de Agricultura de Autlan
Universidad de Guadalajara
KM. 200 Carret Guadalajara-Barra De Navidad
Guadalajara, Jalisco, Mexico

Programa De Graduados
Universidad Autonoma Agraria
Antonio Narro
Buenavista, Saltillo, Coahuila, Mexico
4342443100

Sources of Local Information

Escuela Sup De Agric Hermanos Escobar A.C.
CZDA Hnos Escobar No. 3650
Col La Playa
Ciudad Juares, Chihuahua, Mexico 32310
64991 y 64990

Centro de Entomologia y Acarologia
Col de Postgraduados
C.P. 56230
Chapingo, Edo. de Mexico

Index

Index